the humanities and the library

the humanities and the library

problems in the interpretation,
evaluation and use of library materials

by
LESTER ASHEIM *and associates*

AMERICAN LIBRARY ASSOCIATION

Chicago · 1957

© 1957 by the American Library Association

Manufactured in the United States of America

Library of Congress catalog card 56-12395

Sixth Printing, September 1966

CONTRIBUTING AUTHORS

Religion
Lester Asheim and Herman Bernick

Philosophy
Lester Asheim, with the assistance of Richard Wynne

Art
Lester Asheim, with the assistance of Theresa Fulton

Music
Lester Asheim, with the assistance of Arthur Byler

Literature
Lester Asheim, with the assistance of Milton Crane and
Herman Bernick

RESEARCH ASSISTANTS

Johann K. Gardner
Wallace Look
Nadine Mack

Edwin Suderow
Frederick Weinstein
Larzer Ziff

preface

In 1948 the Carnegie Corporation awarded a grant to the
Graduate Library School of the University of Chicago to under-
write the preparation of a series of textbooks or syllabi. These
texts were to be used with the so-called "books courses" then
being introduced into American library schools. They were intended for use not only in the Graduate Library School but also by
library schools, students of librarianship generally, and non-
library students in the several subject fields.

The books courses are a central part of the emerging pattern
of library education in this country as it has changed since World
War II. The courses were developed from dissatisfaction with the
too-great emphasis previously given to training in library practices as such. Although they may differ from school to school, the
courses are intended to provide students with more knowledge
about the *contents* of books and the *criteria* for evaluating them
than was provided in the previous system of education. Such book
knowledge is regarded as a supplement and an extension, in terms
of the particular needs of librarianship, of the general or liberal
education that the student brings to his professional training. Primary attention is shifted from the book as a separate physical

object to its content and its relationship to its field. The student will thus be taught not only the usual library methods of organizing and managing books and similar materials, but also something of the general nature of the books with which he will be dealing.

The faculty of the Graduate Library School began discussions on the establishment of its courses in this area in the tenure as dean (1945-46) of Ralph Beals. Discussions were continued and the first courses set up in the deanship (1946-47) of Clarence Faust. The grant for these materials was obtained and the first drafts completed in the deanship of Bernard Berelson (1947-51), and the final work was done during the present tenure of Lester Asheim. The general aims of these textbooks may be summarized in the basic objectives of the courses as established at the University of Chicago Graduate Library School:

1. To extend the background knowledge of students about books and other materials of communication, about authors, and about publishers

2. To give students some understanding of the classification of knowledge and the relation of the content of materials to this classification

3. To provide students with the ability to evaluate and interpret books and other materials critically with particular reference to the provision, interpretation, and use of materials in libraries

4. To provide students with some knowledge of the development of the literature of different disciplines, and of the growth of significant ideas, forms of expression, and scholarship

5. To acquaint students with the nature and functions of the interpretive aspects of librarianship: reference work, readers' advisory work, bibliographical method, etc.

6. To direct students in the acquisition of certain skills essential in the performance of the interpretive aspects of library work: analysis of questions and problems; determining the needs of users of the library; selecting or adapting materials to meet their needs; etc.

A more extended statement of the rationale of these materials was prepared by Mr. Faust as a consultant to the project in its early years. Parts of his memorandum follow:

> The general purpose ... is to increase the future librarian's grasp of the subject matters represented in libraries so as to enable him to engage more intelligently in the activities of librarianship. Without some grasp of the content of the books he handles, the librarian is bound to perform his functions in a purely mechanical way. He needs some knowledge of the matters with which books deal if he is to engage

intelligently in such activities as the selection of books, the cataloging of them, the handling of reference problems, and the advising of users of book collections.

It is obviously impossible, however, for the librarian to acquire a specialist's mastery of the wide range of subjects which even the meagerest of libraries presents. He cannot become an economist, a political scientist, a sociologist, an anthropologist, a musicologist, a metaphysician, a physicist, a chemist, a geologist, and an astronomer. Yet without some knowledge of these and many other fields, he can function merely as a custodian of books. The answer would seem to be that in order to function wisely and effectively, in order to engage in what might be properly regarded as professional activity, he must acquire a knowledge of at least the *literature* of the various subject matters represented in libraries. More knowledge of bibliography will not, however, serve his purposes. What he needs is not bibliographical information solely, that is, elaborately classified lists of titles, but such knowledge of the nature of the literature of the various fields represented in libraries as will enable him (1) to make out the distinguishing features of a given book in any one of these fields; (2) to locate it in the tradition, school, or trend to which it belongs; and (3) either by personal examination of it or by proper interpretation of the judgments of others to appraise its value with respect to its treatment of its subject and its usefulness to different kinds of readers.

This course is not intended, then, to duplicate the work of survey or general courses offered in subject-matter departments of colleges, nor simply to carry such work beyond the points these courses reach. It is planned for students who have already acquired the kind of general education available in the better American colleges and is designed to supplement and build upon such general education for the purposes of librarianship by providing an elementary and practical overview of the nature and history of the literature of the major fields of human study and imaginative construction. To lay the base for the insight into the significant characteristics of kinds of literature which the librarian needs in order to describe a given instance of a kind, or to compare several such instances, or to exercise the judgment about the relative merits of several pieces, it is necessary the student acquire a knowledge (1) of the nature of the subject matters of each kind of literature; (2) of the ends or purposes exhibited in that

literature; and (3) of the range of methods of investigation,
exposition, and construction employed in it ....

It is one of the purposes of the syllabus to present librarianship as a co-ordinated series of functions which are all
parts of one major function — interpretation, evaluation, and
preservation of library materials for the most effective use
by the library patron. The majority of textbooks intended for
library school use in the past have dealt with its functions —
book selection, reference work, etc. — separately and in iso-
lation. The result of such an approach is still apparent in
many libraries where specialization has become compart-
mentation, and processes — which should be only means to an
end — have become ends in themselves. This syllabus departs
from the traditional organization and emphasizes the interrelation of library functions and the co-ordination of the
several aspects of these functions into an integrated whole.
Thus, book selection, reference principles, theory of classification, etc., are considered together throughout the syllabus.

It is hoped, in short, that the syllabus will provide the
basis for co-ordinating and integrating the professional with
general education by studying librarianship in the light of the
major characteristics of each of the variety of kinds of literature presented in libraries. In addition to seeing library
processes in their relation to each other, the syllabus attempts
to point up the interrelation of the processes with the subject
materials to which they are applied. Thus, although librarianship is the primary object of study, the point of departure is
the subject matter. Librarianship is studied as conditioned by
the nature of the materials which make up the library collection, and these in turn as they are conditioned by the nature of
the subject field out of which they spring. The overview of the
several disciplines is designed to throw light on the library's
activities in the fields by developing the student's knowledge
of the nature of the literature in each of the major trends of
human study and acquainting him with the major trends in that
literature, as well as with the needs of its readers which
shape the kinds of services libraries do or should supply, the
kinds of materials they make available, and the separate techniques for each discipline which they have developed in the
past or must develop in the future to serve most efficiently
both the specialist and the non-specialist user of subject materials. The syllabus thus forms a bridge between "pure"
librarianship and "pure" subject matter which, while it allows

the student to move easily both within and between the two
areas, serves to stress the connection rather than the separation between the two. Such an emphasis, it is believed, should
lead to the librarian's understanding of both areas and enrich
the libraries' services and value for the users.

No single library school faculty is qualified to prepare such
materials alone. Therefore, although the project was under the
direction of members of the Graduate Library School faculty, it
was undertaken with the active participation of certain faculty
members of the University of Chicago. Members of the faculty
were selected for this project on the basis of their interest in the
problems of general education; their breadth of outlook (i. e., their
lack of narrow preoccupation with a special field or a segment of
it); and their experience with the preparation of syllabi and texts
of this sort in their own educational program. Such people supplied the subject knowledge on the basis of which the materials
were prepared.

The original intention was to produce a volume in each of the
three major subject areas: the humanities, the social sciences,
and the sciences. A variety of problems arose in the preparation
of the work, some deriving from the differences in subject matter
with which the writers had to deal. The plan of operation, adapted
without too much difficulty to the field of the humanities, did not so
adequately meet the problems involved in the preparation of a text
on the sciences or the social sciences. Several modifications were
introduced in an attempt to salvage the work already accomplished
and to bring the total volumes to completion, but only in the case
of the humanities was a satisfactory syllabus produced. The work
dealing with the social sciences has been brought together in a
volume which places its emphasis almost exclusively on the social
sciences per se, and more properly should appear under some
other imprint than that of the American Library Association; steps in
that direction have been taken. Although a good deal of exploratory
work was done in the sciences, a volume in that field has not mate-
rialized.

The volume on the humanities, therefore, stands as an example
of the kind of syllabus originally projected. The purpose of the
volume is to provide a sample textbook for such a course in the
fields of the humanities (philosophy, religion, art, music, and literature). It is hoped the book will illustrate how the humanities
collection, its users, and service to them are related to the nature
of the subject discipline itself.

The humanities volume although based upon the kinds of materials presented in the books courses taught at the Graduate Library

School of the University of Chicago is not a complete reflection of those courses. An attempt was made to keep the text flexible enough and broad enough to be of use to other schools and other programs. The instructor of the humanities course at Chicago utilizes only so much of this volume as is useful to the objectives of his program in any given academic quarter and supplements it as he sees fit. Because the text was designed with the Graduate Library School courses in mind, a word should be said about the organization of these courses for the guidance of teachers and students in other programs who may wish to use these materials.

The Graduate Library School courses, entitled "Interpretation, Evaluation and Use of Library Materials," form a four-quarter sequence within a core curriculum of seven courses. These four quarters are devoted respectively to one quarter of general introduction to basic principles, practices, and tools and one quarter each to the adaptation, extension, and application of these and similar principles, practices, and tools to the fields of the humanities, the social sciences, and the natural sciences.

The present text accompanies the second quarter of work in this sequence. It is used after the quarter of introductory work and does not attempt to supply the basic knowledge of principles and tools which an introductory course is assumed to cover. The student user of this text is assumed already to have learned something about the general sources of information about books; the general methods of book selection and ordering; the "why" of cataloging and classification and something about the "how"; the criteria of evaluation for general and reference materials; and the general procedures of reference work and readers' advisory services. The omissions of certain basic information, titles, and procedures from this book are deliberate. Such general reference tools as the *Encyclopaedia Britannica,* the *United States Catalog* and *Cumulative Book Index,* or the *Readers' Guide,* essential as they are to any librarian in a humanities department, are not treated. Neither are beginning training in the form of the catalog card and the kind of information it contains, nor the general principles of classification, nor general practice in the routines of order work, principles of filing, book selection, etc. The purpose of the volume is not to provide such basic instruction, but *to build upon it,* emphasizing the way in which the nature of the subject matter of the humanities field and of the audience for library materials in that field dictates adaptations of the general principles.

In some places in the text, possible assignments are suggested.[1]

---

[1]See the "Turn of the Screw" assignment, p. 231, for example.

These do not constitute all of the assignments necessary in a books
course. They are included as examples of the types of assignments which combine the subject content and the content of librarianship in a single exercise. It is assumed that the individual instructor will wish to assign considerable additional reading outside
of this volume and many exercises and problems beyond those
suggested here. All that can be said for these particular suggestions is that they have, at one time or another, been used by the
instructors of the humanities courses at the Graduate Library
School and have been found useful in illustrating to the student the
interactions between the subject field and library practice and
problems in that field.

It will be noted that the same scheme of organization is not
used in each chapter; a section on the selection of books for children in the field of religion is not balanced by a section on the
selection of books for children in each of the other areas. This
seeming inconsistency is a reflection of the fact that the humanities volume is seen as part of a *series* of texts to be used with a
sequence of courses. It is assumed that particular problems in
the interpretation, evaluation, and use of materials will be handled
at that point in the sequence where they are most serious, or most
clearly illustrated. The problem of selection of children's books
in the religious field introduces some basic principles which can
most graphically be dealt with there and selection of books for
children is not repeated where it is less pertinent and less illustrative. The humanities volume considers only some of the problems of book selection, reference, and cataloging work. If the
original series of three volumes had been completed, those problems peculiar to science and social science materials would have
been treated in the framework of the subject, e. g., corporate entry
in social science, treatment of scholarly journals in science, etc.

The Table of Contents uses a broad subject breakdown so that
the focus will remain on the general discussion areas and course
units and not on specific facts. An index which would provide a
small subject analysis was contemplated but deliberately rejected
to discourage the idea that the work can be used as a source book
of factual information.

A word should be said also about the references that appear
in the body of the text and in the bibliographies. It will be noted
that complete bibliographical references are seldom given. This
apparent bibliographical laxity was permitted for the following
reasons:

1. In the case of examples cited in the text itself (see "The
Organization of Literary Histories", p. 216, for example) titles
are merely illustrative and are not meant as models for the students' particular attention. The whole purpose of the citation is
served by the mention of the self-explanatory title.

2. In the case of the reference bibliographies it is assumed that these titles will be checked by the student in the latest edition of Constance Winchell's *Guide to Reference Books* and its supplements, and that copies of the works listed in the bibliographies will be available at reference desks or in library school collections for student use. Full bibliographical references were considered nonessential for this purpose, especially since it is assumed that the reference list will be constantly revised and will be adapted to the facilities of the individual collections to which the student has access.

A final word of caution to the users of this volume: the book is not seen as a definitive textbook for this field. It is the intention of the writer that it be used not as a master plan in itself, but as a basis for individual planning of courses — an example of an *approach* to the materials of librarianship through the subject matter with which they deal.

A work of collaboration like the present volume presents a very misleading picture in carrying a single name on its title page. The "associates" are every bit as important as the designated "author," although full recognition is often denied them. I should like to acknowledge my very real debt to all those who worked with me throughout the history of this volume, most particularly those whose names appear in this introduction, and on the page of contributors and assistants. Of these, Bernard Berelson, who continued to assume the obligation of directing the project after his departure from the Graduate Library School, is the one person most responsible for keeping the project alive and encouraging its eventual completion.

The members of the office staff of the Graduate Library School who typed drafts, cut stencils, revised lists, and otherwise did the "dirty work" without which such a volume never can be written should also be mentioned, as should the students in my classes who used the work in its several draft versions as a syllabus and made constructive comments about its value.

Finally, of course, I wish to express my thanks to the Carnegie Corporation of New York whose generosity made the project possible, and whose patience far exceeded my own during the long period of mishaps and setbacks that delayed the publication of it.

Lester Asheim
August 1956

contents

Contents

chapter one

religion

INTRODUCTION

Of the several fields of knowledge which have here been designated as the humanities, that of religion is the most logical one with
which to start, for it is, historically, the soil out of which all the
others grew. Philosophy, for example, came into being when men
began to attempt to understand ultimate reality in rational rather
than emotional terms, but it has always been associated with religion, either by derivation or by way of criticism, for both are
concerned with the same object. The earliest literature which we
possess for any civilization is invariably connected with religious
belief. Music and the dance both originate in early religious ritual;
the earliest graphic arts depict religious ceremonies as well as
the everyday incidents of the hunt and battle; and the earliest monuments were erected to glorify the gods.

Religion has thus influenced many fields which are apparently
unrelated to its specific province and has been instrumental in the
development of many arts and sciences which no longer reflect
their religious origin. In addition to the impetus given by the zeal
to please the deities to architecture, the plastic arts, music,

1

poetry, and the dance, progress has been accelerated in other
fields even more remote. The desire to hold ceremonials at certain specified times led to more precise computations of time intervals and to the development of a calendar based upon astrologi-
cal and astronomical observation. Inspection of the slaughtered
animals used in ritual sacrifices gave the first ideas about anat-
omy. The alchemistic speculations of the priest as medicine man
led to the study of chemistry. The use of the temple as the earliest seat of law made jurists of the priests whose practices left
their imprint on the science of law. The emphasis upon the special
divine grace which is visited upon the poor and the weak has made
Judaism and Christianity leaders in the cause of social betterment.

Quite apart from his specific religious convictions, the well-
educated man in any subject field is more or less indebted to the
knowledge which is classified as religious, and his understanding
of the history and development of his own discipline is enriched by
his understanding of the history and development of religious
belief. The religious influence, like the influence of philosophy
and other shaping forces, has not always been one in the direction
of what we today call progress. Strictures against idol worship
retarded the development of Hebrew art; restrictions of the church
on the subject matter and style of medieval painting and sculpture
were thrown off only gradually and after a long "dark" period; and
attacks upon "profane" literature, art, and science have blocked
advancements in those fields in many famous and notorious instances. Although it is true the monasteries were centers of what
learning existed in the Middle Ages and guarded what remains of
earlier writings, it may also be true that more might have endured
but for religious censorship and disapproval. The significance in
these influences, both positive and negative, is that much of our
thinking and many of our predispositions and expectations even in
nonreligious fields have been shaped by religion. That means that
the literature and materials of religion cannot be isolated from
those of other fields, nor can the thought of other fields be ignored
in the library collection nominally devoted to the area of religion.
Therefore, the study of the interpretation, evaluation, and use of
materials in the field of religion is important not only to the students who plan to work in a theological library, but also to the
general librarian and even to the special librarian in other fields.

DEFINITION OF RELIGION

The area of religion, broadly speaking, is concerned with
man's beliefs and practices in relation to a god, gods, or the supernatural. There are differences among the basic concepts and

the rituals to be followed and among the attributes of the object of
worship or fear, but in essence religion is related to the beliefs
concerning some ruling force or forces and the ways in which
these forces are worshiped and obeyed. This entails a body of
belief concerning the wishes, rules, and precepts set forth by the
object of worship or designated by his representatives as desirable
or obligatory. The field of religious literature proper includes
theology, which is the systematic presentation of the teaching of
some positive or historical religion, methodically formulated; the
philosophy of religion, which relates religious experience to other
spheres of experience in an attempt to determine its "real" meaning in exact terms of thought; the *science of religion,* which is a
purely historical or comparative account of the various manifestations of the religious instinct without pronouncing on their relative
truth or value; and purely *personal religion,* which is not dependent
upon historical data or controlled methodology, but which analyzes,
often in enthusiastic terms, the nature of individual religious experience as subjectively experienced.

THE LITERATURE OF RELIGION

Most libraries, except for a few special libraries connected
with a particular religious group, are concerned with the literature
of religion as literature; they are not concerned with establishing
the rules of religious conduct or the bases for a single "true" belief. Religion is represented upon the library's shelves as a subject for investigation and study; its sacred books, its regulations,
its decrees, exhortations and testimonials, its defenses and the
attacks upon it are of interest to the librarian as documents. The
library does not act as advocate or prosecutor, but as an impartial
source of information.

This is the library's concern in all fields of knowledge, but it
is not possible in this area to apply the criteria of scientific truth
and impersonal scholarship as guides to selection, for many of the
leading documents in the history of any religious belief are those
which are grounded in faith, which is, by definition, nonrational.
Faith is literally a *super*natural phenomenon and defies the proofs
demanded by the natural sciences. The indispensable documents
in the area of religion are quite frequently completely nonscien-
tific; their importance rests on the influence they have exerted,
the reverence in which they are held by their adherents, the
beauty and cogency of their language, and the historical significance
of their position. The library is not charged, as it is in the science
and social science fields, with representing on its shelves the
latest established truths which men have discovered in the field of

religion, but in tracing and detailing the search for those truths. The scientific and scholarly studies of religious belief make up only a small part of the basic religious collection, for religion is not really an academic discipline in the sense that history or science is, with a controlled methodology and a defined procedure. When these techniques are introduced, they are borrowed from other fields which *are* disciplines.

Types of Religious Literature

The literature of religion consists of a number of types of material. There are the sources for belief and practice advocated by the individual religious authorities themselves. These include the holy documents which have the greatest authority in establishing and determining points of belief and practice, like the Bible for Judaism and Christianity; and the manuals of religious worship which record the practices accepted over a period of time and having the sanction of religious authorities, like the *English Book of Common Prayer* or the Catholic *Missal*. Closely associated with these are the books which record controversies and discussions of doctrine and practice, like Calvin's *Institutes of the Christian Religion*, or the Jewish talmudic writings. All of these are addressed to communicants of one given faith.

The religious literature addressed to those of other faiths or of no faith takes on a different character. It starts from the premise that the writer is of the true faith and that the reader is in error. These writings may attack other religions, or defend the writer's own, but the purpose is to convert the reader to the "true" faith. Those of false faith to whom such writings are addressed can be distinguished into two groups: those who are completely misdirected and those of a wrong religion which contains the rudiments of the true one. The temper of Christian polemic and apologetic literature, for example, is one thing when directed toward the pagans, another when directed toward the Jews.

It is in the area of attack upon other faiths that the first steps are taken towards a true *study* of religion. Disinterestedness is usually lacking, of course; some descriptions are predetermined proofs of the falsity of other religions (as is Augustine's treatment of pagan religion in *The City of God*) or studied attempts to show the rudiments of the true religion in earlier ones (as in Pascal's treatment of Judaism in the *Pensées*). Such studies do lead the writer to an investigation of practice and belief, to sequential history, and to the examination of documents and the accumulation of evidence. Combined with objectivity, this methodology produces the "science of religion," but objectivity was at first possible only in studies of other religions, because of the religious considerations imposed on students of the faith in which they believed. Thus much of the contemporary scholarship of the religious field consists of studies which are not governed by religious principles but by those of other disciplines — such as sociology, psychology, or history.

The several techniques described above of dealing with single religions may also be used in a comparative study of several. The field of comparative religion has been particularly fruitful to those students who seek to trace the development of religious beliefs. The investigation of parallels, borrowings, and migrations of practices and beliefs has opened vast areas of research in the field of religion which depend upon the methods and findings of other fields for assistance. Comparative philology has contributed enormously to the understanding of biblical texts in historical context and to tracing the interdependence of early religions and the thematic unity of widely scattered legends and beliefs. The findings of anthropologists, of historians, of archaeologists compose an ever-increasing part of contemporary scholarship in the religious field. While these scholarly studies are becoming more and more an essential addition to the well-rounded collection, it should be recognized that exegetical texts upon the Scriptures, personal accounts of mystical experiences, and polemical arguments still loom large on the shelves of books on religion.

Religion is the largest subject area in contemporary publication excepting fiction and juvenile books (and many titles in these categories are concerned with religious themes). Religious publication includes writings in every literary form and on every level of worth. A vast literature exists related solely to the sacred scriptures; histories of individual sects and groups of faiths are numerous; biographies of biblical characters, of leading personalities in the development of certain religions, and personal accounts of religious experience abound. There are the polemical publications already mentioned; guides to living according to religious principles; and interpretations of religious teachings in contemporary terms. There are sociological investigations of the place of religions in many societies including our own; anthropological studies of comparative practice and belief; and psychological studies of religious experiences. There are poems, plays, and novels dealing with religious themes which cover this same wide range of approaches: historical, biographical, polemical, exhortatory, and scientific. Perhaps no other single force has moved so many pens as that of religion.

Regardless of subject matter, there are four major ways in which books in a religious collection treat the material. First, there are the *historical* studies, which, whether scholarly or popular, trace the development through time of institutions, practices, and beliefs, or place them within their temporal context. Religious biography, compendiums, and textbooks belong in this category as well as the conventional histories. Second, there is the *devotional and inspirational* literature, which contains the contemplative writings and the expositions of personal religion. This group includes writers as diverse as St. Francis and Basil King, or Thomas a Kempis and Dorothy Sayers. It has always had a wide following and has often been extremely important in the history of religious literature. Many of the works in this area (those of Thomas Browne, for example) rank very high as literature in their own right. Third, there are the *interpretative and doctrinal* works, which also cover a range from the extremely scholarly to the widely popular. Biblical commentaries form part of this group, as do the expositions and interpretations of creeds and systems of faith, the encyclopedias and specialized reference works, and the controversial writings exemplificative of special viewpoints. Last, there is the *practical and informative* group: the "how to" books for churchmen which may deal with administration of religious organizations, religious education, aids in counseling, material for sermons, and other professional literature of the field.

In the nineteenth century, the books of major popular interest were those which dealt with religious faith and doctrine. Today this theological approach has lost favor; the emphasis is now placed upon books that deal with problems of living, which act as inspirational guides toward self-adjustment or self-development, or which stress social, ethical, or scientific aspects of thought. This trend away from theology and towards individual and personal religion is not a twentieth-century development. The Protestant Reformation is based upon just such a tendency, and its seeds go back to pre-Christian history in the conflicts between the priests and the prophets in early Judaism.[1] The present age has increased the attention given by leading theologians to the questions raised by sociology, psychology, and the study of human relations, as shown by the growing socialization and secularization of religious activities, as well as by the changing emphasis in religious publication.

---

[1]Yet the concept of religion as a purely private affair is alien to most (although not all) primitive religions, and institutionalization characterizes even the most highly personalized religions. Despite the historic break of Protestantism from the church, non-Catholic Christianity also is highly institutionalized, and so is orthodox Judaism. Indeed, the question may be raised whether the distinction between religion and philosophy does not rest upon this very factor — the concept of a mediator (church or priestly caste) between man and ultimate truth.

The Scholarship of Religion

The classics in the field of religion, even though they do not
meet the requirements of contemporary scientific methodology,
present a concise history of the changing scholarship of succeeding
periods in time. In Augustine we have the characteristic blending
of Hellenistic Platonism with Christian mysticism which marks
the best of early Christian scholarship. In Aquinas, we find the
Aristotelian orderliness which organizes all knowledge into a
single great unity — the medieval synthesis which is the crowning
glory of the scholarship of the Middle Ages. The humanistic emphasis of the Renaissance is epitomized in such a scholar as
Erasmus. This emphasis, carried to a logical extreme in its insistence on the importance of the individual rather than upon any
institution or any traditional authority, finds its religious expression in the revolt from the church of such men as Luther, Calvin,
Wyclif, Zwingli, and Hus, although each reflects the spirit in his
own way. With the Enlightenment, skepticism enters religious
writing, and a rationalist approach to the materials is introduced.
As the influence of scientific method grew, its techniques were
borrowed by the scholars of religion, while the reaction to rationalism which characterized the Romantic movement brought into
religious research the methods of literary and historical study.
After the publication of Darwin's *The Origin of Species,* the devel-
opmental theory appears in the studies of religion, with Christianity seen as just one of the institutions which reflect man's slow
progress towards perfection out of crude and barbarous beginnings.
The technical scholarship — in the sense of serious, intellectual application of a precise procedure to some specific research
problem in the field — has concentrated mainly on the history of
the church, on comparative religions, on biblical criticism, and on
the psychology of religious experience. In each of these, the
methods employed have been borrowed from other subject fields,
and the discipline has developed as a part of the larger one.
Church history, for example, has used the methods of secular
history and has paralleled its trends. Comparative religion as a
subject of scholarly research grew out of the findings of the anthropologists and the philologists. And the psychology of religious
experience is still of more concern to psychologists than it is to
churchmen.

Church history

Until the Reformation, the Latin Church was content to limit
itself to excerpts and translations from the *History of the Christian*

Church by Eusebius, which was published about 325. In 1559-74,
however, the first history from the Protestant point of view — the
Magdeburg Centuries by Matthias Flacius — appeared and ushered
in a new era of historical writing about the church. The twelve
volumes of the *Ecclesiastical Annals* of Baronius, the first of which
appeared in 1588, were meant as a Catholic answer to Flacius, and
from that time forward a constant flow of histories issued from
the presses. Each presented the denominational point of view of
the writer and reflected not only the difference between the Protestant and Catholic interpretations of religious history but also the
differences within the denominations themselves, conservative,
liberal, and radical. In all of them, however, church history was
seen in terms of historical reconstruction.

Modern historical method was introduced into church history
by August Neander, whose *Allgemeine Geschichte der Christlichen
Religion und Kirche,* published from 1825-52, earned for him the
title of "Father of Church History." Neander turned from the so-
called "Pragmatic" school which dealt with the development of the
church in terms of doctrine and tried to deal with it as history. It
was he who introduced the biographical emphasis into religious
history — an emphasis which continues today in attempts at the
psychological interpretation of individual personalities. With
Neander, church history begins to appeal to documentary evidence
and attested fact to support its authenticity. Official documents
both ecclesiastical and civil (acts of councils, church laws, papal
bulls and encyclicals, etc.); writings of individuals, like the Church
Fathers, the reformers, and other actors in the history itself; and
artifacts, relics, and inscriptions are introduced as supporting
evidence. Despite this facade of authority, the objectivity which is
the goal of contemporary scientific method in secular history is
seldom achieved in religious histories. As is so frequently the
case in the field of religion, the evidence is marshaled to support
a conclusion already predetermined, and facts are interpreted in
the light of doctrinal bias. The tests of accuracy and reliability
usually applied in the evaluation of political or social histories are
seldom met. This does not eliminate these volumes from consideration, but the librarian should be clear in his own mind as to
what the particular bias is, whether it is admitted or not by the
author. With the bias known, the special viewpoint of a Catholic
history, a Protestant history, or a Jewish history has its own value
to the student of religion.

Examples of such biases as they enter the scholarship may
readily be examined by comparing the accounts of a single incident,
concept, or person in the encyclopedias of Protestantism and
Catholicism: Hastings' *Encyclopedia of Religion and Ethics* and

The Catholic Encyclopedia.[2] The articles on the life and significance of Martin Luther will serve as an instructive if somewhat
exaggerated example. While in general agreement on the basic
facts, the two articles illustrate graphically the selective character of the presentation. Both articles are copiously documented,
both present extensive bibliographies, and both attempt to demonstrate their neutrality by concentrating on authorities in the opposite faith. Yet *The Catholic Encyclopedia* pictures Luther as a
"tense and neurotic" hypochondriac, whose "terrible temper"
eventually "drove from him his most devoted friends and zealous
co-laborers," culminating in publications of such "unsurpassable
and irreproducible coarseness" that "a common impulse of de-
cency demanded their summary suppression by his friends."
Hastings, however, presents him as a great professor, author,
translator, and theologian whose "intensity, concentration, earnest-
ness, directness and action" illustrate his versatility and whose
deep "Pauline" Christianity lead him "deeply into the treasures of
Holy Scripture to find therein the solution of the problems of human
life." The value of the two accounts lies, obviously, not in their
absolute historical accuracy, but in their clear presentation of a
partisan view.

Comparative religion

The study of comparative religion in any real sense was long
delayed by the prejudices inherent in an orthodox acceptance of
doctrine. While the existence of other beliefs was known from the
earliest Christian eras, they were long considered as mere superstition and mythology and therefore beneath serious consideration
as religion. Even after the Renaissance opened up new worlds
through increased travel, the cosmopolitan sophistication obtained
made little change in the description of non-Christian or non-
Jewish belief, which was still couched in terms of derogation and
prejudgment that destroyed any possibility of scientific detachment.
The first steps in the direction of objectivity were taken in the Age
of Reason when men like Herder on history and Hegel in his investigations of primitive practice and belief, reflecting the influences of Newton and Locke, opened the way for serious consideration
of other cultures. The real beginnings of comparative religion as
a study followed the nineteenth-century rise of scientific anthropology and comparative linguistics — disciplines unfettered by

---

[2]*The Jewish Encyclopedia* illustrates its particular bias by treating the subject only in relation to Jews and Judaism and so admittedly omits much that
would make a comparison with the other encyclopedias meaningful.

doctrinal loyalties which would blind them to parallels and mutual borrowings in the several systems of belief. Important in this development was Max Müller's publication of the *Sacred Books of the East* in which the investigation of purely linguistic materials — roots and changes of words and structure of language — threw a new light on the development of religious ideas.

The philologists' chief interest lay in tracing the development of grammatical forms. To do this they resorted to a system of methodical comparison which led to the recognition of the community of languages. With the acceptance of a common source for Indo-European languages and the establishment of laws governing phonetic change and the development of idioms, all literatures became equally important as subjects of study, and a more objective analysis of content could be made. The study of Sanskrit led to a serious consideration of the vedic literature, not only for its grammatical construction, but for its religious ideas, and the inevitable result was an acceptance of a common source of belief as well as of language. The discoveries of the anthropologists, whose studies of both ancient and contemporary primitive cultures added data concerning religious practice and belief, contributed further evidence that other cultures and other religious systems reflect an affinity with the Christian and European and are no less worthy of consideration. The sixteen volumes of Sir James George Frazer's *The Golden Bough,* published from 1890-1915 (although modern scholarship has moved beyond both its methods and its conclusions), is still a notable example of a pioneering study of ancient myth and folklore which attempted to trace the evolution of many contemporary religious beliefs to their sources in primitive magic and culture.

Biblical criticism

Out of the study of comparative scriptures grew the critical study of the Christian Bible. Here again the philologists opened the way, as sounder interpretations of the ancient texts became possible. While the students of linguistics were concerned only with reconstructing the text grammatically, their findings illuminated circumstances under which the books were written. It became possible not only to correct the errors of translators and editors, but also to date the books more accurately, to recognize interpolations, and to identify different styles of composition. Concurrent with textual criticism, which endeavored to reproduce the original text without accretions, distortions or corruptions, there grew up the so-called "higher criticism" which aimed at a true interpretation of the original text in its historical context.

The relation between "lower" and "higher" criticism, it should be noted, is sequential, not normative. "Lower" criticism (textual criticism) is the preparatory study of the authentic text upon which the "higher" criticism (inner study) is dependent; both are equally important in establishing the "true" sense of the biblical text.

Biblical textual criticism was not, in itself, an invention of the nineteenth century. As early as the third century, Origen compiled his "hexapla" which arranged the various biblical texts in six columns: the Hebrew text, the Hebrew in Greek letter, three Greek translations other than the Septuagint, and his own version of the latter. The several synods and councils which addressed themselves to the problem of determining canon also were engaged in textual criticism of a sort. According to one legendary account, all the books under consideration at the Council of Nicea were placed under a table and prayers were offered to God that the inspired writings rise to the top of the table, leaving the spurious works underneath. The prayers were answered, and the canonical books, so the story goes, separated themselves with God's aid from the false ones. That such an account could be circulated and believed, even though it is not likely to describe the actual procedure employed, gives a clue to the nature of the task of determining canon and the approach of the churchmen to it. The distinction between these efforts and those of modern scholars is that the modern scholar is no longer concerned with identifying the touch of Divine inspiration but with tracing accurately the human authorship. The starting point today is intellectual curiosity; in the past it was faith.

Semler's *Treatise on the Free Investigation of the Canon,* published in 1771, epitomizes the new rationalistic approach. In Semler the canon is viewed as an historical accumulation which grew through the centuries, rather than as a single-stroke creation of Divine dictation. Once this view was accepted, the way was clear for intensive study of the individual books to determine their authorship, date, and authenticity. In the early nineteenth century, most of the biblical studies centered on the separate parts of the Bible. Schleiermacher's studies of Timothy I and Luke, and Bretschneider's investigations of the Gospel of John are typical. The Romantic reaction, on the other hand, started a trend back to the study of the Book as a whole; Coleridge, for example, demanded that the Bible be studied like any other book, as a literary work. By 1835, the literary approach had gained favor, and Baur's *Totalanschauung* called for a view of the Scriptures as a spiritual total — an entity rather than a piecemeal collection of individual books. It was in 1835 also that David Friedrich Strauss, in his *Life of Jesus,* introduced the mythological interpretation of the scriptural account and pointed the way to a historical-sociological reconstruction of the Jesus story. This "destructive" criticism of Strauss's was bitterly attacked in his day and resulted in his professional ostracism. Contemporary sociological study of religious belief, however, continues in this tradition — a tradition which begins to lead away from the Scriptures themselves toward a study of the society which produced them. The advances made in the fields of anthropology, philology, and sociology in general were reflected in the special field of biblical study, and the leadership taken by German scholars in the three fields was paralleled by the leadership taken by the Germans in textual and higher criticism. With American education in the nineteenth century heavily dependent upon the German universities and German practice, it is not surprising that American emphasis in religious scholarship has also been primarily upon biblical criticism.

Throughout the nineteenth century, and down to the present day, the discovery of manuscripts — either of portions of the Scriptures themselves or of writings which help us to understand the Scriptures and the times in which they were originally set down — has led to constant revision of the biblical text and reinterpretation of its probable original meaning. The discovery in 1947 of the Dead Sea Scrolls, for example, seems to some scholars to shed new light on the origins and meaning of many of the concepts in the New Testament and to call for a re-evaluation of many of our current ideas about the source of certain Christian precepts. The controversy over the implications of the Scrolls serves to illustrate the continuing concern of the scholars with establishing accurately and authoritatively the authentic biblical text and its meaning.

The Psychology of religion

One of the aspects of mental life to which psychologists early addressed themselves was that of religious experience. Since religious experience consists of sensations, sentiments, and emotions issuing in action, it has been taken by the psychologists to be as proper an object of psychological investigation as any other part of conscious life. Their insistence upon finding "natural" explanations for phenomena which are considered by most religionists to ɔe evidences of divine and extrahuman action (premonitions, visions, revelations, sudden moral conversions, mystical experiences, etc.) has cost them the support of most churchmen, and psychological research in the field of religion is almost exclusively the work of psychologists rather than of students of religion. William James's *Varieties of Religious Experience* is one of the most famous of the early attempts to apply the critical and inductive methods of empiricism to a study of religious experience.

James approaches the problem like a scientist but, having factually described the phenomena he is investigating, he concludes that only extrahuman causes can explain some of them. This has made James acceptable to many religionists, but not to his fellow psychologists. As early as 1912, James Leuba spoke for the nonreligious psychologists in these terms:

> William James's effort to find in religious experiences phenomena warranting the hypothesis of divine action is a *fiasco* which, despite his own preference announced in the conclusions, should be felt as a severe blow by the supernaturally inclined.[3]

The quarrel has continued to the present day, with the religious scholars insisting that "inner" and "immediate" experience is not susceptible to scientific measurement, and the psychologists claiming that until scientific method is applied to the study of inner experience it cannot lay claim to serious consideration. In effect the controversy resolves itself into a claim by the psychologists that religion is really psychology, and a claim by the religionists that what psychology is attempting to do, religion has long since done — and better.

The studies of religious psychology undertaken by churchmen have, in general, been of a type of "applied" psychology called "pastoral," which deals with practical problems of adjustment. Churchmen are beginning to recognize the value of psychiatric help; many theological students are required to undergo a course of analysis to prepare them for the ministry; and several churches have established combination pastoral and psychiatric clinics. Whether this pastoral psychology is acceptable scientifically is a moot question, but that it is acceptable to the general public has been overwhelmingly demonstrated. The continued publication and popularity of such books as Rabbi Liebman's *Peace of Mind,* Monsignor Sheen's *Peace of Soul,* and the works of Norman Vincent Peale (some of them based on experiences in the psychiatric clinic of the Marble Collegiate Church where he is pastor) testify to the present-day appeal of such solutions to soul-sickness and neurosis.

Another application of the findings of psychology to the study of religion is that used by the sociologists of religion, who attempt to find an explanation of the rise and spread of religious beliefs through a study of the needs and drives of the societies which hold them. The emphasis here is upon society rather than upon religion; belief, practice, and doctrine are interpreted in terms of the social pattern of the particular time and place. In these studies, a

---

[3]James H. Leuba, *A Psychological Study of Religion: Its Origin, Function, and Future.* (N. Y., MacMillan, 1912), p. 274.

combination of disciplines is applied to the problem, and religion becomes merely one of the many aspects of total social experience. Pareto, Malinowski, and Durkheim are interested in religious belief only as it throws light upon human action as a whole. Durkheim, in *The Elementary Forms of the Religious Life,* for example, in attempting to discover the reality for which sacred objects are the symbol, finds it in the solidarity of the social group — society itself becomes for him the real object of religious veneration. More familiar, possibly, is Max Weber's thesis in *The Protestant Ethic and the Spirit of Capitalism,* in which he states that the religious philosophies of different civilizations reflect the socially sanctioned values and goals in their secular life. It is not surprising that such propositions and conclusions ill-accord with the beliefs of those who seek to discover Divine truth and revelation as the basis of religious belief and that the psychology and sociology of religion have been the concern of the social scientists rather than of the churchmen. From the standpoint of the library classifier, it must be admitted that such studies of religion are frequently placed in the Dewey 300's rather than in the 200's as a more accurate reflection of the author's intention and probable reader interest. With the subject matter of religion a part of the scholarship of the social sciences, we have an example of the need for wider knowledge even among the religious specialists.

Contemporary writing in the field of religion more and more utilizes the *methods* of all the disciplines to cast light on the development of religions, the progress of church history, and the meaning of the Scriptures. Biblical theology is definitely established as a historical science, and higher criticism is firmly. entrenched as a legitimate study in religious schools which formerly opposed it as heretical. Christianity is now seen as a movement within history, not as an isolated phenomenon unrelated to the time, place, and events which surrounded it. The Gospels are seen as a product of that movement which reflects these conditioning factors. Skepticism, agnosticism, and the questioning attitude in writers about religion no longer lead to ostracism, denunciation, or death; they are an accepted part of the modern temper in the field of religion as well as in other fields of men's concerns. Questionnaire studies were ultilized as early as 1899[4] to obtain quantitative data about conversion experiences. The findings of the anthropologists, psychologists, biologists, geologists, and many others whose fields would seem remote from the area of religion are utilized by students of religion to clarify, to explain, and — sometimes — to

---

[4]E. D. Starbuck, *The Psychology of Religion.* (N. Y., Scribner, 1899).

support religious belief. Where formerly it was the scientist who was forced to defend himself on the grounds that his findings supported religious belief, it is the man of religion who now defends *himself* on the grounds that science verifies his revelations. The unity of science and religion is claimed in both instances, but the authority to which appeal is made has changed camps.

Yet a constant remains in religious writing by religionists: the conclusion is known in advance, and where scientific methods fail to turn up the desired answers, science is repudiated. For truly disinterested application of scientific method, one must turn to the other disciplines where religion is merely the object of investigation, and not the guiding principle.

THE "LITERARY" RELIGIONS

All of the so-called "higher" religions — those which continue today to exert an important influence over a large segment of the world's population — have two characteristics in common. All of them arose on the continent of Asia (Hinduism, Buddhism, Confucianism, Taoism, Zoroastrianism, Judaism, Christianity, Mohammedanism, and Sikhism), and all of them possess "holy" documents which are their basic authority.[5] Earlier, no-longer-living religions also had their literature — the *Code of Hammurabi,* the *Book of Ptah-Hotep* ("the oldest book in the world"), and the *Book of the Dead,* for example — upon which our knowledge of them depends. By the time civilization has reached the place where religious belief is written down and codified, it is in a relatively sophisticated and advanced stage. For a study of the really primitive religions we must rely on histories written later (the Bible itself discusses heathen beliefs and suggests, in Ecclesiasticus, a theory of the genesis of idolatry), or on the anthropological studies of contemporary primitives, as in Africa, Australia, and the Far North. Nevertheless, we can trace even through the written records of the major religions a growth and change in religious beliefs and concepts which provide enlightening historical insights. (Between the earliest books of the Old Testament, for example, and its later ones, the one God has developed from a purely tribal deity to a universal Father and a completely new ethical concept has entered: the jealous God of vengeance and wrath of the Pentateuch [the first five books] has become a God of justice and mercy in Amos and Hosea.) In addition, most of the controversies,

---

[5]Religions without a literature find little place in library collections of religious materials. In general they are represented only by anthropological studies which deal with religious practice as only one aspect of the total culture with which they are concerned.

discussions, and developments throughout the history of the individual religions have found their way into written records. A vast literature has accumulated covering the shifts in tradition, the changes in doctrine, the alteration of emphases which have marked the development of religious belief from the earliest times to the present.

No one library can attempt a complete documentation of the growth of religious tradition, but every library can acquire the basic books out of which this voluminous store of knowledge has developed. For Christianity and Judaism this sacred doctrine is contained in the group of books known as the Bible, and since so much of the literature of these two important religions is based upon these Scriptures — as commentary, interpretation, elaboration, retelling, refutation, or defense — a short history of the development of the Testaments should be useful for any librarian, however limited the collection of religious materials in his library may be.

THE JUDEO-CHRISTIAN BIBLE

Development and editions

Both Judaism and Christianity accept the sacred character of the Old Testament. To the Jews, however, it alone constitutes scripture; Judaism has never expanded its sacred canon beyond the text set in the second century A.D. When Christianity began as a cult within Judaism, it naturally based its teachings upon the Old Testament; but when Paul saw in Christian teaching not a vague heresy within the older religion but a way of salvation for all mankind, he added to it the books of the New Testament which relate the history of the Nazarene movement and expound the teachings of Jesus. Taken together, the Old and New Testaments present a roughly chronological narrative of the progressive development of Judeo-Christian ideas and ideals.

Despite its status as Holy Writ, the Bible as we know it today, both Old Testament and New, is the result of many revisions, interpretations, translations, and accretions. Different Christian sects disagree in their opinions on the authenticity of certain books, the order and numbering of the books, and the interpretations to be placed upon the words contained in them. Although contemporary scholarship has provided many insights which help to bring us closer to the probable sense of the original, the Bible has undergone many changes and alterations between the original text and the one we know.

As noted above, the text of the standard Hebrew Bible of today

was set, according to the evidence we have, by the second century
A.D. The greater part of this text of the Old Testament was produced about the fifth century B.C., but Scriptures continued to
appear through the production of the New Testament, and many of
these are included in the semi-canonical portion of the Bible called
the Apocrypha.

A special guild called the Masoretes (from Masorah, meaning
"tradition") was entrusted with the preservation of the text, and
every effort was made to keep it constant, as the word of God.
The original Hebrew, however, had no vowels and no separations
between words, which led to many bitter controversies over meaning and interpretations. The Masoretic text, therefore, added linguistic aids and divided the original into books and verses, so that
even this carefully guarded text has undergone interpretations and
revision which weaken its claim to absolute authenticity.

The dispersion of the Jews to various communities brought
biblical translations from the Hebrew to the language of the country. The first translation into Greek, for example, was made by
the Jews of Alexandria, and is known as the Septuagint, or LXX.
This translation was accepted by the Hebrew community for a
while, but exegetical controversies finally led to its condemnation
and to the making of other translations. In the Christian Church,
on the other hand, the Septuagint became the basic text. All early
translations outside the Jewish community were made from it, and
it is still the authentic version in the Greek Orthodox Church.

Meanwhile the new book called the New Testament entered the
domain of Holy Writ. It is a collection of writings by many hands
over a considerable period of time and details the life of Jesus and
the rise of the Christian religion. Since it so clearly is the product
of so many writers, the New Testament presented the church with
the problem of establishing authoritative canon. As early as 382,
a synod drew up a list of canonical books; in the fifth century, Pope
Gelasius ratified the list; and finally in 692 formal unanimity was
established for the Christian world in this matter by the Quinsex-
tine Council.

The New Testament thus established contains the four Gospels
of Mark, Matthew, Luke, and John; a Book of Acts which related
the history of the Nazarene movement; various Epistles written by
Paul and others; and a book of apocalyptic revelations.

An important influence in settling the New Testament canon at
the Synod in 382 was the Church Father, Jerome, whose Latin
translation of the whole Bible from the Hebrew rather than from
the Septuagint or other translations gradually came to be accepted
as the exclusive text of the Church. This version, known as the
Vulgate, was declared by the Council of Trent in the sixteenth

century to be the authentic Bible for public reading, disputation, and preaching. It is not, however, the text as originally set down by Jerome, for corruptions crept into it as it was transmitted from generation to generation, and revisions were made several times. The official edition of the Catholic Church today is that translation of the Vulgate made by Clement VIII in 1592, called the Clementine Edition.

The Protestant revolt naturally led to new translations of the Bible to repudiate translations made within the Church and to make vernacular editions available to Protestants who could not read Latin. Martin Luther's translation was completed in 1534. Wyclif and his followers, basing their translation on the Vulgate, produced the first complete rendering of the Bible into English. William Tyndale's translation utilized Hebrew and Greek texts as well as the Vulgate. Miles Coverdale's translation was the first to separate the noncanonical books into a unit of Apocrypha. The "Great Bible" of 1539 was the first authorized English translation, but continued efforts were made to make new and better translations. In 1611 the edition we now know as the Authorized Version, or the King James Version, was completed and published, and the beauty of its language has established it as one of the great works of English literature, quite apart from its standing as religious canon.

The talk of further revisions did not end with the King James Version, however. In 1870 the Convocation of Canterbury appointed a committee to undertake a revision to be done by separate groups of scholars for the Old and New Testaments, with assistance from American scholars. This Revised Version came out in parts: the New Testament in 1881, the Old Testament in 1884, and the Apocrypha in 1895, and is the most generally used version in England. The committee formed in this country to assist in the revision continued to work after its publication and in 1901 published the American Standard Version which is the version most easily available and widely used in this country.

In 1928, a committee of fifteen scholars was appointed by the International Council of Religious Education to revise the Old and New Testaments in the light of the discovery of much additional manuscript material, Greek papyri, and papyrus fragments contemporary with the New Testament itself. In 1946, the committee's translation of the New Testament, called the Revised Standard Version, appeared, and the Revised Standard Version of the complete Bible was published in 1952. The then newly discovered documents used in this translation throw light on the meanings of Greek words and phrases as they were used at the time of Jesus, and this revision is considered a triumph of modern biblical knowledge in its fidelity to the sense of the original Greek.

The above story of English translations of the Bible is primarily the story of the Protestant tradition. The great Catholic translation of the Old Testament was undertaken at Douai and of the New
Testament at Reims; the complete work, known as the Rhemes and
Douay Version (1635) was revised by Dr. Challoner in 1749-50 and
is the revision, known as the Douay Bible, which is used today by
Catholics in English-speaking countries. Recent translations or
revisions in the Catholic tradition include those of Monsignor Knox,
whose New Testament was published in 1945 and Old Testament in
1948, and that of the Catholic Biblical Association of America,
sponsored by the Episcopal Committee of the Confraternity of
Christian Doctrine.

Differences among the editions

This outline of the development of the various editions and
versions of the Bible has been included because some understanding of the differences in the editions will clarify the need for the
several versions in a good library collection. Certain of the Old
Testament books, which are part of Catholic canon, are not accepted by the Protestant Church. These books, known as the Apocrypha, are printed under that title in the King James Version, and
as a separate book in the Revised Version. In the Douay Bible they
are printed as part of the regular Old Testament and are not designated as apocryphal in any way. Certain books, which are not
accepted as canonical by either the Catholic or Protestant Churches,
are available only in the Protestant Apocrypha, since the Douay
Bible omits them completely and does not recognize an Apocrypha.
The number of the books in the Old Testament also differs in the
Protestant, Catholic, and Jewish versions: there are thirty-nine
books in the Jewish and Protestant versions of the Old Testament;
forty-six in the Douay. This means that there are different names
for the books and that the divisions of the books are not always
identical. The order of the thirty-nine books in the Protestant and
Jewish versions also varies. For example, the Book of Ruth follows Judges in the Protestant version; in the Jewish version it
follows the Song of Songs (called the Song of Solomon in the Protestant Bible), and similar variations occur among several other
books in the two canons. The Jewish version, of course, does not
include the New Testament.

Library selection of editions

This short summary of differences among Bibles, simplified
though it is, reveals the problem of selection of Bible editions by

libraries. Even the small general library, used only by laymen without scholarly motivation, will find it necessary to supply several different versions, and the librarian must be aware of the inclusions and omissions represented by each. The King James and the Douay versions, the Revised Version based on the King James, the Revised Standard Version, and the Jewish Version are essential, as representing the standard texts accepted by the three major religious groups in the United States. In addition, the librarian should consider the needs of his particular community which might be served by such special editions as those in basic English, the "American Translation" by Goodspeed, the several "shorter" Bibles, and the *Bible Designed To Be Read as Living Literature*. In the scholarly library, the many versions and revisions and the early Greek, Latin, and Hebrew texts will be essential.

All of these editions are *translations* of the basic text. The problem of selection of story versions based on the Bible and of retold stories and tales from the Bible, both for children and adults, will be considered later as part of the total problem of popularization in the field of religious literature. Even in the realm of translations (not adaptations or retellings), judgment must be exercised by the librarian. Many modern English versions of the Bible exist which attempt to translate the Scriptures into the language of the common man, and the librarian's desire to reach a wider audience should be tempered by a sensitivity to the literary quality of the means. While it is true that much of the language used in standard translations of the Bible is archaic and may lead to misunderstanding and confusion, the librarian should consider seriously whether he is justified in accepting editions which include such renderings as "The Lord is my shepherd I should worry" or the translation of the Garden of Eden as "Eden Park."

The apocryphal writings should be represented in any basic collection of religious materials. As has been pointed out in the history of the development of the canon, not all versions of the Bible include it, nor do all denominations designate the same materials as apocryphal. The Douay version includes books which the Protestants consider apocryphal, but they are not designated as Apocrypha in the Douay, since they are part of Catholic canon. On the other hand the King James is the only standard Protestant version of the Bible which includes the apocryphal writings in its single volume. There are at present separate editions of the Apocrypha (in the Oxford World's Classics series; in the Everyman editions, and many others) which might well need representation on the library shelves in addition to the Bible versions which include it.

Bible publishers

For the librarian charged with the responsibility of selecting, ordering, supplementing, or replacing editions of the Bible in his collection, a knowledge of the Bible publishers and their specializations is essential. A. J. Holman Company is the oldest Bible publishing house in America, and carries Bibles of all kinds, but there are special editions and special kinds of Bibles for which other publishers are noted. Benziger Brothers, for example, are publishers of the Douay Bible; P. J. Kenedy and Sons, of Roman Catholic Bibles of all kinds; the Jewish Publication Society, of the Jewish Version. Thomas Nelson and Sons are the authorized trade publishers of the American Revised Version and the Revised Standard Version. The University of Chicago Press is notable for the Goodspeed translations in modern English and for shorter Bibles. The American Bible Society is the best source for Bibles in foreign languages of all kinds — not merely in the familiar European languages, but in such tongues and inventions as Choctaw, Esperanto, etc. Where format is a consideration, librarians should be aware of such specializations as those of the Oxford University Press, with its opaque Indian paper; the John C. Winston Company, with its "self-pronouncing," large-type Bibles, with passages marked in different colors (red for salvation, green for the Holy Spirit, etc.); and the World Publishing Company, with its teachers' and readers' reference Bibles.

Reference Aids to the Bible

Because of the Bible's importance in the fields of literature and history, as well as in the field of religion, an important reference literature has grown up around it. Quite apart from the general tools of reference in the field of religion, there is a group of volumes concerned solely with the Bible which forms a basic core for any reference collection, whether general or special.

One of the best known and most widely used of such tools is the concordance. A concordance is an alphabetical index of principal words in partial contexts, showing the places where the words occur in their full contexts. Concordances may exist for any literature — there are concordances to Shakespeare, Wordsworth, and many other writers, for example — but "Bible" is generally understood when the term "concordance" is used. Bible concordances differ in many features, and should be known for their individual advantages and limitations. One concordance may differ from another in completeness, in the version of the Bible concorded, or in the inclusion or exclusion of the books of the Apocrypha, and such variations may require the library to provide more than one in order to meet the several kinds of demand which a concordance serves.

One of the most famous of Bible concordances is that of Alexander Cruden, *A Complete Concordance to the Old and New Testaments*. Originally compiled in 1737, it has been completely revised and frequently re-edited. All editions have at least two alphabets: one for common words and one for proper names; and earlier editions devoted a third alphabet to analysis of the Apocrypha. Robert Young's *Analytical Concordance to the Bible* is the most comprehensive, giving the various shades of meaning of related words represented in the English by one word and the original Hebrew or Greek for them. James Strong's *Exhaustive Concordance of the Bible* is limited to the canonical books of the Old and New Testaments, but provides a comparative concordance of the Authorized and Revised Versions. Thompson and Stock's Concordance is for the Douay Bible; J. B. R. Walker's is based on the Authorized Version; M. C. Hazard's concordance, published by Nelson, is to the American Standard Version. *The Oxford Cyclopedic Concordance,* published in a new edition in 1947, is a concordance and Bible dictionary combined.

A Bible dictionary differs from a concordance in that it defines instead of locating words and includes many words which are not in the Bible itself although related to Bible concepts and subjects. The leading Bible dictionaries are the *Westminster,* edited by John D. Davis and Henry S. Gehman; the one-volume dictionary compiled by James Hastings; and the cooperative work of M. W. Jacobus, A. C. Zenos, and E. E. Nourse. All of these dictionaries are based on scholarly research in biblical history, geography, archaeology, and philology and are reliable and accurate. The Hastings is perhaps the most popular, the *Westminster* the broadest in scope, and the Jacobus the most scholarly.

Other reference aids to the Bible include historical atlases, like the *Westminister Historical Atlas to the Bible,* which contains maps and text incorporating the findings of recent archaeological and geographical research in the Near East; the Millers' *Encyclopedia of Bible Life,* an informal encyclopedia dealing with social and economic conditions in the early Christian era; Frank S. Mead's *Who's Who in the Bible;* and Burton Stevenson's *The Home Book of Bible Quotations*, which gives complete quotations by subject.

Books Based on the Bible

Although it is the world's best seller — or rather, *because* it is the world's best seller — the Bible is not a major item in library circulation, even in the circulation figures of the religious book collection. Its major use in the library is as a reference tool — a basic source book in its field. Of much greater importance, in circulation terms, are the books which use the Bible as a point of departure, either as the subject matter of a new book designed to clarify and interpret the Sacred Book, as inspiration for a book on an entirely different subject, or as source material for elaboration and adaptation.

Adaptations of the Bible stories themselves are the most closely allied to the original source and are always a popular form of religious publication. Bible stories retold for children will be discussed later, but the retelling technique is not limited to juvenile literature. The modernization of the language, the elaboration of details, and a general simplification of the concepts (usually accomplished in the case of the Bible by expansion of the narrative rather than its contraction) are the characteristics of this approach. Fulton Oursler's *The Greatest Story Ever Told,* a top best seller in 1949-50, is typical of this kind of presentation, frankly setting out to popularize the New Testament story by injecting into it the kinds of appeals which have proved effective in winning audiences for nonreligious literature. The depths to which such treatment can descend were illustrated by the newspaper serialization of the Oursler book (repeated twice in one year by popular demand) in its use of the standard journalistic headline technique: RIOTS IN GALILEE!; AGED, DYING CRAWL TO LOOK AT JESUS; or JOSEPH KEEPS FAITH IN MARY, with subheads: "Only Her Word," and "Very Curious." This illustrates in a startling way the manner in which the dramatic qualities inherent in the biblical narrative are explicitly emphasized in such popularizations. In addition, many details are introduced to fill out the simple scriptural story to make certain that no point will be lost and to make the whole approach more closely that of the modern cinema or historical novel pattern.

This expansion of the spare details into full-scale treatment is characteristic, too, of the biographical studies of biblical characters. In the scholarly reconstructions of the life of Jesus, for example, every attempt is made to establish authentic social, economic, and political background out of the oblique references in the Gospels and to fill out the terse biblical account with details supplied by historians, anthropologists, philologists and others. Also characteristic of scholarship in religious biography is the attempt to understand the psychology of the subject; to apply the data of the latest psychological research to illumine the motives, drives, and personality of the biographee. Renan's famous *Life of*

Jesus is important as an early example of the serious, if romantic, attempt to fill out the human attributes of Jesus as a man. Popular biography follows the same pattern, but does not always restrict its conclusions to logical inferences from a strictly controlled investigation. A book like *The Man Nobody Knows* by Bruce Barton is unfortunately fairly typical of some popular treatments which succeed, without scholarly basis, dignity of manner, or depth of insight, in vulgarizing and degrading the original story. It is interesting to note how even the best of the "modernizations" tend to recreate Jesus in terms of the ideals of the time in which the biography is written. The Jesus of the eighteenth-century rationalists was the perfect man of reason and common sense; the Jesus of the nineteenth century is a typical romantic. Albert Schweitzer's *The Quest of the Historical Jesus* is a brilliant account of the attempts of the nineteenth-century scholars to interpret the teachings of Jesus in the terms of the "liberal" ideas of religion current in their own time. Mr. Barton's Jesus becomes, following this pattern, the hard-hitting, go-getting advertising executive. The *mot* ascribed to Voltaire well describes much of this literature: "God created man in His own image, and man has been returning the compliment ever since."

Bible scholarship is concerned also with the history of the composition of the Sacred Book. Closely allied to the study of its historical period, the study of biblical origins sees the Bible arising out of the times, reflecting its surroundings and conditions, and both affecting and being affected by the "spirit of the age" of its composition. Mention has already been made of the philological studies which led to the recognition of multiple authorship and to the dating of individual books. A popular literature now exists which attempts to make available to the general reader the findings of this scholarship and to assist in the appreciation and understanding of the Bible itself. Such studies as William C. Bowers' *The Living Bible* or Edgar J. Goodspeed's *The Story of the Bible* are excellent examples of scholarship made readable in this field. From such studies it is but a short step to the commentaries and interpretations of the Bible which attempt not merely to retell the stories but to reach their inner meanings. Through the study of the historical and cultural events of biblical times and a knowledge of the composition of the several books, the modern reader can come to a clearer understanding of the meaning of the biblical narrative and its implications. In Mary Ellen Chase's *The Bible and the Common Reader* and Goodspeed's *How To Read the Bible* the layman finds a combination of sound scholarship and charm of manner that leads to a greater appreciation of the Bible in personal terms.

Modern biblical criticism and interpretation emphasize the popular, vernacular appeal of the language, the literary character of the writing, the development of religious thought through the succeeding books, and the comparison of biblical precepts with those contained in other "bibles" like the Koran. Parallel with the literature of higher criticism there has always been a resistance group which attempts to stand firm against what seems to them to be the scientific onslaughts against traditional faith. The early rationalists were able to accept miracles and the supernatural, and succeeding writers have often continued to stand on this ground and to repudiate nonmiraculous explanations of the events described in Scripture. The Divine inspiration of the Bible is the keynote of this school of thought, which defends the inspiration theory on the grounds of the majesty of the doctrine itself; the purity, simplicity, and dignity of the style which ill-accords with the known illiteracy of its human writers; the antiquity of the books and the failure of their enemies to destroy them; the prophetic oracles, the testimony of martyrs, and the attested miracles. Not all of these arguments are used by all defenders of Bible inspiration; there is a slow but growing tendency for such writers to accept scientific findings but to reconcile their acceptance with continued faith. Henry S. Nash's *History of New Testament Criticism*, for example, devotes the major portion of the text to an apology for his use of the scientific method and ends by finding higher criticism itself to be a product of Divine inspiration: " ... can we doubt that the Lord intended Germany to be the country which would lead in the higher criticism of the Book?"

Completely nonreligious studies of the Bible are also popular. The Bible as literature, for example, rather than as religious teaching or ethical guide is frequently the subject. Richard Moulton's *The Literary Study of the Bible* discusses the Bible in terms of the several literary forms which occur in it, and Miss Chase's book, mentioned above, includes a literary evaluation of the work as well as an historical and ethical one. The King James Version is studied as an example of English literary composition in college literature courses on the basis of its language and rhythm. The influence of the Bible on literature also has been the subject of study. Lawrence E. Nelson's *Our Roving Bible* traces the effect of the Bible on English literature, and Nathalie Wright's *Melville's Use of the Bible* is, as its title clearly suggests, a study of Melville and not primarily a study of the Bible at all. Similarly in the realm of the plastic arts, the Bible becomes incidental to the main interest of the study. A. E. Bailey's *Christ and His Gospels in Recent Art* is a book about art which is interested in the Bible only as the source of the subject matter in the paintings, and the work of Houston Hare and Guy Rowe entitled *In Our Image* is a book of portraits of biblical characters which subordinates the biblical text to the illustrations.

Fiction based on the Bible

The Bible has also provided the source material for much fictional writing, both good and bad. As in nonfiction, the biblical story may merely be retold, enlarging the details, clarifying motivations, and adding implications which may or may not be found in the original story. This is not necessarily bad: Milton's *Samson Agonistes* is an example of such a retelling which stands as literature in its own right. A much more prolific field of fictional creation, however, takes the Bible as a point of departure and adds a series of incidents to expand the original account and give new values to it. Sholom Asch's series, *The Nazarene, The Apostle,* and *Mary*, is such an elaboration, while Thomas Mann's Joseph series recreates the biblical stories in a new context which makes it more than an elaboration and closer to an independent creative work. Others take a biblical incident as only a small part of the book and weave a series of fictional incidents around it as did Lew Wallace in *Ben Hur*, or conjecture as to possibilities of subsequent action stemming from some incident in the Bible, as did Lloyd Douglas in *The Robe* or Manuel Komroff in his *Two Thieves*.

All of the examples noted here are directly dependent upon biblical accounts for their inspiration. Since any book dealing with a Christian theme must in one sense or another ultimately stem from biblical materials, the more remotely connected types of fiction and nonfiction will not be dealt with here. It is clear, however, that literature in almost every possible form has been created out of the incidents, the teachings, or the morality of the Bible. The common source does not, however, impose a common manner; materials as diverse as *Paradise Lost* and *The Green Pastures; In His Steps* and *Elmer Gantry; The Brothers Karamazov* and *Magnificent Obsession,* and writers from Augustine to Toynbee have, in one way or another, translated biblical precepts into other literary forms of great power and influence.

OTHER SCRIPTURES

The Judeo-Christian tradition is not the only one with a sacred book. Most of the so-called "higher" religions are "bible" religions in the sense that their teachings are embodied in writings which rank as divine revelation. The individual librarian must decide how large a collection he will have of scriptures of other faiths, basing his decision on the makeup of the community he serves, the use to which his religious books are put, and his definition of what his library should be. Certainly he should recognize the right of non-Christian and minority faiths to find their own sacred books in a public library. Where such faiths are not represented in his community, the librarian should recognize the needs of students of comparative religion and the requirements of a book collection which pretends to any degree of completeness.

The scriptures of other religions, many of them of greater antiquity than the Jewish and Christian Bible, deserve a place on the library's shelves as world literature. The sacred lore of Hinduism, which is the oldest living religion, goes back almost four thousand years in its collection of hymns, prayers, and liturgical formulas called the Vedas. The Sanskrit "veda" is the ancestor of the German word "wissen" and the English "wit," and roughly translates as "knowledge" in the sense of the kind of wisdom needed to propitiate the gods and succeed in life. The oldest and most important part of the vedic literature is the Rig Veda, which contains over 1000 hymns. With the growth of urbanization and a more settled existence, the Hindus began to develop a priestly caste and to demand a modernization of the Vedas to fit the changed conditions of their lives. Accordingly the first of the commentaries upon the Vedas, about 1000 B.C., interpreted the ancient literature in ritualistic terms and placed the key to salvation in the hands of the priests. These commentaries are called the Brahmanas, and as might be expected from our knowledge of the history of other religions, there soon arose a collection of philosophical commentaries to challenge the ritualistic concept and to put salvation in the hands of the individuals. This literature of the sages, as opposed to the priests, is called the Upanishads, of which over two hundred are supposed to be in existence, although they are little known to western scholars. The most famous piece of Hindu literature is the great epic of 100,000 verses called the Mahabharata, which contains within it the famous "Song of God," the Bhagavadgita. This famous ethical and religious dialogue has been called the "Gospel of Hinduism" and is the most widely known and translated of all Asiatic documents.

Four great religions arose in the sixth century B.C.: Buddhism, Confucianism, Taoism, and Zoroastrianism. Of these, the most virile and widespread is Buddhism. Starting originally as a Hindu sect founded by Siddharta Gotama who became known as the Buddha ("Enlightened One"), it was made a state religion in the third century B.C. By this time it had developed into two forms, each with its own scriptures. The earlier of these was written in Pali, which was the language of Gotama himself, and the other was

written in Sanskrit and Chinese. The Pali texts are primarily
ethical, teaching salvation through renunciation of the world and
treating Buddha as altogether human. The most famous of these
writings is the "Benares Sermon," which has been likened to the
Sermon on the Mount and has been called "a turning point in the
religious history of man." The scheme of salvation contained in
this sermon is completely devoid of superhuman elements; its key
lies in an inward change of heart, and it is unconcerned about the
soul, the gods, or an afterlife. The major collection of Buddha's
doctrine is contained in the Dhammapada, an anthology of 423 sayings in verse, which were probably written by many hands and at
different times.

The Sanskrit scriptures are less an ethical system and more
a way of worship. In them, Buddha is accepted as divine, and other
legends and gods are absorbed into the Buddha legend, making
them earlier manifestations of Buddha. The most renowned of the
Sanskrit writings is called the Surangama Sutra, which dates from
about the first century A.D. It sets out to prove that all perceptions are transient and illusory and that truth can be known only
through the intuition that comes from living a life of morality and
kindliness. Lin Yutang has called the work a combination of Locke's
Essay on Human Understanding and the Gospel According to St.
John.

The major scriptures of Confucianism are contained in the
Classics, compiled and edited by Confucius himself; the Sayings of
Confucius, which were compiled later by his disciples; and The
Great Learning, which is a capsule summary of his teachings that
has been the subject of endless subsequent annotation, commentary,
and debate by Chinese scholars. Two later writings have virtually
attained the status of sacred literature in Confucianism; one, called
The Golden Mean of Tsesze, is ascribed to the grandson of Confucius and is devoted to an exposition of the philosophy of the middle
way; and the other, the *Books of Mencius,* deals with a theory of
benevolent government based on the teachings of Confucius and
until recently was compulsory reading in Chinese schools for com-
mission to memory by all Chinese pupils. Like Buddha, Confucius
emphasizes proper conduct on earth rather than religious rites or
concern with life after death, and his Classics testify to his reverence for tradition and the past which is considered to be so characteristic of the Chinese attitude towards life.

Taoism arose out of the same period of chaos and political
upheaval that gave rise to Confucianism. Its history is similar to
that of many other religions: initiated by a sage (in this case,
Lao-Tze) as a philosophical system, it did not gain wide currency
until much later through the efforts of a follower (Chuang-Tze in

Taoism, Mencius in Confucianism, King Asoka in Buddhism, Paul in Christianity) who changed the philosophy into a regular religion, with Lao-Tze as chief god. The major scriptures of Taoism are the Tao Teh King of Lao-Tze, which is an entirely mystical advocacy of complete withdrawal from the world into a kind of primeval spirituality (a strain running through many philosophies and religions which has been called by Aldous Huxley "The Perennial Philosophy" in his book of that name); and thirty-three books by Chuang-Tze, which are a witty and entertaining exposition of the ideal of nonaction. Taoism recently has fallen into neglect, but the number of adherents is impossible to estimate, since nearly all Taoists are Confucianists and millions are Buddhists as well.

Zoroastrianism is the ancient religion of Persia. Although it barely numbers 100,000 adherents today, almost all of them among the Parsees of India, its importance lies in its great influence on Judaism, and through Judaism, on Christianity and Mohammedanism. Zoroaster (or Zarathustra) lived during the great age of the Persian Empire's domination of the civilized world, when Judea was part of that empire. The influence of the Zarathustran beliefs upon Judaism was later carried over into both Christianity and Mohammedanism, and from it stem such aspects of belief as heaven, hell, Satan, Armageddon, the final judgment, the general resurrection, and the messianic age. Most of the scriptures, called the Avesta, were destroyed during the Greek, Mohammedan, and Mongol invasions of Persia; the few fragments which remain consist of psalms, some of which probably date from the time of Zoroaster himself, a priestly code, and certain later apocalyptic writings.

To the devout Jew, the Talmud has a status of authority almost equal to that of the Old Testament. The Talmud (meaning "Teaching") is an interpretive extension of the first five books of the Old Testament, which are called the Pentateuch, or the Torah ("Law"). These first five books (attributed to Moses by the Jews but clearly proved to be of multiple and later authorship by subsequent scholarship) contain the Ten Commandments and are the most hallowed part of the Bible to orthodox Jews. After the Fall of Jerusalem (70 A.D.), the rabbis attempted to hold the homeless and nationless Jews together with rules through which they could continue to serve the Lord by obeying his commandments. Six hundred and thirteen ordinances were originally set down as guides to conduct based upon the Torah, but they were continually subjected to reinterpretation and dispute until a vast conglomeration of discrepant and repetitious legal decisions resulted. Around 200 A.D. these were digested into about 4000 legal decisions called the Mishna ("Repetitions"), but immediately upon the release of the Mishna, another body of interpretation came into being. This too was finally reduced to writing in 500 A.D., and called the Gemara ("Learning"). The combination of the Mishna and the Gemara forms the present Talmud.

Mohammedanism is the youngest of the world religions and almost the most widespread. Muhamed (570?-632) taught that he was the last and greatest of the prophets in the line beginning with Abraham; he therefore accepts the Old Testament as the historical basis for his claim. The Koran is the scripture of Mohammedanism, which is more accurately called "Islam," meaning "Surrender" (of the self to Allah). It is a body of rhymed prose taken down by the followers of Muhamed and gathered into a volume about twenty years after his death. Muhamed is looked on by the Western world as primarily a political leader, but the Koran includes not only civil and criminal laws, but theological passages emphasizing the Oneness and Righteousness of God, and many moral reforms as well.

Two other religions, while not world-wide in influence, are of importance to American communities — Mormonism and Christian Science, and their basic books may also require representation on the library's shelves. The scriptures of Mormonism are *The Book of Doctrine and Covenants;* the *Book of Mormon,* translated by Joseph Smith from a record "made by the prophets of ancient peoples who inhabited the American continent for centuries before and after the time of Christ";[6] and the revelations purportedly made by the Angel Moroni to Joseph Smith, contained in the volume, *The Pearl of Great Price.* Mary Baker Eddy's *Science and Health with a Key to the Scriptures* is not truly a scripture of Christian Science, but a textbook interpretation of its scriptures which are, as in other Christian denominations, the Old and New Testaments.

Sources for Other Scriptural Writings

Most of the major religious writings of the world have, at one time or another, been translated into English. Many of these translations, however, are scholarly works of philological interest which were made in the late nineteenth and early twentieth centuries when philological interest in comparative texts was at its height, and very few of them are still in print. Occasionally new editions of the more widely known of the religious writings are brought out; notable examples are the recent translation of the Bhagavadgita by Swami Prabhavananda and Christopher Isherwood,

---

[6] James F. Talmadge, *The Articles of Faith.* (Salt Lake City, The Deseret News, 1899), p. 255.

with an introduction by Aldous Huxley, and a translation of the
twelve most important Upanishads, translated by Swami Prabhavananda and Frederick Manchester. Usually the small library and
the general library will find that their needs are served adequately
by selections from the literature, or by certain useful series which
include most of the major works in this field. In the "Viking Port-
able Library" series, for example, the volume edited by Robert O.
Ballou called *The World Bible* contains selections from the sacred
writings of the several world religions; Selwyn G. Champion is the
compiler of a volume entitled *Eleven Religions and Their Prover-
bial Lore* which contains selections from the several scriptures;
Mirza A. Schram includes translations from the sacred books of
nine religions in *The Bible of Mankind,* and Lin Yutang's *The Wisdom of China and India* includes selections from the Rig Veda, the
literature of Taoism, the books of Mencius, and others, in addition
to much nonreligious literature of the two great Oriental countries.
Two of the most useful series in this connection are "The Wisdom
of the East" series, edited by L. Cranmer-Byng and Dr. S. A. Ko-
padia, which began publication in 1911 and is still issuing volumes;
and the very excellent *Sacred Books of the East,* translated by various oriental scholars, edited by F. Max Müller and published in
fifty volumes by the Oxford Press from 1879-1910. Most of the religious literature of the non-Judeo-Christian religions is contained
in the two series.

In a scholarly library where the study of comparative religion
is pursued, the provision of these additional scriptures is mandatory. Texts in the original language as well as complete scholarly
translations in Latin, German, and other languages as well as English will have to be supplied. In such cases, the library is merely
meeting the obvious needs of its "community." In general libraries, such needs will not appear so obvious. Many smaller communities will contain few, if any, members of the non-Judeo-
Christian faiths, and scholarly interest in comparative studies
will be limited. The very fact that such groups do not exist in
large numbers in the community should cause the library to consider its position as a repository of the world's knowledge. In
most communities, the library will be the only agency where such
materials could conceivably be found, and the librarian should
consider carefully his responsibility to have such materials available. There is probably a greater need for the library to represent
such hard-to-find important materials on its shelves than there is
for it to provide in many duplicate copies currently popular and
ephemeral titles which are also available in the local bookstore, in
the railroad station, at the newsstand, and in rental collections.

SELECTION OF RELIGIOUS BOOKS FOR THE LIBRARY

In the general public library, the average patron is a layman rather than a clergyman, his interests in religious materials are much less highly specialized, and his background is usually more limited. This does not mean that the public library has no need for the "practical" books, for clergymen are heavy users of library materials and — as community opinion leaders — an important segment of the library's clientele. What it does mean is that the extremely scholarly and specialized materials will be little used; that popular treatments will be in much greater demand; and that the public library cannot possibly assume the obligation to provide a well-rounded professional collection for the clergyman any more than it can for the lawyer or the doctor. Theological students do not form a major group among the users of the religious collection, even though students comprise a large segment of total users of most subject areas, mainly because religious schools and seminaries generally have their own libraries. The average patron will want simply written, emotionally satisfying works of general appeal, works that will console, convince, and support him in his already established beliefs. The most used items in the religious collection will be much like the most used items of general fiction — popular, talked-about, easy to read, and not too challenging to the general temper of belief. When the findings of scholarship are of general interest, they may have to be diluted through popularization before they can be made palatable.

Popularizations

Popularizations, per se, are not necessarily bad. Quite frequently the academic demands for detail, for explanation of methodology, and for specialized vocabulary impose a pedestrian presentation upon material which could readily, and without falsification, be presented in a much more readable fashion. The results of many scholarly investigations are of great interest to the average reader even though he has no interest in the research methods employed nor in the problems of search, control, and organization which fascinate the specialist. Recognizing this, many of the scholars themselves have rewritten their studies in terms more acceptable to the nonspecialist reader. The works of Edgar J. Goodspeed — *The Story of the Bible, How To Read the Bible,* etc. — are excellent examples of readability and general appeal which do not in any way destroy the scholarly accuracy of their information. In the area of comparative scriptures, the form and language of the original texts may prove too difficult, too unfamiliar, and too figurative for the

average reader, and too dependent upon a full understanding of
their historical context to be meaningful to the uninitiated in the
field. Popular discussions of these materials which will supply
the necessary glosses upon the scriptural text are therefore often
more informative than the original scriptures themselves. Such
popularizations as those of Lewis Browne in the field of comparative religion *(This Believing World, The World's Great Scriptures)*
make highly interesting reading for the average man while serving
an admirable ethical purpose in their lessons of tolerance and
understanding. Certainly the librarian is justified in opening his
shelves to popularizations which broaden the minds and increase
the knowledge of many of his patrons who, without them, would not
have access to such educational forces at all.

The difficulty lies in determining which popularizations actually accomplish these noble purposes and which so badly over-
simplify or distort the material as to be blocks rather than aids to
learning. To discover the characteristics of the popularization
which twist and impoverish the facts, one must compare the popular
treatment with the best of recent research on the same subject. This
is not always possible for the librarian who may have neither expert knowledge of the field, access to the scholarship, nor the time
to compare texts. In order to analyze some of the characteristics
of popularization in the field of religious writing, a small research
project was undertaken by a recent class in the Graduate Library
School in which several admittedly popular and best-selling discussions of comparative religion were compared with the accepted
scholarship concerning several religious histories. By identifying
the characteristics of the genre "popularization," it was hoped
that criteria might be established which could be applied to any
subject matter. It was found that the popular books under investigation were marked by certain weaknesses, some of which are peculiar to the special subject field itself, and some of which seem
to be inherent in the form, no matter what its subject matter.

Generalizing from the categories devised in this analysis, we
can draw attention to the following characteristics which mark the
transition from scholarly research to popularized presentation:

1. *A biased attitude.* In the field of religion this manifests
itself often in an attitude of smug superiority towards other beliefs
and practices and in a tone of derision or derogation wherever
non-Christian religions are described. The result is a presentation which stacks the evidence (either in overt statement or by im-
plication through stylistic treatment) in favor of the Judeo-Christian tradition. This kind of editorializing is probably more
outspoken in the religious field than in others because of the
emotional involvement of the writers in the subject matter, but

it is this failure to maintain objectivity that the scholars condemn in popularizations in general.

2. *Oversimplification.* The popularization is, by definition, a simplification of scholarly presentation; the danger lies in *over-*simplification which goes beyond clarification to misrepresentation. The tendency to reduce the complicating factors in order to avoid confusing the reader often results in a false picture which misinforms him instead. Such oversimplification is apparently based upon the belief that the nonspecialist reader wishes to have all his doubts resolved rather than to have additional questions raised. But in subject areas where questions still exist, the elimination of questions is a distortion of fact.

3. *Omission of wider implications.* One of the results of oversimplification is the single-line thematic development which eliminates all aspects of the problem not pertinent to a predetermined theme. The economic, social, and political implications of the study, for example, may be minimized or omitted in a religious history in order to maintain the emphasis upon the one aspect of the study. If the reader wants a book on religion, religion is what he gets, and no extraneous material is admitted which will divert his attention, even though a knowledge of these relationships is essential to a full understanding of the subject.

4. *Manipulation of the material.* The attempt to give artistic unity to the presentation through the adherence to some single-line plan of development often leads the popularizer to rearrange his materials to give the "best" total effect. This differs from the scholarly use of a guiding hypothesis in that true scholarship uses the evidence gathered to discover *whether the hypothesis is correct,* while the unscholarly technique uses the evidence to *demonstrate the correctness of the hypothesis.* The latter method reaches its conclusions before the evidence is in, and leads frequently to an arrangement of the facts as they "ought" to be rather than as they are.

5. *Dogmatic statements.* The material can be simplified also through the use of an absolute answer which ignores the uncertainty, confusion, and disagreement among the "known facts." Where the scholarship qualifies its statements with "it seems" or "it would appear," the popularization often says merely that "it is." While the scholars also take stands and minimize the cogency of arguments with which they disagree, they generally present their own stand as the "best" in an admitted argument, whereas the popularization minimizes the existence of disagreement and presents its stand as indubitable truth.

6. *"Dramatic" presentation.* Popularizations show a tendency to select the more sensational and lurid incidents which, even

though they may be true, are not necessarily representative of the total picture. In the presentation of primitive religions, for example, blood sacrifices are more colorful and striking than periods of solemn meditation, and the former are much more likely to be emphasized in a popular treatment. Relationships, motives, and cause and effect are often rearranged, too, to fit a dramatic situation rather than to conform to less theatrically-effective facts and to create a dramatic unity rather than to reflect the patternless complexity of reality.

7. *Biographical emphasis.* Because personalities are considered to be of more general interest than things or ideas, many popularizations interpret the material in terms of personalities, emphasizing aberrant behavior or colorful individual quirks above the play of social forces and historical movements. A popular history of religions is usually the story of the individual leaders rather than an analysis of the social and ethical needs which the religious systems satisfied.

8. *Unsubstantiated "insights."* One of the weaknesses of the biographical approach is that it leads the writer to an omniscient analysis of motivations and drives without sufficient evidence. Popular biographers frequently enter the minds of their subjects, detailing the whisperings of conscience and the struggles of the soul as though they were fact rather than conjecture. To deal with historical figures as though they were fictional creations is to run the risk of finishing with fictional creations.

Popularization, as can be seen from this list, is mainly a matter of style and treatment. Very few errors of fact were found by the analysis upon which this list is based; the discrepancies between the popular and the scholarly book arise mainly out of the technique of presentation and the manner of interpretation. It was not so much that the popular treatment did not tell the truth in so far as it is known but that it told only a part of the truth, or that it told the truth in such a way as to lead to distorted impressions and false implications, or that it presented what *may* be true as though it were subject to no doubts. An awareness of these characteristics makes possible an evaluation of popular presentations of fields of knowledge in which the librarian is not an expert. If objectivity is absent, if substantiating evidence is lacking, if all the factors fall too neatly into a predetermined pattern with no loose ends, the librarian has fair presumptive evidence that a check against more scholarly reports is required to establish the reliability of the account.

If the librarian is committed to a policy of giving the public what it wants in so far as that is at all possible, as many public libraries do, he will have to accept many popular treatments of religious material that can lay little claim to distinction on literary, scholarly, or educational grounds. If, on the other hand, he decides to fix a qualitative minimum beneath which he will not select popularizations no matter what the demand, he creates the very difficult problem for himself of establishing some reliable standards and criteria. This is particularly difficult in the fields of the humanities, and especially in religion, because arbitrary rules of scientific accuracy and scrupulous objectivity cannot always be applied to all fields of writing in this area.

Standards will often have to be stated in terms of subjective judgment and the standard of literary excellence is one of these. Fairly high standards of readability and style should be applied to the books in this field, but the evaluation of style is often dependent upon individual taste rather than established rules, and nowhere is individual preference a less reliable gauge than in cases where the evaluator has strong personal convictions and emotional ties. Sincerity of presentation should be another criterion, but sincerity is another characteristic that cannot be determined by objective measures. And even truth, which ought to be an absolute if it is to be used as a yardstick, is as yet a moot matter in the religious field.

Originality — of viewpoint or of presentation — should probably also be considered in the selection of popular works in this field, but it introduces additional problems concerning the library's aims and objectives. To what extent should the library supply the unfamiliar rather than the familiar? To what extent should the library excite rather than soothe, disturb rather than reassure, move to an attitude of questioning rather than of acceptance? Certainly the librarian will wish to supplement the "popular" titles with material of more lasting quality whenever possible. The library is an educational institution by definition and proud boast, and some of the popularizations it feels called upon to stock cannot be designated "educational" by the wildest stretch of the meaning. Many educational books are educational precisely because they do disturb and shock. The traditional classics are often writings which in their day were considered radical and even heretical. Yet in matters of faith the usual rational arguments have little effect, and the field of religion is one of the most difficult in which to introduce the new and the unconventional, even though the lessons of history testify to their value. Against the salutary effects claimed for thought-provoking materials, the librarian must weigh the bad effects which may result from alienating many of the library's staunchest supporters.

Polemic Literature

Selection becomes a particularly difficult question in relation to the polemical literature which forms such a large part of religious writing. Here certain standards of objectivity and disinterestedness should be applied. The librarian, since the library does not act as advocate of one sect or creed or set of beliefs against another, is obligated to weigh carefully the apologetic and censorious literature which constantly comes to his attention. When titles in this field are selected, they should satisfy stringent standards of truth; there should be no distortions or misrepresentations of fact which do not arise out of legitimate error; there should be no deliberate attacks on emotional grounds without substantiating data. This is extremely important, not only because of the dangerous effects of such inflammatory material upon the community, but also because those groups who are under attack will naturally seek an explanation of the library's stand. Its reasons should be valid ones.

This is not merely a hypothetical situation presented to illustrate a pedagogic point. The problem arises constantly in the library world, and librarians in the field are constantly called upon to define and justify their position. In 1929, Edwin Franden Dakin's biography of Mary Baker Eddy was denounced by Christian Science groups, and pressure was brought to bear on libraries to remove it from their shelves. In 1948, a series of articles about the Catholic Church in the *Nation* magazine resulted in the banning of the magazine from New York school libraries. In 1949, Paul Blanshard's book based on these articles, *American Freedom and Catholic Power,* was bitterly denounced by Catholic groups and repudiated in many articles and in other books. After half a century, the *Protocols of the Learned Elders of Zion* are still the center of controversy in many libraries.

That the latter were proved conclusively to be spurious forgeries circulated with the intent to incite anti-Semitic sentiment is a fact that should be seriously weighed by the librarian who is faced with the problem of representing them on his shelves. In this instance there is a clear-cut case of scientific accuracy versus deliberate misrepresentation. The other cases are not yet quite so clear. Blanshard's book and articles appear to be documented, but footnotes do not necessarily insure reliability, and the reviewers, even in the non-Catholic media, have not been unanimously convinced of their authenticity. The biography of Mrs. Eddy was a serious attempt to get at fact rather than to attack a group, but again the group concerned denied the truth of the account and posed a problem for the library selector. Great care should be taken by the librarian that personal biases do not enter into such selection and

that his own involvement on one side or the other in the controversy
does not blind him to distortions and misrepresentations which happen to support a personal prejudice. While the librarian may legiti-
mately take a stand supporting factual material which happens not
to please all of his patrons, he does have the obligation to demand
certain standards of accuracy and sincerity in such publications.

Unfortunately, the practical politics of functioning successfully
in one's own community forces many librarians to make compromises with these ideals. A predominantly Catholic community
might well withdraw its financial support from a local library which
stocked the Blanshard book over the protests of certain influential
civic leaders, for example, just as the Christian Science groups
threatened to do in the case of the Dakin biography. Whether such
pressures have ever successfully curtailed a library's budget or
cost a librarian his job has never been proven, but most public
librarians hesitate to play the part of guinea pig in a test case.
Book selection quite frequently consists in anticipating unfavorable
reactions and avoiding them by negative selection. Thus the report
in the *Library Journal* on the Blanshard volume reads:

> Recommended, but local decisions after careful reading against
> consideration of local temper required.

The accuracy or truth of a publication, it seems, is not the only
criterion which the practicing librarian applies in selection. While
he might deny that his desire to please special interests could ever
force him to suppress truth, his compliance with outside dictation
in such matters often seems susceptible to such an interpretation.

But jesting Pilate's question still cries for an answer. The
ideal of truth makes a fine-sounding abstraction in general discussion, but it is not always so readily defined and identified as one
could wish. In the instances cited above, which is the truth: the
Blanshard book or the books that refute it? The Dakin biography
or the official rebuttals from the Christian Scientists themselves?
The librarian can only apply his tests for objectivity, documentation, and sincerity and weigh the facts as he knows them. There is
no guarantee that to demonstrate he is supporting truth will necessarily win the librarian favor with the groups to whom the particular truth is distasteful.

Another consideration must be recognized. In areas of tension
and high feeling — and the area of religious belief has always been
one of these — the truth may sometimes be more than distasteful,
it may well prove dangerous and harmful. In communities where
anti-Semitism is prevalent, a true statement about a single "bad"
Jew may result in disorders which harm many of the innocent; in

anti-Catholic communities, a true report of a single corrupt act by a Catholic may incite violence and destruction. In weighing the truth of a book, the librarian should take into account whether it is the whole truth, whether it is presented in such a way as to foster misinterpretation, and whether the readers who will use it are capable of reading it correctly and using it constructively. The library's neutrality in religious matters does not absolve it from the responsibility to select, evaluate, and judge.

In selecting books in this area as in any other, the librarian will feel obliged constantly to refer to reviews and evaluations by others for assistance. For the scholarly works in the field, the reviews will appear mainly in the more scholarly journals — and often so much later than the book's publication as to be of little value at the time when the book should be purchased. The less specialized books are reviewed in the major general reviewing media, with occasional special issues devoted primarily to religious books and their comparative evaluation. The *Saturday Review* and the *Publishers' Weekly* both issue special "Religious Book" issues in February which provide a fairly comprehensive listing of the general books in the field, with specially selected lists for Lenten reading, and lists for different denominations. The Religious Book Committee of the American Library Association issues an annual list of "Fifty Leading Religious Books" in the September 1 issue of the *Library Journal.* Frequently, as illustrated in the review quoted for the Blanshard book, the reviews shift the responsibility to the librarian, forcing him to decide whether the book is suitable for his particular library.

The principle of "neutrality" is often invoked by the librarian to avoid making a decision in such cases. On the grounds that the library takes no sides and that the patron must make the ultimate decision, libraries frequently provide an equal number of books on both sides of a controversial religious question: exactly the same number of copies of the reply to Blanshard as of the Blanshard book itself. Or, in instances where no official reply is available, an equal number of pro-Catholic titles as of anti-Catholic titles. Such a procedure is only a minor salve to the librarian's conscience, however, and a very small contribution to broader understanding of issues. There is no way to guarantee that the balanced reading thus tacitly recommended will actually be done by the library's patrons; indeed, experience with reading habits leads one to anticipate either that the more sensational aspect of the question is the one most likely to attract wide readership, or that the argument closest to the reader's predisposition is the one that he will choose, ignoring or discrediting the arguments for any other point of view. To justify substandard materials on the grounds that they keep a balance in the collection is short-sighted and dangerous; actually, the library is disseminating — and giving its apparent approval to — materials which frequently have no place in the library. Such "balanced" selection in reality is a failure to select.

The librarian must be prepared to hear the label "censorship" applied to his policy of selection in this area. The word should not frighten him. If refusal to spend public funds for untruths, poor writing, irrational attacks, and unsubstantiated polemics be censorship, then the librarian has the right to censor. His position demands the exercise of his judgment in shaping the book collection, and the public which supports the library assumes that its personnel are qualified. Legitimate differences of opinion may arise in certain specific instances, but in most cases, the librarian's judgment, based upon specialized training, constant work with the materials, and familiarity with sources of information not available to the average layman, will probably be accepted. It should always be remembered that a few complaints are not necessarily the expression of public opinion, so that even if the librarian takes "demand" as his criterion, such pressures should not be given more weight than they deserve. Where these pressures do represent majority opinion, the librarian still has the responsibility of evaluating the worth of the requested materials to the book collection. Demands by patrons should be weighed, not in terms of the amount of noise made but of the merits of the case presented.

Religious Literature for Children

In the selection of religious literature for children, these considerations become of even greater importance. The child is much more susceptible to suggestion and influence; his opinions in matters of religious faith are not yet formulated; his emotional loyalty to predispositions is less, but his emotional susceptibility to new ideas is greater. Polemical literature therefore has little place in a collection of religious books for children; constructive ideas can be inculcated without the necessity, as there often is with adults, of destroying earlier notions and false beliefs. The library should carefully preserve its position of neutrality and avoid special pleading for one creed or sect. In recent years there has been an increasing emphasis upon the "liberal," comparative religion approach in children's literature: an attempt to point up the similarities in religious beliefs and the universality of religious concepts. Such titles as *One God: The Ways We Worship Him,* by Florence Mary Fitch, or *The Tree of Life,* stress the unity rather than the dissension that exists between religious denominations and ememphasize ethical principles above specific formulas and creeds.

The "children's literature" of an earlier day — like Foxe's
Book of Martyrs or Mrs. Mortimer's *The Peep of Day* — which
sought to frighten the child into conformity and to impress him
with the horrors of hell and the pain of punishment is no longer
acceptable. Modern religious literature for children attempts to
lead the child naturally along the lines of his own questions and his
own interests. It applies the latest findings of the child psychologists who see religious belief as part of a total experience and not
as an isolated good in itself to be sought without counting the cost
in other facets of the personality and adjustment. Religion is made
attractive and interesting, speaking to the child in his own language
of the things he wants to hear. A book of prayers designed especially for children, like Emilie E. Johnson's *A Little Book of
Prayers,* avoids the "if-I-should-die-before-I-wake" approach and
supplements original prayers with selected Bible verses which
serve to introduce the child easily to the poetry of the Sacred Book.

The established standards for selection of children's literature
in any field must also be applied in the field of religious writing.
Language that is suitable to the child's maturity level and vocabulary span; absence of condescension; suitable type and page size;
appropriate illustrations; and recognition of children's interests
should all be looked for in this area as they are in any other. Because of the need for simpler concepts and language suitable to the
child mind, a much better case can be made for the retelling of
biblical stories for children than for adults. Great care should
be taken to see that a high level of literary quality is maintained
in adaptations, for in this reading the child is forming his literary taste as well as his religious beliefs. The sense of the original should be retained too, so that the retelling leads the child
eventually to an appreciation and understanding of the original
rather than to a preference for the modified and diluted form of
the simplified version. The closer the adaptation can remain to
the original language and incident of the Bible, the better it serves
its broader, long-term purpose.

A good example of what can be done with retold Bible stories
for children is the book arranged and illustrated by Nancy Barnhart, *The Lord Is My Shepherd.* The familiar tales, from that of
the Garden of Eden to the story of Saul on the road to Damascus,
are told simply and briefly, with excerpts from the King James
Version introduced in appropriate places. The drawings which
illustrate the book were made in the Holy Land and are both decorative and authentic. The interest of the child is retained without
sacrifice of literary quality, authenticity, or inspirational values.

In addition to retold stories based upon the Bible, special
Bibles — like *A First Bible,* illustrated by Helen Sewell — are

designed to meet the child's particular needs and interests. For older children, *The Junior Bible* is a selection from the Goodspeed American translation which introduces the child to an adult Bible without plunging him too quickly into concepts that are beyond him.

The primitive and pre-Christian religions play a larger role in the children's department than they do in the adult section because children read the legendary tales as stories rather than as systems of belief, wherein they classify. The Greek, Roman, and Norse myths, legends of the American Indians, tales from the Mahabharata, and many other stories with religious significance are an essential part of literature and deserve a prominent place on the shelves of the children's collection for their literary value alone. Many excellent editions and adaptations from this literature exist, and general guides like the *Children's Catalog*, the *Standard Catalog for High School Libraries*, or May Hill Arbuthnot's *Children and Books* evaluate them with intelligence and discrimination.

Periodicals

Religious periodicals cover a range of interest and of quality almost as broad as that embraced by the book literature of the field. The 1956 edition of Ayer's *Directory of Newspapers and Periodicals* listed 1385 titles published in the United States and Canada under the category of "Religious Publications." This total includes newspapers as well as magazines and special subjects within the broad category, such as "The Bible," "Church Management and Supplies," "Zionist," etc. Ulrich's *Periodicals Directory,* a selected list of magazines only, listed 287 titles including foreign language periodicals under "Religion and Theology" in its 8th edition, 1956. These are publications of sufficient worth to demand consideration for purchase for any reasonably complete religious collection.

These magazines range in appeal from the learned journals to the frankly nonintellectual, popular type; from those intended for clergymen to those intended for laymen; from adult magazine to juvenile; and from narrowly denominational to broadly universal. Each of the individual denominations has at least one magazine of its own, and most of them have magazines which cover all of the types mentioned above. There are the *American Hebrew,* the *Catholic Record,* the *Christian Science Quarterly,* the *Lutheran Church Quarterly,* the *Mennonite Quarterly Review,* and the *Muslim World,* to mention but a few of the obvious denominational titles. An interesting phenomenon in the field of religious periodicals is presented by the magazines which are devoted to nonreligious subjects but which interpret them in the light of certain religious attitudes. The *Christian Century* for its Protestant viewpoint and *Commonweal* for its Catholic viewpoint are extremely valuable magazines in the general collection as well as in the religious one. The scholarly journals in the field compare favorably with the learned journals in any other discipline, often providing the first hearing for current research and scholarly debate. Titles like the American *Journal of Biblical Literature* or the *American Catholic Historical Society Records and Monographs;* the British *Hibbert Journal* or *Journal of Theological Studies;* the *Canadian Journal of Theology,* and many foreign language periodicals are limited in their appeal to only the most scholarly libraries, but they must certainly be represented there. Of the other extreme it is probably not necessary to speak. The standards set by the library for its book purchases should be as rigidly applied to periodical literature, and those which do not satisfy the requirements of literary quality, importance of content, or seriousness of purpose should be excluded.

Of the 1385 religious publications listed in the 1956 Ayer's, 62 are juvenile or Sunday school publications. In general the public library need not supply the Sunday school releases in its children's collection, but certain of the higher quality children's magazines may deserve representation. In reaching decisions concerning periodical subscriptions for the children's shelves, selective lists like Laura K. Martin's *Magazines for School Libraries* are extremely useful.

Gifts

A constant problem in all departments of the library, but particularly in the religious collection, is that of gifts and donations. Small sects, crackpot groups, and fringe denominations of all types are especially generous in their contributions to public library collections and especially vociferous in crying "discrimination" when their donations are refused. While it is true that the library does not assume responsibility for all opinions expressed in the volumes it contains and that many points of view are given a hearing with which the librarian himself does not agree, he cannot allow his collection to become top-heavy with badly written, low-quality minority reports. To lower standards because the material is free is a poor economy; the same literary and educational standards should apply to gift materials as to those which come out of the library's funds. The criterion should be the contribution of each title to the quality of the total collection and not merely the money saved in the particular transaction.

It becomes a nice exercise in diplomacy to refuse gifts without alienating the groups who offer them, and only a blanket rule against any donations can answer the accusation of discrimination. Many libraries do not wish to close the door on any and all gifts, for often these are a valuable source of worthwhile additions to the collection. Some compromises have been tried, with varying degrees of success. Librarians have tried to accept all gifts and then to hide in inaccessible stacks the items not meeting the standards of the general collection. The groups who disseminate such literature, however, are the ones most apt to check the library's disposition of their gifts, so that this technique has not proved particularly satisfactory. Other librarians have salved their consciences with a nameplate in the book which identifies the donor and explains the presence of certain substandard titles on the shelves; but this is of dubious value if the shelves become overbalanced with poor books. Other libraries try to refuse excessive donations of this kind of literature on the grounds of public demand, attempting to point out to the would-be donor that the proportions of each religious group in the community's total population should be reflected in the proportions of its literature on the shelves.

But demand is a dangerous guide to selection; first, because the library wishes to lead opinion to a certain extent, not merely to reflect all of the elements, good and bad, in the community; second, because demand can be manipulated too easily by pressure groups who can make it seem to exist where it does not. It is instructive to read the frank advice of Father James Keller in his book *You Can Change the World:*

> It might be well to point out ... that libraries make it a practice to order books which seem to be in demand — a fact of which many library users are not aware. If your library does not have a copy of a particular good book, you and your friends, with a Christopher purpose, can bring friendly pressure to bear upon the order department simply by putting in a "reserve" for it.

Such "demands," purporting to reflect a general interest but really reflecting only that of a particularly aggressive group, must be evaluated carefully if the librarian wishes to keep his collection representative of the needs of the entire community. The pressure group is a legitimate instrument of communication between the public and the librarian, but a book selection policy should provide also for the needs of those who are not so efficiently organized to make their wants known.

RELIGIOUS LIBRARIES IN THE UNITED STATES

Despite the importance of religion in the history of man and in his intellectual life and the large number of religious books published annually, religious literature is a minor part of the general library's circulation and use. Usually, nonfiction books in this field (the Dewey 200's) constitute about 2 to 3 per cent of the total annual circulation, and queries related to religion form a similar percentage of reference questions.[7] This is due, in part, to the fact that users of religious books purchase them for personal ownership. Certainly this is the case with the Bible, the world's number one best seller, but not a leading title in library circulation. A very real market exists for individual purchase of religious books which is proved by the existence of so many religious bookstores in every large community in addition to the general bookstores which also carry religious titles. Most of the major Christian sects support bookstores of their own. Catholic, Methodist, Presbyterian, Lutheran, and other specialized bookstores account for the continued sale of a large number of titles in this field, and for the continued publication of religious titles, both by general publishers and by special publishers for individual sects and creeds. The existence of parochial schools, seminaries, and other training institutions for those who go into the church as a profession also explains the small use made of general libraries by many users of religious materials. Special librarianship in the field of religion, therefore, has long been recognized as an important aspect of library activity.

The development pattern of formal theological libraries in America follows that of theological education, which may be roughly divided into three major eras. The earliest is that of theological training in the general college, such as Harvard. In the seventeenth century, while the colleges were not designed solely for ministerial preparation as is now commonly believed, Latin, Greek, and Hebrew were required; the college curriculum did emphasize theological subjects; and about half of the student body were ordained. In the second era, that of parsonage or tutorial preparation, aspirants to the ministry took instruction from successful pastors who offered to tutor them informally. The upset conditions during the French and Indian Wars and the Revolution tended to foster this unorganized kind of arrangement. The third era is that of seminary education. Although the Roman Catholics had had a seminary since 1791 at Baltimore, it was not until the early nineteenth century that

---

[7]Bernard Berelson, *The Library's Public.* (N. Y., Columbia Univ. Pr., 1949), pp. 57 and 75.

the Protestant seminaries began to appear. They arose at first
with the designation of some one minister as sole approved tutor,
around whom soon gathered an institution and a faculty.

Library development corresponded to the three eras. The
library of the early college was a collection of books, but their
housing was not thought of as part of the library concept. The theologians coming to America in colonial days brought their own
books with them, and these private collections only eventually became the nucleus of what was later to be the college library.
Yale's collection was begun in 1701, for example, by requiring
each of the brethren to donate one valuable book from his own
collection. In the second period — that of the tutorial system —
little reliance was placed upon books. The single shelf of volumes
owned by the teacher was the main source of textual material, and
no effort was made to centralize or develop the book collection.
The seminaries from the beginning, however, had separate rooms
devoted to the library and soon recognized the need for a separate
building to house their growing collections. The great number of
theological students who went to German institutions to study during
the nineteenth century opened the field of German publication to
American attention, and the importation of foreign works and the
purchase of complete libraries of deceased German professors
became of major importance in building the theological collections
in America. The emphasis on philological study and textual criticism of the Bible which characterizes American theological scholarship reflects the influence of the German theologians.

Separate religious libraries, as they exist today, are generally
of three types. In the first group are the libraries of theological
seminaries which are attached to larger educational institutions,
such as the Princeton Theological Seminary or the University of
Chicago Divinity School. The second group is composed of the
libraries belonging to seminaries which are not attached to any
other educational institution. The libraries of the General Theological Seminary in New York City, of the Jewish Theological
Seminary, or of the Pacific School of Religion in Berkeley are of
this type. The third group consists of completely independent libraries which are not attached to educational institutions. These
libraries follow the pattern of special libraries in other fields,
generally being maintained by publishers of religious materials or
by religious organizations and associations; the library of the
American Bible Society is an example in this category.

Each of the three types of libraries will make slightly different demands upon its librarian. In the theological seminary attached to a university or college, the librarian is likely to give
much more specialized and limited service than in the library of

an independent seminary. On a larger campus, the library collections and facilities of the rest of the school are available to the
theological students, and the librarian of the theological library
can concentrate solely on the specialized materials directly related
to his field. Most of the technical processes — acquisition, cataloging, classification, etc. — are handled by the central library in
many cases, with the theological library operating as a special
branch of the main system rather than as a separate institution.
The major duties of the branch librarian then are book selection in
the special field and reference service and special research for
the students and faculty. In such a position, subject knowledge is
much more important than a knowledge of library techniques.

In seminary libraries, the librarian is called upon to perform
many general library duties as well as the specialized ones in the
subject field. Book selection will have to take cognizance of the
related and allied fields of interest as well as of the special field
of theology itself. Books on religious architecture, music, and
painting; books on social problems not religious in content but with
which the minister has to deal; political and economic histories
which impinge in any way upon the history of religion; and literary
works with religious implications, may have to find a place in the
seminary library since the art, sociology, history, and literature
collections of a larger institution are not available to supplement
the theological concentration of the special branch. Reader services, too, will cover a broader range of interests, since the single
library is called upon to assist in the work of all the courses in
the curriculum and not merely in those directly related to theological subjects. In such a library, the librarian will have to be both
a general librarian and a special one, and he will have to handle
all of the library processes as well as the subject problems of the
field.

In libraries of the third type — those not attached to an educational institution — the demands made upon the librarian will vary
with the particular organization maintaining the library. If the
library is operated solely for the personnel of the organization, its
services will be more highly specialized than if the library is open
to the general public. The particular aspect of religion or theology
with which the organization is concerned will dictate the emphasis
in the library collection and in the kinds of services rendered.
Often these libraries are highly specialized, using the collections
of other libraries in the community to assist in any researches
requiring materials outside their defined field. All of the library
processes in such libraries, however, must be handled by the librarian, and library training should supplement subject training if
the materials are to be organized and administered with maximum

efficiency. Often the subject knowledge required is of so special a nature that it can only be acquired on the job; in this case, the knowledge of librarianship is the major requisite.

Special Collections

It is to be expected that theological schools would develop special collections of materials, especially materials related to their denominational affiliations. The special librarian needs to be familiar with these special collections; to know where the best materials on some phase of the subject can be found; to borrow on interlibrary loan where scholarly needs warrant; or to direct the researcher to other collections better suited to his needs. While one might presume that materials of particular denominations would be best represented in denominational institutions, he might not know that Saint Mary-Of-The-Woods College in Indiana has an outstanding collection of Old French religious books; that Drew University in Madison, New Jersey, has a notable collection of patristics; or that the University of Colorado owns the excellent library of the late Bishop Mandell Creighton which is strong on the Conciliar Movement and the Protestant Reform. Nor should he forget that public libraries, too, often house special collections in the field, like Cleveland Public Library's collection on Mohammedanism; Tulsa Public Library's file of religious music; and the fine collection of Judaica in the Free Library of Philadelphia.

The infinite variety of religious subjects and the unexpected sources of materials in the field can be learned only through constant use of source materials, personal knowledge of collections, and through such indexes to special collections as *The American Library Directory's* index and the Special Libraries Association's *Special Library Resources*. A glance through the index to the latter set is an excellent introduction to the complexity of the field and to the many facets of the subject matter which have been collected, many of them in unpredictable places. Thirty-eight special collections are listed under the heading "Religion," with cross references to "Christianity," "Theology," and the names of churches. "Religion - History," "Religion, Comparative," and "Religious Education" are the headings which follow alphabetically in this section of the index, with a cross reference also to "Church History." Under the names of the churches, further cross references appear. Following the listing of eleven special collections on the subject, "Roman Catholic Church," are found cross references to "Canon Law," "Jesuitica," and "Renaissance Papacy." Other subjects also appear as one thumbs through the index: "Christian Symbolism in Art," "Church Music," "Oxford Movement,"

"Wesleyana," "Zionism" — hardly a page lacks a subject related to the field of religion in one context or another.

CLASSIFICATION OF RELIGIOUS MATERIALS

The classification of materials as diverse as these constitutes a real problem — a problem which has not been solved completely by the Dewey Decimal scheme. In Dewey the 200's have been divided into four distinct sections which are not necessarily discrete, and the philosophical writings in religion are separated from the theological on the basis of their approach. The Dewey breakdown is as follows:

210   Those works which are philosophic rather than Christian in their approach to the subject matter: treatises on fatalism, religion and science, good and evil, etc., when dealt with as general concepts.

220   The Bible and the books about it.

230-289   Christian religion solely, in its several aspects:

        230   The doctrinal works — theology
        240   The devotional and practical works
        250   Homiletics, and parochial materials: sermons, church finance, parish work, etc.
        260   The institutions and work of the Christian church: public worship, missions and religious organizations, sunday schools, etc.
        270   General history of the Christian church.
        280   Churches and sects within Christianity.

290   Non-Christian religions, including comparative religion, and general histories of religion where an equal or minor place is given to Christianity.

The bias of such a scheme is readily discernible at a glance. Only about one third of the human race are actual or nominal Christians, but seven tenths of the Dewey classification of religion is devoted to Christianity. Where an entire tenth of the 200 classification is devoted to Christian church history alone, other religions are given one one-hundredth of the classification to cover every aspect of their belief, history, and practice. It can be noted in defense of the system that the bias of Dewey is also the bias of

most American communities and that popular demand will exist
for materials on Christianity much more than for materials on
Brahmanism or Judaism. The distortion in favor of Mr. Dewey's
own religion, however, is not an accurate reflection of the state of
the literature — and it is the literature which must be made to fit
the classification scheme.

Actually, the Dewey scheme is a classification, in many instances, of religious concepts rather than of books and is of very
little practical usefulness in the arrangement of materials upon
the shelf and the succinct description of content. An example of
the kind of conceptual breakdown which Dewey uses is his 230 section on theology:

230		DOCTRINAL DOGMATICS THEOLOGY
	231	God
	232	Christ
	233	Man
	234	Salvation
	235	Angels Devils Satan
	236	Eschatology Last Things
	237	Future State
	238	Creeds Confessions
	239	Polemic Theology

The schematism is a neat one, beginning with God, working down
to Man through Christ, and back up the scale through death, resurrection and judgment to the future state, of heaven or eternal punishment; but the literature in the field does not follow this kind of
pattern. To books on the life of Christ, which form an extremely
large part of religious publication, Dewey gives no more space in
his classification than he gives to discussions of conditional immortality; and to Greek and Roman religion and mythology he devotes a segment of the whole no larger than that assigned to reviv-
als and parish missions. In large libraries where extremely
precise classification is required, such division of the decimal
system results in extremely complex numbers following the decimal point, which destroys the major advantage of the scheme — its
simplicity and mnemonic character. Most special libraries in the
field have found it necessary to work out special expansions of the
Dewey classification to take care of much that now is inadequately
handled or to devise entirely new classifications better suited to
their needs. The best of these thus far is that created by Julia
Pettee, then librarian of the Union Theological seminary, *Classification of the Library of the Union Theological Seminary in the City
of New York*, 1939.

For smaller libraries, and for general public libraries whose religious collections do not warrant classification more precise than the third summary of Dewey, the Dewey scheme is probably adequate. The difficulty in classification here arises not out of the weakness of any particular classification scheme but out of the overlapping between subject areas. The librarian's problem is not that there is no place in the classification for a particular book, but that the book can fit in so many different places. Religious history, for example, often is as much political and social as it is religious: histories of the Reformation, of the Holy Roman Empire, and — to bring the problem into the present — of the new nation of Israel, may well fit as logically into the Dewey 900 classification as into the 200. The problem of whether a book is philosophy or religion is also a nice one. What makes a discussion of freedom of the will a religious book instead of a philosophical one? Where do discussions of moral questions classify? What is the proper subject field of the psychological study of religious experience? If one wanted to find a book on the attitude of the Catholic Church toward socialized medicine, would he expect to find it with the books on religion, on social legislation, or on medicine? Books on the relationship between the church and civil government could classify in 261.7, or 322, or 172.3, depending on whether the particular treatment emphasizes the church, politics, or state ethics. Books on ecclesiastic discipline and courts could be religious or legalistic in their treatment, and books on ecclesiastical furniture might well relate more directly to art and design than to ecclesiology, although there is a place for them in either subject area.

The deciding factor in such cases is usually the intent and major emphasis of the author. The nature of the collection to which the book is added may sometimes dictate the most logical classification from the standpoint of use. In a collection entirely devoted to religious materials, books on religious architecture could be classified in the 700's since the religious orientation is assumed, whereas a general collection might find it necessary to keep religious architecture with the rest of the books on religion, rather than with the volumes on secular architecture. In college and university libraries, the source of recommendation for purchase often determines the classification. If the funds of the music department are used to purchase a book on sacred music, it will probably be classified for the music collection since that is presumably where it will be most in demand; the same book purchased by the theological school would be classed with the religious books. In highly departmentalized systems, it is often necessary to purchase more than one copy and to classify the copies differently to meet conflicting demands. When a book is equally important in more than one field but can only be classified in one, the library's answer to obtain maximum use for the volume is to indicate its additional facets through subject headings in the card catalog.

CATALOGING OF RELIGIOUS MATERIALS

Cataloging of religious materials also raises some difficult problems for the librarian. For scholarly purposes, subject headings and main entries reflect special and professional terminology which would be meaningless to the average layman user of the catalog. A comparison of the *Subject Headings Used in the Dictionary Catalogs of the Library of Congress* with *Sears' List of Subject Headings* serves to illustrate the differences. For example, the Library of Congress list includes both "Bible — Hermeneutics" and "Bible — Criticism" as headings, because of the necessary distinction to be made between books of biblical criticism and books about biblical criticism in a large collection; Sears uses the heading "Bible — Hermeneutics" only as a cross reference and files all titles of both kinds under the single heading "Bible — Criticism." Library of Congress has a separate heading for "Dialectic (Theology)," whereas Sears omits "Theological Dialectic" completely and uses "Dialectics" only as a cross reference to "Logic." In the Library of Congress, "Theophanies" is a separate subject heading; in Sears it is not even listed. In Library of Congress, "Patristics" is listed with a cross reference to "Fathers of the Church"; in Sears, no entry for "Patristics" is considered necessary, although "Fathers of the Church" is used.

As has already been shown, the point of departure for most Christian scholarship is the Bible. But the Bible itself presents serious difficulties to the cataloger, both as a main and as a subject entry. Filing of entries for the Bible is an extremely complex problem, even in a comparatively small collection. An arbitrary main entry has been set for the Sacred Book, following the procedure used for anonymous classics, which is simply "Bible," with "Bible. O.T." for the Old Testament and "Bible. N.T." for the New. For individual books of the Bible, the older plan, still followed in most scholarly libraries, was to file the several books in canonical order based upon the English Authorized Version, under "Bible. O.T." or "Bible. N.T." as the case might be. To find a commentary on the book of Esdras the patron must know where it appears in the Bible in relation to the books preceding and following it. Since there are 122 different groups that could be made according to this plan, the difficulties it raises for the average

user are obvious. Many libraries prefer to file the names of the
several books alphabetically within the major entry, "Bible. O.T."
or "Bible. N.T.," although the *A.L.A. Rules for Filing Catalog
Cards* recommends this practice only in the smaller libraries.
Many larger libraries follow this system, however, since the user
can then look alphabetically within the major subject group for
"Esdras" in this instance, without having to be familiar with the
sequence of books in the canon.

The many entries for "Bible," even with this kind of simplification, become an extremely confusing matter for the user of a collection of any size. In the catalog of the University of Chicago
library — admittedly complex because of the theological schools on
the campus and its arrangement for scholarly use — there is a total
of eighteen card drawers labeled "Bible." The layman user, seeking to locate — let us say — a copy of the Douay Bible, would find
himself faced with this series of drawer labels:

```
Bible - Bible f
Bible g - Bible (subj) a
Bible (subj) b - c
              etc. through the alphabet for Bible (subj)
Bible (subj) stu - Bible. O.T. Selections
Bible. O.T. (subj) a - g
Bible. O.T. (subj) h - O.T. Octateuch
Bible. O.T. Pentateuch - Genesis
Bible. O.T. Exodus - Job
              etc. through the books of the Old Testament
              in canonical order
Bible. N.T. a - Selections
Bible. N.T. (subj) a - c
Bible. N.T. (subj) d - z
Bible. N.T. (groups) - Bible. N.T. Gospels
Bible. N.T. Gospels (subj) - Bible. N.T. Matthew
              etc. through the books of the New Testament
              in canonical order
```

The average nontheological student is likely to be completely
baffled by such an array of possibilities. If he is well-informed in
the use of the card catalog it may occur to him to look up "Douay
Bible" in the hope of finding a cross reference to the proper entry,
or if he is completely uninformed, he may naively assume that a
Douay Bible would be listed under that entry. In either case, if he
tries that approach, he will find:

Douay Bible
   see
Bible. English
   Arranged with other Bibles by date

Even the librarian must admit that the guide does little to
dispel the patron's confusion. In which of the several drawers
listed above does one find "Bible. English"? And what "date" is
referred to? The user, if he is interested in finding a particular
version of the Bible (in this case, the Douay), might assume that
all of those versions will be brought together under "Bible.
English" in chronological sequence at 1750 when that version was
made. This is not the case, however; in accordance with the *A.L.A.
Rules for Filing Catalog Cards* the date used in filing cards for the
Bible is the imprint date of the particular edition. Different print-
ings of the Douay Bible will be filed wherever they fall in chronological order; one wishing to check on the holdings of a given library for a particular version would be forced to go through the
entire set of Bible listings, picking out the wanted version under
each date on which new (not necessarily revised or altered in text)
editions had been published. This regulation for filing brings the
latest imprints of all the several versions together at the end of
the file of cards for Bibles in English. It disrupts the usual alphabetical arrangement of cards in the dictionary catalog in order to
serve another purpose, but in so doing, it undoubtedly causes some
confusion in the minds of catalog users who do not know this special
variation of the library's usual filing rules.

Smaller libraries will pose less complicated problems in the
cataloging of Bible entries, but with the many books about the Bible
which require "Bible" to be used as subject heading as well as
main entry, and with the great number of commentaries on individual books which constantly appear, even a small collection can
present a confusing array of catalog entries. Reference work in a
religious collection often consists mainly of guiding the users
through the inevitable intricacies of the library's own tools and
keys.

REFERENCE WORK IN THE FIELD OF RELIGION

In reference works the average patron will want tools to lead
him through the more difficult aspects of the basic literature, to define terms and to identify people, places, and teachings, and to orient
him generally without requiring serious historical study or scholarly
application. The most frequently asked questions in the field of
religion are requests for (1) exact wording, usually of biblical

quotations; (2) historical facts; (3) biographical facts; (4) illustrations; and (5) lists of book titles on special aspects of reading in the
field. Of major importance, then, will be the reference aids to the
use of the Bible, particularly the dictionaries, concordances, and
tools for identification of persons and places. Similar quick-reference aids for nonbiblical materials are also much in demand,
particularly encyclopedias, dictionaries, and yearbooks, both general in scope and oriented about particular creeds and churches.
Selective bibliographies, and indexes to periodical literature, to
illustrations, and to parts of books are also very useful.

In scholarly libraries, the emphasis will be less on isolated
facts and more on broader concepts and the original scholarship.
The more scholarly encyclopedias are of great value here, not only
for their monographic articles but also for their bibliographies,
for the bibliographic tools are probably the single most important
type of reference aid for the researcher. To survey the state of
scholarship, past and present; to discover what has already been
done; to open up possibilities for needed research; and to guide in
the most fruitful reading, the bibliography is indispensable. Another extremely important area of reference work for the scholar
is that of philology. In his study of comparative texts and original
manuscripts, the theological student will have frequent need of
philological grammars, dictionaries, and concordances, especially
in the Semitic languages and in medieval Greek and Latin. For
very scholarly research, original manuscripts, church documents,
and primary materials of various kinds are basic.

REPRESENTATIVE REFERENCE TOOLS
IN THE FIELD OF RELIGION

The accompanying bibliography is a highly selective list of the
most commonly used and needed reference tools. It is by no means
a definitive selection, but it does serve as a guide to the types —
and to the more familiar examples of each type — of reference tools
with which the general librarian should be acquainted if he ever is
called upon to answer questions which deal with religion.

The librarian of a theological seminary will need to know many
more basic tools than the few scholarly titles mentioned here. The
7th edition of *Guide to Reference Books* by Constance Winchell, its
supplements, and references in the bibliographies mentioned on
the list, will serve to introduce the novice to some of the many
other important titles in the field. The librarian in the small library, on the other hand, may find that many of the general tools
will be as useful as the specialized aids. As can be seen from the
list, the few special periodical indexes for general and scholarly

publications in the field of religion must be supplemented by the
Readers' Guide and the *International Index to Periodical Literature*
which list many of the most widely read articles in the field. Similarly the *Essay and General Literature Index,* the general encyclopedias, the traditional "Who's Who" publications, and the bibliographies which cover humanities fields are often all that the
average small library needs to answer the majority of questions
which deal with religious subject matter. Where the amount of
emphasis on religious materials is limited, the librarian should
check carefully the distinctive features of the specialized publications to see if they are likely to be used by his patrons.

Bibliographies

Barrow, John Graves. *A Bibliography of Bibliographies in Reli-
     gion.* 1955.
Diehl, Katharine Smith. *Religions, Mythologies, Folklores: An
     Annotated Bibliography.* 1956.
The Guide to Catholic Literature. Vol. I: 1888-1940; vol. II: 1940-
     1944; vol. III: 1944-1948; vol. IV: 1948-1951 (in progress).
Hurst, John Fletcher. *Literature of Theology: A Classified Bibli-
     ography.* 1896.
International Bibliography of the History of Religions. 1952-
For annual lists of new religious books, see the special issues of
     Publishers' Weekly, Library Journal, and *Saturday Review*
     devoted to religious books.

Encyclopedias

Catholic Encyclopedia; An International Work of Reference on the
     Constitution, Doctrine, Discipline, and History of the Catholic
     Church. 16 vols. 1907-14. Rev. and enl. edition: vol. 1, 1936.
————— Supplement I, 1922.
————— Supplement II, 1950.
The Encyclopaedia of Islam: A Dictionary of the Geography, Eth-
     nography, and Biography of the Muhammadan Peoples.... 4
     vols. and suppl. 1913-38.
————— New ed., vol. 1- 1954-
Shorter Encyclopaedia of Islam. 1953.
Ferm, Vergilius, ed. *An Encyclopedia of Religion.* 1945. (Desk
     size)
Encyclopaedia of Religion and Ethics. James Hastings, ed. 13 vols.
     1908-27. (Frequent reissues)
————— ————— 2d ed. 13 vols. in 7. 1951.
The Jewish Encyclopedia; A Descriptive Record of the History,

Religion, Literature, and Customs of the Jewish People from the Earliest Times to the Present Day.... 12 vols. 1901-06.
————— New ed. 1925.

The Universal Jewish Encyclopedia; An Authoritative and Popular Presentation of Jews and Judaism since the Earliest Times. 10 vols. and Reading Guide and Index. 1939-44.

Schaff, Philip. *The New Schaff-Herzog Encyclopedia of Religious Knowledge;* Embracing Biblical, Historical, Doctrinal, and Practical Theology, and Biblical, Theological, and Ecclesiastical Biography from the Earliest Times to the Present Day. 12 vols. and Index. 1908-14. (Reprinted 1949-50)

Supplementary volumes have title: *Twentieth Century Encyclopedia of Religious Knowledge;* An Extension of the New Schaff-Herzog Encyclopedia of Religious Knowledge. 2 vols. 1955.

Dictionaries

Attwater, Donald, ed. *A Catholic Dictionary.* 2d ed. 1949.

The Book of Saints; A Dictionary of Servants of God Canonized by the Catholic Church. 4th ed. 1947.

Brewer, E. C. *A Dictionary of Miracles, Imitative, Realistic, and Dogmatic.* 1884. (Reissue 1934)

Ferm, Vergilius. *A Protestant Dictionary.* 1951.

Hughes, Thomas P. *Dictionary of Islam;* Being a Cyclopaedia of the Doctrines, Rites, Ceremonies, and Customs, together with the Technical and Theological Terms, of the Muhammadan Religion. 2d ed. 1896.

Julian, John. *A Dictionary of Hymnology.* Rev. ed. 1907. (Reprinted 1925)

Mathews, Shailer, and Smith, G. B., eds. *A Dictionary of Religion and Ethics.* 1921.

Biography

Religious Leaders of America; vol. 2, 1941-42. (Volume 1 had title: *Who's Who in the Clergy,* 1935-36)

Yearbook of American Churches. 1932- Most yearbooks, almanacs, and annuals in this field carry biographical sections. Specific denominations also have biographical dictionaries, as well as their own yearbooks. For example:
American Catholic Who's Who. 1934/35-
Baptist Who's Who.... Great Britain and Ireland. 1933.
Who's Who in American Jewry. vol. 1, 1926; vol. 2, 1928; vol. 3, 1938-39.

Mythology

Frazer, Sir James George. *The Golden Bough;* A Study in Magic
and Religion. 3d ed. 12 vols. 1911-15. (Reprinted 1952)
────── ────── One volume edition. (Frequently reprinted)
────── *Aftermath; A Supplement to the Golden Bough.* 1937.
*Funk & Wagnalls Standard Dictionary of Folklore, Mythology and
Legend.* Maria Leach, ed. 2 vols. 1949-50.
Mythology of All Races. 13 vols. 1916-32.

Indexes

American Theological Library Association. *Index to Religious
Periodical Literature 1949-52.* Comp. and ed. by J. Stillson
Judah. 1953.
Catholic Periodical Index; A Cumulative Author and Subject Index
to a Selected List of Catholic Periodicals. 1930/33, 1939/43-
Richardson, Ernest Cushing. *An Alphabetical Subject Index and
Index Encyclopaedia to Periodical Articles on Religion, 1890-
1899.* 1907.
────── *Periodical Articles on Religion, 1890-1899 . . . Author Index.*
1911.
See also:
  International Index for articles in the major scholarly journals
  of religion.
  Readers' Guide for articles on religion in the general maga-
  zines.

Miscellaneous

Clark, Elmer T. *The Small Sects in America.* Rev. and enl. ed.
1949.
Ferm, Vergilius, ed. *Forgotten Religions.* 1950.
Mead, Frank S. *Handbook of Denominations in the United States.*
Rev. and enl. ed. 1956.
U.S. Bureau of the Census. *Religious Bodies: 1936.* 3 vols. 1941.
Yearbook of American Churches; A Record of Religious Activities
in the United States. (1915-32: Title varies); 1932-
See also:
  Yearbooks, annuals, and biographical dictionaries of specific
  denominations, as
    American Baptist Yearbook
    American Catholic Who's Who
    Official Catholic Directory
    Jewish Yearbook, etc.

SPECIAL REFERENCE AIDS TO THE BIBLE

Bibliographies

"Elenchus Bibliographicus Biblicus." Regular Department in *Bi-blica*. vol. 1- 1920-
New Testament Literature; An Annotated Bibliography, ed. by
William Nelson Lyons and Merrill M. Parvis. vol. 1- 1948-

Dictionaries and Encyclopedias

Davis, John D. *The Westminster Dictionary of the Bible.* Rev.
and rewritten by Henry S. Gehman. 1944.
Hastings, James, ed. *Dictionary of the Bible.* 5 vols. 1898-1904.
—— —— One volume version. 1909. (Reprinted 1927)
Jacobus, M. W. and others. *A New Standard Bible Dictionary;*
Designed as a Comprehensive Help to the Study of the Scrip-
tures, Their Languages, Literary Problems, History, Biogra-
phy, Manners and Customs, and Their Religious Teachings.
3d rev. ed. 1936. (Reprinted as *Funk & Wagnalls New Standard
Bible Dictionary*)
Miller, Madeleine S., and Miller, J. L. *Harper's Bible Dictionary.*
1952. Same with title: *Black's Bible Dictionary.* 1954.
—— *Encyclopedia of Bible Life.* Rev. ed. 1955.

Concordances

Cruden, Alexander. *A Complete Concordance to the Old and New
Testament and the Apocrypha.* Reprint of 10th London ed.
1864. New clear-type ed. 1951.
Hazard, M. C. *A Complete Concordance to the American Standard
Version of the Holy Bible.* 1922.
Oxford Cyclopedic Concordance.... New ed. 1949.
Strong, James. *The Exhaustive Concordance of the Bible.* 1894.
(Frequently reprinted)
Thompson, N. W., and Stock, Raymond. *Complete Concordance to
the Bible.* (Douay Version). 4th rev. and enl. ed. 1945.
Walker, J. B. R. *The Comprehensive Concordance to the Holy
Scriptures.* 1898. New ed. 1936. (Frequently reissued)
Young, Robert. *Analytical Concordance to the Bible.* 22d Ameri-
can ed. rev. by Wm. B. Stevenson. 1947. (Reprinted 1955)

Miscellaneous

Kittel, Gerhard. *Bible Key Words.* Tr. and ed. by J. R. Coates.
6 vols. 1949-52.

—— —— One volume ed. 1951.

The Interpreter's Bible   (12 v. to be issued two volumes a year, 1951-). Vols. 1-5, 7-11 have appeared to date.

Stevenson, Burton E., comp. *The Home Book of Bible Quotations.* 1949.

Wright, George Ernest, and Filson, F. V., eds. *The Westminster Historical Atlas to the Bible.* 1945.

chapter two

philosophy

INTRODUCTION

To define philosophy is not easy. The classification of disciplines, including philosophy, is in itself a task of philosophy, and different philosophers approach that task in different ways; therefore, any single definition of philosophy may be in disagreement with those of a good many philosophers.

A more specific difficulty in the way of a discrete definition arises from the fact that all knowledge is the province of philosophy. In practice, this does not mean that the philosopher seeks to rival the specialist in every field. Since any discipline, whether well developed or unexplored, may be the object of philosophical investigation, the layman often finds it difficult to draw the line separating philosophy from the matter with which it deals. The pseudo sciences and the moral studies constitute two of the fields which illustrate this difficulty.

Philosophy is the mother of unborn sciences. Psychology emerged from it as a separate discipline only within the last century, the physical sciences several centuries earlier. Semeiology, the science of signs, is even now struggling towards birth, but

many of the forms are monsters that will never survive. When a
man thinks he has discovered a new science and writes a book describing it with a vague and grandiloquent enthusiasm, the work is
usually classified as philosophy. Indeed, it may be not unlike some
of the early works in the physical sciences (alchemy) or psychology
(mesmerism). One has reason to feel contemptuous toward most
of such works, but one also has reason to be lenient in judgment.
When such works, both of the present time and of the past, are put
under the heading of "philosophy," their variety and incoherence
make the field a hard one to define.

Philosophy, like religion, is also concerned with moral problems. It might be distinguished from religion and preachment by
describing it as the "critical examination of problems" as opposed
to the dogmatic assertion of opinions were it not for the fact that
many of the men who have made significant investigations of moral
problems have been at the same time either staunch adherents of
an established religion or vigorous prophets of new ones. This
makes it difficult to fix a boundary and as a result practically any
book with a moral subject matter which does not plainly belong with
one or another established religion is called "philosophical."

The reasons for listing pseudoscientific tomes and platitudi-
nous handbooks as philosophy tell more about the essential nature
of philosophy than do the contents of such works. The former are
included because it is philosophy's task to fill, or at least to point
out, the gaps in knowledge. The latter are included because it is
philosophy's task to discover, or at least to investigate, the interrelations of different bodies of knowledge; the relationship between
moral knowledge and knowledge of nature is one of the great continuing problems of philosophy.

We have said that all knowledge is the province of the philosopher, but that the philosopher does not attempt to rival the specialist in every subject field. What he does try to do is what the specialist, being a specialist, fails to do — study the unexplored regions
and the borderlands between developed regions. The philosopher
cannot neglect the well-developed disciplines; although he does not
concern himself with their masses of detailed information he is interested in the basic principles, the methods, and the logical structure of the theories in each such field.

These separate tasks — (1) the exploration of new areas; (2) the
examination of interrelations among all areas; and (3) the dissection
of the logic of developed areas — are subordinate to the basic task
of philosophy, which is the systematization of all knowledge. When
a scientist, an artist, or a politician leaves his special preoccupation
behind and begins to deal with problems which embrace several fields,
he is beginning to do philosophical work and his results must be

judged by philosophical standards rather than by those of his original speciality. If he broadens his interests far enough, he becomes a philosopher, good, bad, or indifferent.

A few philosophers, like Aristotle and Kant, have produced complete systems, but their systems are not in agreement. It has been evident from the time of the Greek philosophers that there are certain serious difficulties in the way of the systematization of all knowledge, and many philosophers since that time, instead of working out complete systems, have dealt with one or another of these problems. So it is that in the antispecialist discipline of philosophy there are specialists: ethical thinkers, metaphysicians, philosophers of science.

Another type of specialist in philosophy is the logician, who studies and tries to improve the tool used in systematizing knowledge — logic. To the layman, logic consists of a few rules of correct thinking, but to the professional logician, it is the study of the nature and structure of thought. The theories and arguments developed in every field are the subjects of its investigations, and as a result there are works on the logic of physics, the logic of psychology, the logic of the social sciences, and so forth.

Concern with unsolved problems and concern with logic are historical characteristics of philosophy. Ever since Socrates it has been a virtue among philosophers to admit ignorance, which is to claim to recognize the limits of one's understanding. The sins abhorrent to philosophers are contentment with easy, inadequate solutions to problems and confused, disorganized thinking.

To these characteristics may be added one more which also sets philosophers apart from the practitioners of other disciplines and that is the reflexivity of their thinking. In other fields, men think about subject matters such as the stars, human history, microbes, slum clearance. But in philosophy, men think about thinking, they theorize about theory, and it is common practice for them to turn about and investigate their own investigations and analyze their own analyses. This feature, perhaps more than any other, gives work in the field that complexity which newcomers find so bewildering.

If philosophy's task is the systematization of all knowledge, as here asserted, it follows that the classification of disciplines is a part of that task. And if various philosophers disagree as to the nature and place of philosophy, it follows that the foregoing delineation of the field is not in agreement with the views of many philosophers. This is a paradox typical of those which frequently result from philosophical reflexivity. To continue in a philosophical vein, no solution to the paradox will be given, but only the assurance that, although this description of philosophy might not be subscribed

to by all philosophers, it does apply fairly well to the bulk of their
works.

HISTORY OF PHILOSOPHY

Only the briefest kind of surface survey is attempted in this
outline of the history of philosophy. The student should not imagine
that it is meant to substitute for a thorough account of the subject,
and certainly not for readings in the major philosophers themselves.
It is designed mainly to stimulate the student's interest sufficiently
to send him to some of the important primary and secondary writings in the field and to introduce him to some of the approaches to
the history of philosophy.

Greek Philosophy

The natural beginning for a study of Western philosophy lies in
Greece. Not only does the name come from the Greeks ($\phi \iota \lambda o \varsigma$, "fond
of," and $\sigma o \phi \iota a$ "wisdom"), but also the conventional divisions of the
subject which still form the basis of contemporary philosophical inquiry were made by the Greeks. Logic, cosmology, metaphysics, ethics, and aesthetics were all designated the material of philosophy by
the Greek philosophers, and continue to be so designated to this day.

Greek philosophy began as a criticism of religious belief and
practice. Greece, free of a priestly caste which had political authority, was a favorable soil in which rational investigation of religious
belief could flourish. The earliest philosophy is a rational reaction
against the explanations of the nature of the universe contained in
the mythologies of popular religion. The emphasis in the earliest
philosophers — Thales and others of the Milesian school — was
therefore on that branch of philosophy called cosmology; the orientation was, in its way, scientific, and the first important philosophers
were primarily scientists — geographers, astronomers, geologists,
and meteorologists. Much of this aspect of philosophical concern has
now been assigned to the natural sciences, but cosmology is still
oriented around physical interests. (The ideas of matter, motion,
and energy, of atoms, of evolution, of planetary motion, and many
of the hypotheses which were later verified scientifically have been
stated also as pure theory by philosophers quite remote from the
scientific laboratory.)

The Greek city-state left its impress upon the philosophy of the
later Greeks. In Socrates and Plato the emphasis is upon right living among citizens and upon such social principles as goodness,
honesty, and justice. Plato sees the state as an organ of morality
whose structure expresses its ethical ideas and qualities and

conceives of the attainment of the highest human good through the community. This emphasis upon political philosophy, as exemplified in Plato's concept of the ideal commonwealth in *The Republic,* is one of the dominant themes in the Greek philosophy of the period.

Aristotle comes at the end of the great creative period in Greek thought; he is essentially a conservative, summing up what is already known. He is the great encyclopedist and researcher, summarizing in a single massive work the extant knowledge of his time. His eminence as a thinker, compared to the men who followed him in the Hellenistic and Roman periods, established him as absolute authority to the generations that followed, and fixed as permanent, many concepts that were essentially a description of the status quo. Great as Aristotle was, it cannot be denied that in certain areas (notably the sciences) the unquestioning acceptance of his dicta (or even worse, the misinterpretation of the principles he enunciated) blocked progress for centuries.

Many of the ideals of Greek democracy represented by the city-state were lost in the period of the Macedonian domination, and the disillusioned, subjected people felt more need for a way of life which would help them to endure the world than for a complete philosophical system. The popular "philosophies" of the time were incomplete ethical systems which classify more properly as preachments than as philosophies, but they provided prescriptions for conduct which made life bearable for the individual and so gained a following. The best known of these doctrines, more important for their longevity than for their philosophical profundity, are Cynicism, Skepticism, Epicureanism, and Stoicism, all of which came into being during the time of Philip and Alexander.

Cynicism originally advocated indifference to fortune and the rejection of worldly goods, emphasizing virtue and the emancipation from fear. As the doctrine became popularized, it moved away from abstinence and emphasized merely the attitude of indifference. Our modern connotation of cynicism as a sneering disbelief in rectitude and sincerity stems from the distortion of Cynicism which applied its indifference not merely to things of this world, but to debts, commitments, and moral obligations as well.

Skepticism is a system of dogmatic doubt. According to this belief, no one knows nor can ever know; nothing can be proved except by the instrumentality of something else, which means that all argumentation is circular and without possible end. To the Skeptic there is no reason to believe in one course of action more than in any other and he is unconcerned with problems of right or wrong.

Epicureanism set up pleasure (defined essentially as the absence of pain) as the good that should be sought. The ideal was conceived of as a state of equilibrium; violence in any form, even

violent pleasure, was to be avoided. While this belief was materialistic, it was not deterministic; Epicurus felt that the natural laws
which rule the world could be understood so that one could exercise
his will to adjust to them. The popular idea of Epicureanism as a
doctrine of luxuriousness and voluptuousness stems from later and
less philosophical definitions of the meaning of pleasure.

Stoicism sought virtue as the highest good and minimized the
importance of health, happiness, or possessions. Stoicism, however, is deterministic; there is no chance, but only rigidly operating natural laws which work in constant cycle. Everything that
happens has happened before and will happen again, but virtue lies
within and cannot be destroyed by external forces. Man, therefore,
can rise above circumstance by willingly submitting to natural law
and cultivating indifference to the pains and pleasures of the world.

These so-called philosophies of endurance are very much like
the kind of doctrines which today qualify as philosophy in the popular mind, and it is interesting to note that for many laymen, the
term "philosophical" is still felt to be synonymous with the term
"stoical" or "cynical." Apparently what has always been demanded
of a "popular" philosophy is that it outline a way of life which will
make simpler an adjustment to the world rather than that it establish a complete and rational system which synthesizes all knowledge
into a harmonious whole. It can be seen that there is a long-standing
historical precedent for the popular misconception of what philosophy consists, and the librarian should be flexible enough to adjust
to the different connotations which the word philosophy may have
for different members of the library's public. Classification, cataloging, book selection, reference services, and readers' advisory
work may all have to make room for materials in the field of philosophy which the academic philosopher would repudiate.

Philosophy of the Middle Ages

The early Christian Era is marked by a period of transition
from Greek philosophy to Christian belief. The attempt to synthe-
size the philosophical concepts of Platonism with the Oriental beliefs of Judaism and Christianity is called Neoplatonism and is illustrated most clearly in the writings of such men as Origen,
Plotinus, and Augustine. The belief in the immortality of the soul,
which is implicit in Plato since ideals are eternal, becomes explicit
in Plotinus, who sees the soul as the creator of the visible world
which is the best possible copy of the eternal world and its beauty.
He emphasizes freedom of the will through which man is led into
sin, and encourages men to look within rather than to the world out-

side, thus putting limits upon scientific inquiry. The greatest of the Neoplatonic philosophers is Augustine, whose *The City of God* was extremely influential throughout the Middle Ages. It holds that all men are equally guilty of the sin of Adam; therefore damnation is evidence of God's justice, while salvation can come only through God's mercy. With this as a dominating philosophy, much of the superstition and cruelty which mark the Middle Ages is more easily understood. Later, this austere Augustinian belief was revived and disseminated through the teachings of Calvin to bring to the seventeenth century some of the superstitions and excesses which characterized the so-called Dark Ages.

An intellectual revival occurred in philosophical thought in the eleventh century with the rise of the movement called Scholasticism. Scholasticism set out to show that the truths of religion — although they may be above and beyond reason — are not contrary to reason. The movement reflects the dominance of the organized church, with its use of rational thinking to support the divinely revealed truths established by the church. It is important in the development of philosophical thought because it helped preserve the methods of Greek philosophy, emphasizing logical procedure and dialectical method. Within the framework of doctrinal orthodoxy, the better philosophers were able to raise many of the major questions which lie at the heart of philosophical inquiry. The leading philosophers of the period include St. Anselm, who gave early expression to the ontological argument for the existence of God and was extremely influential upon such later philosophers as Descartes, von Leibniz, Kant, and Hegel; Abelard, who stressed the importance of dialectic and the ultimate authority of reason in cases where other authorities disagree; Roger Bacon, who anticipated the arguments for empirical method which were to be given currency three hundred years later by Francis Bacon; and William of Occam, whose insistence on separating logic from metaphysics and theology did much to encourage scientific research.

The Scholastic philosopher whose influence was most widespread and lasting was undoubtedly Thomas Aquinas. St. Thomas is still a living influence, for in all Catholic educational institutions teaching philosophy, that of Aquinas is taught as the only correct one. It is based on Aristotelian method, which is carried over into Christian dogma with a minimum of alteration. The appeal to reason which will demonstrate the truth which the Catholic faith professes typifies the attitude of the Christian philosophers to whom the truth was felt to be known in advance and by whom reason is used to support a foregone conclusion rather than as a tool in a quest for an ultimate truth not yet revealed.

"Modern" Philosophy

The reaction against Scholasticism, ushered in with the Renaissance, is revealed in the movement called Humanism, which places its emphasis upon man on earth and the pleasures of this world rather than on a life after death. Humanism was much more important to literary men than it was to the philosophers and its outstanding figures are men like Petrarch and his followers. Classical literatures rather than logic became the object of study in the new movement; the "New Learning" arose to challenge the trivium and quadrivium of the universities. This emphasis upon the individual and the liberation from authority which characterizes it resulted in a new approach in philosophy. But for a time philosophical inquiry was retarded rather than advanced in this period for two reasons: Plato was disinterred and became a dominating influence; and the Reformation threw philosophy back into the realm of theological argument similar to that of the medieval period. The important factor in shaping a "new" philosophy was the rise of science, which forced men to think in terms which would fit the findings of the scientists. In men like Francis Bacon, with his plea for inductive method and the systematization of scientific procedure; Hobbes, with his argument from logical premises and consequences rather than from religious mythology; and Descartes, strongly influenced by the new physics and astronomy, we find the beginnings of modern philosophy.

Descartes is often considered the founder of modern philosophy. His famous "Cartesian" doubt with which he set about to doubt everything it is possible to doubt and which ends in his famous *Cogito ergo sum* typifies the new approach which accepts no authority and no previous tenets of belief. Descartes with his belief in the rational soul of man which is outside the mechanistic rules regulating the rest of the world, foreshadows the rationalism which was later to characterize one phase of the Enlightenment. This appeal to reason and universal truth, found also in other seventeenth-century philosophers like Spinoza and von Leibniz, summarized a whole facet of the thought of the period. In von Leibniz, particularly, we get the optimistic rationlist at his most extreme. Even nonphilosophers today are familiar with the von Leibniz credo of the "best of all possible worlds," which gained a dubious immortality through the merciless lampoon of Dr. Pangloss in Voltaire's *Candide*.

One reaction to rationalism took the form of what is called empiricism. In empiricism, experience — not reason — is the basis of all knowledge. It may take two forms: in Berkeley and Hume, it becomes an emphasis upon sensation and perception as the only source of knowledge; the entire world is in the mind. In the materialists, it becomes an emphasis upon matter as the source of sensation; even mind becomes merely material motion, as in Hobbes. This reduction of man to a bunch of atoms subject to deterministic mechanical laws eliminates the need for a belief in gods, immortality, and free will and explains in part the atheistic tendencies which appear in many of the thinkers of the eighteenth century.

From Locke to the present, English philosophy reflects the prejudices of the rising commercial middle class. Locke's liberalism, his democracy, his emphasis upon prudence, experience, and the innate ability of the "honest man" to know what is just and right, usher in the era of the upper-middle class. The divine right of kings is gone; the philosopher as elite intellect disappears; property rights and individual self-interest become the guides to general welfare. Lockeian liberalism was extremely influential upon the founders of American democracy, with their belief in gradual reform, free discussion as a guide to the solution of problems, the theory of checks and balances, and the rights of property.

The compromise between rationalism and empiricism was effected by Kant in his *Critique of Pure Reason*. Founder of the so-called Critical Philosophy, Kant sets out to prove that none of our knowledge can transcend experience, but that it is nevertheless in part a priori, and not inferred inductively from experience. Knowledge comes from sensation (empiricism), but is organized by the mind (rationalism). The best from both systems is thus saved. Kant is important too in his analysis of morals; his concept of the "categorical imperative" as the guide to conduct places responsibility upon the individual to act only in accordance with principles which he would be willing to have made the law for all. Virtue thus does not depend upon the intended result of an action, but only on the principle of which it is itself a result.

A forecast of Romanticism can be seen in much of Kant's philosophy. Romanticism comes as the reaction to rationalism; not reason — but feeling, emotion, and sentiment — become of major importance. Our "natural" feelings are the best guide to virtue and right; the "noble savage," the "natural man," unspoiled by civilization and man-made inhibitions, comes nearest to obeying the voice of untrammeled conscience which is an infallible guide to right action. Carried to its farthest extreme in the later Romantic philosophers like Fichte and Schelling for whom everything in the world is God, this belief in the spiritual nature of reality becomes pantheism: the entire universe is a growing, dynamic whole; in plants and rocks and every part of the material world the unconscious impulse exists which moves upward until it reaches man in whom it becomes conscious and seeing.

After Kant, and with the introduction of Romanticism, philosophy

took turns in several different directions, reacting in different ways
to the stimuli of romanticism, idealism, and science. The eternal
will as the center of belief could lead to optimism in a philosopher
like Fichte, or pessimism in one like Schopenhauer. Science and
romanticism are combined in an evolutionary concept in such philosophers as Hegel ("Life is an endless becoming") and Bergson
("Life constantly moves upward"). The place of man in the center
of the scheme of things becomes, in Nietzsche, a justification for
the concept of the superman; in Schopenhauer, the will becomes
superior even to knowledge; in James, the only truth is that which
is pragmatically useful to man. To reconcile the power of the individual with the apparent determinism of science, the concept of
scientific control of the universe appears: in Bentham and Mill,
the mental and physical world both are deterministic, but their
laws can be discovered experimentally and man can learn to control them; in Bergson, the new romanticism finds expression in
his belief that it is the function of science to present the true nature
of reality to man so that he may rise above the downward pull of
matter and continue his inevitable upward climb.

Trends in 20th Century Philosophy

The closer one comes to his own time, the more difficult it becomes to characterize the period in all-embracing terms. The
variety and complexity of thought become more and more apparent
and to summarize it in terms of some single *Zeitgeist* seems to do
too great violence to reality. Whether this means that the present
day is actually more complex than preceding eras is open to question; it is not impossible that an equal variety would have been seen
by a man of the thirteenth or the sixteenth or the eighteenth centuries, and that he would have condemned the oversimplification
with which we now view the characteristic mind-set of his period.
On the other hand, it may be that the perspective of time permits
us to see more clearly the reality of a period and that the apparent confusion comes from being too close to our object of study.
However that may be, a simplification of the current philosophical
situation must be even more tentative than one for preceding periods since we cannot stand off far enough from the subject to be sure
that we see its whole.

Certain strains can be detected, however, in the philosophical
thought of the current century. One of these is the strain of "logical positivism," which, borrowing the methods of the natural scientists, accepts as valid only such statements as can be tested by
"scientific" method. To philosophers of this school, Aristotelian
logic and traditional metaphysical thinking are a waste of time and

concepts like "liberty," "democracy," or "justice" are meaningless. To the semanticist, the lack of a concrete referent seems
to be the source of the confusion, which he hopes to resolve by an
extension of mathematics into a system of symbolic logic. But even
the most extreme of the logical positivists must recognize that
though such a word as "democracy" be vague and meaningless, it
has caught men's imaginations and fired them to action as if it had
concrete meaning. Another strain in contemporary philosophy,
then, is that which attempts to discover how irrational and even
false ideas can have the power and the importance that they do.
Philosophers concerned with this problem become students of culture, employing the data of psychology, history, and the arts to lead
them to an understanding of man and society; many modern philosophers write like social scientists and address themselves to the
subject matter which formerly — in terms of library classification —
was thought of as 300 or 900, rather than 100. Yet this is not a to-
tally new element in philosophy; Plato's *Republic,* Aristotle's *Politics,* Machiavelli's *Prince,* Hobbes's *Leviathan,* and Marx's *Das
Kapital* are also as much social science as they are philosophy.

The objective scientificism of much modern philosophy does
not eliminate the counterstrain which might be expected by any
student of history. This takes the direction of renewed religious
faith, and men like Niebuhr, Maritain, and Toynbee show an apparent leaning towards a new religious revival to counteract the anti-
religious extremists in the logical positivists' camp. Whether,
when the twentieth century is history, it will be characterized as
an Age of Faith, an Age of Godlessness, or an Age of Objective
Reason, we cannot now predict. Such characterizations seem too
easy and oversimplified in view of the contradictions which pres-
ently confront us. What now seems like confusion may well, with
the perspective of time, resolve itself into a clear and orderly pattern to which a single all-embracing descriptive phrase may be
properly applied.

American Philosophy

The history of American philosophy is almost inseparable from
the history of American theology. American philosophy from the
beginning has been marked by two opposite strains: the theistic,
Calvinist in its theology, Berkeleyan in its idealism, and Augustinian in its medievalism; and the deistic, with its rational and pragmatic morality stemming from the philosophies of Hume and Adam
Smith. The otherworldly, anti-individualist belief in the absolute
sovereignity of God flourished side by side with the businessman's
puritanism of "thrift and righteousness": Jonathan Edwards and

Benjamin Franklin were contemporaries. The first publication of Jonathan Edwards' *The Insufficiency of Reason as a Substitute for Revelation* occurred within a decade of Ethan Allen's *Reason, the Only Oracle of Man.* By the end of the century, however, it was Allen's viewpoint that was the more congenial to the time and the place; the rationalistic materialism of the Enlightenment more adequately suited a new and democratic state with apparently unlimited opportunity than did the ecclesiastical class rule and the doctrine of special election of the earlier Calvinism. The Calvinistic influence did not completely die out; throughout our history its influence has been felt in anachronistic and anomalous deviations from the anticipated pattern of freedom, tolerance, and rationalism.

Meanwhile, as in Europe, a reaction against the empiricism of Locke and the Enlightenment found expression in a romantic movement in philosophy. The most striking contribution of American philosophy to this development was the transcendentalist movement, which combined Neoplatonism, the ethical (not the materialistic) side of Calvinism, and romanticism. The transcendental emphasis upon the divinity of nature, the worth of man, and the capacity of man to know the truth directly, maintained the ideal of democracy although it was harsh in its denunciation of the crassness of the rising commercial class. In such philosophers or preachers as William Ellery Channing, Theodore Parker, Emerson, and Thoreau, transcendentalism, for all its European roots, took on an American flavor that was reflected in literature as well as in philosophy.

As in Europe, so in America, the introduction of the theory of evolution caused a revolution in philosophical thought. There was here, as elsewhere, a group of writers who voiced an immediate opposition to the theory, on both theological and scientific grounds. But there was also a group of writers who rose to defend the doctrine. Asa Gray, for example, attempted to show that the evolutionary theory was not inconsistent with the idea of a divine design, and others like James McCosh and John Fiske soon followed with additional philosophical support to hasten the general acceptance of the theory. It should be noted, however, that the evolution with which the scholars were concerned was Spencerian rather than Darwinian.

In opposition to the agnosticism of Spencer, a new movement called speculative philosophy arose, in which the influence of Kant and Hegel was marked. The middle and late nineteenth century was dominated by German scholarship, in philosophy as well as in other fields. The immigration of German scholars to America, the eminence of German universities which attracted the leading American students, and the consequent deference to German ideas and ideals

in the scholarly publications both in England and America served
to perpetuate the influence of Germany on American philosophical
thought. The first learned journal in philosophy in the English language, the *Journal of Speculative Philosophy* — although it also provided an outlet for the early publications of young American philosophers — was primarily an organ through which America could gain
access to English translations from the German idealists, like
Fichte, Schelling, and Hegel.

Hegelianism, carried to its ultimate extreme, often results in
pantheism and solipsism. To counteract this tendency, the concept
of personalism, a theistic doctrine first introduced by Bronson
Alcott in which the person is central and the key to the meaning of
reality, was adopted by such American philosophers as George
Howison and Borden Parker Browne. As the history of philosophy
in every country reveals, the eventual reaction is the rejection of
idealism in favor of realism, which views the objects of perception
as entities existing in their own right and independent of mind and
sensation. This does not mean that idealism has died out of American philosophy. It continues in the several forms which have traditionally characterized it, stemming either from the belief in objective values, as in Plato; the belief that all reality is mental, as
in Berkeley; the belief that only selves exist, as in von Leibniz; or
the belief that the whole is more than the sum of its parts and that
reality is organic, as in Hegel. Nevertheless, the anti-idealistic
philosophies have a wide following. The earliest realism in America was a "common sense" philosophy, based upon established and
orthodox beliefs, that maintained the dualism between God and the
world, body and soul, and mind and matter. Modern realism challenges this dualism. Naturalism begs the question of the nature of
reality and holds that whatever it is, it is subject to natural laws.
Despite the general belief that a naturalistic view of the universe
leads to pessimism, American philosophers like Dewey and Santayana are optimistic naturalists.

National Characteristics

As can be seen from this short summary of American philosophy, there are certain contributions to the development of human
thought that derive clearly and directly from the peculiar conditions
of life and forms of belief called "American." It is equally true
that American philosophy is not a thing apart from the general
stream of philosophic thought and that it cannot readily be understood except as an aspect of the entire history of human intellection.
For other countries a similar historical summary could be made
to show certain apparently national characteristics: the British

emphasize the psychological approach with the main stress on in-
dividualism, as in Hobbes, Locke, Berkeley, and Hume; the conti-
nental philosophers generally are more ontological, like Descartes
and Spinoza, although the Germans emphasize criticism — idealistic
in Kant, Fichte, and Schelling; materialistic in Büchner and Vogt;
pessimistic in Schopenhauer.[1] In general, while certain aspects of
"race, milieu and moment" are reflected by the individual philosopher just as they are by the individual artist, the philosopher's interest in the "science of the whole" tends to direct his attention
less to an introspective interpretation of personal experience (as
in art) and more to the universal truths which transcend personal
and national boundaries. While it is possible to trace the influence
of Hegel upon Marx, or of Schopenhauer upon Nietzsche, and to interpret such strains in terms of a German influence, it is equally
possible, and just as revealing, to trace the influence of a Spencer
upon McCosh, of Descartes upon Spinoza, and of Rousseau upon the
romantics in every country. Nationality thus becomes one — but
only one — of the many influences which throw light upon the personality of the individual philosopher and the character of his philosophical system.

Summary

Shifts in stress have often shown how philosophical concepts
change through time. It is not that philosophy is looked upon as
something different in each period, but that the emphasis is distributed so that different divisions of philosophy dominate. With
the Milesian philosophers, the world of nature was the concern, and
cosmology with its interest in the physical nature of the universe
attracted primary attention. With the later Greeks, social ethics
suitable to the city-state came into greater prominence. In the
Middle Ages, religious experience, not man, was of major importance, and theology was supreme. In the Renaissance, a stress
upon psychology reflected (or was reflected by) the return to the
belief in the central position of man. With the rise of modern science, the organization of methods for ascertaining truth became
necessary, and precedence was given to epistemology. Out of such
an emphasis upon organization there arose the need for an orderly
systematization of philosophical problems which drew attention to

---

[1] National histories of philosophy form a large part of the total publication in
this field and represent an approach favored by many readers. Typical titles in
this class are Yu-Lan Feng, *A History of Chinese Philosophy;* Herbert Wallace
Schneider, *A History of American Philosophy;* Guillermo Francovich, *Filósofos
Brasileños;* etc.

the history of philosophy as a guiding principle. Currently the wide
concern with communication and common understanding is seen in
philosophy in the interest in semantics. With changing times, the
focus of attention shifts.

It is possible, of course, to present the history of philosophical
thought to emphasize the "spirit of the age" and to show the *Zeitgeist* either as shaping the major philosophical systems or being
shaped by them. This approach in Egon Friedell's *A Cultural History of the Modern Age,* for example, provides many interesting
and perceptive interpretations of the interrelations, in any given
period, between the philosophy, the historical events, and the creative works of man. While it will be apparent to the reader of this
book that the ideals and ideas expressed by the philosophers are
also essentially the ideals and ideas expressed by their contemporary artists and scientists, the direction of the influence is less
clear. Do the artists get their ideas from the philosophers and
then reformulate them in accordance with the rules of their art?
Do the philosophers take from art the principles which will shape
the form of their philosophy? Are art, science, and philosophy results rather than causes, stemming from the cultural environment
which influences the individual and his work? And if this be so,
are not art, science, and philosophy a part of the total environment
which affects what is to follow just as they were affected by what
went before? These questions, stressing the interplay and interdependence of the several disciplines, will serve to enrich the
study of any one field and will act as a useful corrective to the
compartmental specialization of interests common in contemporary
education.

It is especially important for the librarian to resist such com-
partmentation and to recognize how an individual's background,
tradition, training, and place in time shape his view of the world.
If he can realize that his own views and preferences are as much
the product of these forces as are the views of others, he may be
able to see more objectively the many points of view which distinguish the several philosophical systems deserving a place on the
library's shelves, however contrary to the librarian's own philosophy they may be.

LIBRARY CLASSIFICATION IN THE FIELD OF PHILOSOPHY

The classification of disciplines which is one of the philosopher's concerns, is, in a slightly different sense, a concern of the
librarian as well. The distinction between the tasks of the two lies
in that the philosopher is occupied with the classification of knowledge, and the librarian with the classification of books. While books

contain man's accumulated knowledge, they are not the same thing
as knowledge.

A comparison of Francis Bacon's "Chart of Human Learning"[2]
with the philosophy classification schemes of Dewey and the Library of Congress clearly illustrates the differences although both
Dewey and Library of Congress are influenced by the Baconian
classification. In Bacon, philosophy is divided into three major
types: divine (natural theology); natural (physical and natural sciences); and human, which is in turn divided into four subdivisions —
(1) philosophy of humanity (nature of man; mind and body); (2) body
(medicine and the sensual arts); (3) soul (sense and reason, including logic and ethics); and (4) civil philosophy (man in his relation
to others, including etiquette, business, economics, and law).

A quick glance at this summary shows clearly that, while it is
a neat and logical arrangement of knowledge based upon "the faculties of the rational soul," it is far from adequate in dealing with
books, which are not written to conform to such an arrangement.
Given Bacon's basic definitions, it is logical that mathematics
should be separated from natural history, theology from revelation,
and literary history from literature itself, while physics, sociology
and economics should be grouped together. Such subject relations,
however, are not necessarily reflected in the writings in these
fields, and to fit the books themselves into such categories would
lead to strange combinations and separations.

Despite the problems it raises, the subject matter approach is
still the most useful one for book classification. "What is the book
about?" is the question the classifier asks himself. A philosopher,
though, may write about any subject in the world: Plato on government; Aristotle on physics; Augustine on theology; Bacon on scientific method; etc. In book classification schemes the dilemma is
resolved by designating in each subject field a place for the philosophy of the field, where the speculative thinking about the field may
be classified. In Dewey, for example, the "01" section is devoted
to the philosophy of the field; thus 201 is for the philosophy of religion; 301 is for the philosophy of sociology; 501 for the philosophy
of science, etc. Philosophy, itself, is that distinctive subject matter which synthesizes the several truths of art, religion, and science into a rational system in the harmony of all its parts.

Modern library classification schemes lean heavily upon Aristotle in their designation of subject matter which may be classified
as philosophy proper, rather than as the philosophy of another

---

[2] Francis Bacon, *The Advancement of Learning*. Ed. by William Aldis Wright.
5th ed. (Oxford, 1900). Also in W. C. Berwick Sayers, *A Manual of Classification for Librarians and Bibliographers*. 2nd ed., rev. (London, Grafton, 1944).

discipline. In Aristotle the subject matters which are the proper
concern of philosophy are logic, metaphysics, physics, ethics, politics and aesthetics. Most of these still remain in the Dewey 100
classification. Logic, metaphysics and ethics are preserved intact.
Politics — although assigned a number in the social sciences for its
practical aspects — still appears in Dewey as "State Ethics," a subdivision under the general topic of ethics. Physics, or natural philosophy, broke away to become a separate discipline in the sixteenth
and seventeenth centuries under the influence of the empirical method
of Bacon, Boyle, and Newton, but Dewey still leaves room for it in
the classification of the natural philosophy of the early philosophers
and the cosmological inquiries of many others. Aesthetics alone
finds no place in the 100 section, except as part of the psychology of
emotions; it appears in Dewey only in the art classification, as 701,
where it relates to the philosophy of the visual arts, but is out of
place for an aesthetics which includes the literary arts as well.
This classification illustrates a quirk in the philosophy of Dewey
more than a weakness in the scheme devised by Aristotle; aesthetics in Dewey's terminology is related to landscape art, forestry,
and city planning.

Strict adherence to a classification of knowledge as a basis for
the classification of books is seldom possible. The classification
of knowledge, since it need not be concerned with the format of the
medium through which that knowledge is presented, provides no
place for general types of books which cut across many fields, such
as dictionaries, encyclopedias, periodicals, etc. A classification of
books, on the other hand, must take such special format considerations into account. Consequently, in both Dewey and Library of
Congress room is left at the beginning of each subject division for
collections and form divisions. In Dewey, for example, the 00-09
section of each group of the ten major classes is devoted to such
general materials: in philosophy, 103 stands for a *dictionary* of
philosophy, 105 for a *periodical,* 108 for *collected works* of a miscellaneous character. These same form numbers are utilized
throughout the Dewey classification: 203 would be a *dictionary* of
religion; 705, a *periodical* in the field of art; 811.*08,* a *collection*
of American poetry.

Particular systems and doctrines are important in the literature also, although they are not subdivisions of knowledge as such,
but merely ways of looking at knowledge. Again, both Dewey and
Library of Congress provide for such works in special subdivisions
of the field of philosophy, whereas the philosopher himself can ignore the individual interpretations of a fact and concentrate on the
fact as such.

For practical purposes it is frequently necessary to classify the books as books instead of in terms of the knowledge with which they deal. The collected works of the individual philosophers must be represented in any collection of the literature of the field, quite apart from the specific aspects of knowledge with which individual parts may be concerned. The epistemologists may set up all-inclusive categories which are not required to adjust themselves to the unphilosophical vagaries of writers, editors and, compilers, but the classifier of books may not. In Dewey, the 180's and 190's are set aside for the collected works of individual philosophers; in the Library of Congress classification scheme this requirement is satisfied by providing a place for works which represent, not specific areas of knowledge, but national and historical categories. Consequently it can be seen that the discipline which is in itself most concerned with the classification of knowledge is not as useful as might be anticipated in providing for the arrangement of the books concerned with that knowledge.

Yet the logic and inclusiveness of the philosophical approach to classification has had a profound influence upon the devisers of book classification schemes, and much of Bacon has been retained in contemporary library systems. Unfortunately, the revision of Bacon to provide for needed categories destroys the basic consistency of his outline and the retention of parts of Bacon does not mean that Baconian order results. Since Bacon's day his method of compartmenting the human faculties has been shown to be psychologically unsound, and his subject groupings no longer reflect contemporary knowledge and scholarship. Changes have been forced upon later classifiers in many parts of the system, although both Dewey and Library of Congress cling to Bacon's category "Mind and Body," and Library of Congress still classifies etiquette and manners with philosophy. Such apparently irrational inclusions become understandable when we see the scheme from which they spring — a scheme whose fundamental unity has not been carried over in such vestiges.

The 100 classification of Dewey

The Dewey Decimal system in particular suffers from certain logical weaknesses that limit its effectiveness as a practical plan of book arrangement. Following the usual introductory section devoted to collections and other general form divisions, the 100's are divided, in the main, as follows:

110 and 120   Metaphysics, including ontology, cosmology,
                      epistemology, teleology, etc.

130   Metapsychology (the holdover from Bacon's "Mind
      and Body" category, which, in Dewey, includes
      the occult sciences)

140   Philosophical systems and doctrines (includes
      only discussions of particular systems as such,
      but not the works of philosophers belonging to
      the various schools. See 180 and 190, below)

150   General Psychology

160   Logic

170   Ethics

180   Ancient and Oriental Philosophers

190   Modern Philosophers (subdivided nationally, and
      then broken down within each national grouping
      chronologically, with individual numbers as-
      signed to individual philosophers)

If one of the purposes of a system of classification for a library
is to keep like books together, progressing from the general to the
specific in logical sequence, certain aspects of the Dewey 100's are
definitely inadequate. That psychology would some day be more
appropriately classed with the social or the biological sciences is
a development which Dewey perhaps could not be expected to foresee.
But it is difficult to understand why psychology (150) is separated
from abnormal psychology (which falls in the 130's), or why philosophic systems and doctrines (140) appears between the two sections on psychology rather than with the sections on ancient and
modern philosophers (180-190) who illustrate the doctrines in their
writings.

Another weakness is inherent in the decimal system itself,
which requires the arbitrary division of the classification into equal
groupings of ten places each. In the 14th edition of Dewey, for example, the 190's are devoted to modern philosophers, with 191 for
American and Canadian, 192 for British, 193 for German and Aus-
trian, etc. Under 191, a special decimal number is given to such
philosophers as Hickock, Noah Porter, and William Torrey Harris,
but once eight places have been used up, all other philosophers
(James, Dewey, et al) must be classed in 191.9 with other American
philosophic writers. The 15th edition drops the specific assignment
of decimals to individual philosophers and merely puts all modern

American and Canadian philosophers in the 191 section. To permit sufficient flexibility within a ten-place system, specificity is sacrificed.

The B-BJ Classification of the Library of Congress

The Library of Congress classification eliminates some of the inconsistencies in Dewey. It too begins with an introductory section for form divisions and collections, which is followed by these major sections:

B53-67	Theory, method, and relations including general discussions of the relation of philosophy to other disciplines
B69-4651	History and systems (divided chronologically up to modern philosophy, which is subdivided geographically with period subdivisions within each national grouping. Individual philosophers and their works are placed in their appropriate national and chronological sequence)
BC	Logic
BD	General philosophical treatises (corresponds to Dewey's 110, 120, and 140 classifications)
BF1-999 1001-1399 1401-1899	Psychology Metapsychology Occult sciences
BH	Aesthetics
BJ1-1699 1801-2199	Ethics Manners, Social Customs, Etiquette

In Library of Congress, psychology is collected in a single place, with metapsychology as a subdivision of the broader field, leading in more logical progression than Dewey to the so-called occult sciences. The historical development of philosophy precedes the treatment of individual philosophical systems, and modern philosophy, in its chronological place in the historical sequence, is divided by country, allowing the works of individual philosophers to appear in their chronological and national place. While this is essentially what the Dewey scheme attempts to do for modern philosophers, the arbitrary necessity of breaking down each section into groups of ten forces an unrealistic selection of philosophers for major emphasis. The greater flexibility of the Library of Congress classification overcomes this weakness.

Summary

Neither Library of Congress nor Dewey is absolutely satisfactory in all its aspects. The jump from metapsychology to doctrines to psychology in Dewey is not much less logical than the jump from occult sciences to aesthetics in Library of Congress, or its retention of manners and etiquette among the works of philosophy, rather than with sociological studies of mores and manners.

It is easier, however, to criticize existing systems than it is to devise new and better ones. The purpose of such criticism here is not to condemn minor weaknesses in schemes that have proved generally useful, but to show the difficulties that inevitably arise when an arbitrary arrangement is imposed upon a constantly changing and growing field. Perhaps no classification scheme can be constructed which will be sufficiently self-revising to keep abreast of the new developments and relationships in evolving knowledge. The student therefore should recognize the limitations of any classification scheme and should attempt to ascertain the extent to which the library patron actually finds the classification of books the useful tool librarians think it is. At the very least, he should recognize the need to supplement his classification with a system of cataloging which will clarify the relationships and bring out connections which classifications cannot convey.

CATALOGING IN THE FIELD OF PHILOSOPHY

The complexity of cataloging in the field of philosophy varies with the particular library and the interests and background of its clientele. In university and research libraries a much more precise system of subject headings is used, employing the special terminology of philosophy which could be completely unenlightening to a layman using a small, general collection. The scholar, for example, will want headings in the catalog for specific systems of philosophy — hylozoism, panpsychism, etc. — whereas the general reader is not likely to require anything more specific than a heading like "Philosophy, Ancient" or "Philosophy, Arabian." Philosophical systems of individual countries are broken down by types in scholarly catalogs — Lokayata, Manichaeism, etc. — whereas again the smaller library will find the heading "Philosophy," subdivided geographically or chronologically, sufficient.

Whether the catalog is detailed or general, the librarian is faced with the problem of translating patron requests into the terminology of the catalog with which he works. He should know under what headings one is apt to find works on monadology, phenomenalism, peripatetics, or cosmology; he should be able to recognize the approximate period and school, the identifying characteristics, the subject emphasis which are likely to be brought out in the catalog. It is useful, therefore, for the librarian to have at least a survey knowledge of the major philosophical systems, and to know, for example, that the "philosophy of happiness" is called hedonism; that the Scholastics were medieval philosophers; and that Existentialism does not begin with Sartre. He should be able to adapt the terminology of the card catalog to the needs of the layman whose knowledge is limited as well as to the specialist whose knowledge is profound. In philosophy then, as in any subject area, the librarian should be familiar with the men, the literature, and the special terminology of the field.

THE LITERATURE OF THE FIELD

It would simplify matters somewhat if it were completely true that the books which librarians classify as philosophy are those written by philosophers. That it is partially true is attested by the Dewey 180's and 190's, which are dedicated to the works of the ancient and modern philosophers, as traditionally accepted. But philosophers, as we have seen, write on many subjects outside the defined field of philosophy itself or on areas of knowledge no longer classified as philosophy; many philosophers are better known in other fields and are more readily available to the public if classified there. Many works about philosophy and philosophers are not written by philosophers themselves; and much peripheral material which classifies in the field stands for philosophy in the minds of many readers but would be repudiated by the greatest of philosophers.

Still the nucleus of any good collection of material in the field of philosophy must be the historic classics and the works that are part of the framework of modern thought. Indeed, there is one school of thought which defines philosophy as the *history* of philosophy only and which sees in the successive stages of the development of philosophical concepts an organic whole slowly revealing itself through this intellectual evolution. Certainly it is true that the great works of the major philosophers are the backbone of the literature of the field and that the commentaries, analyses, and "improvements" introduced by subsequent writers become, if sufficiently profound to be of permanent value, part of that literature of philosophy in their own right.

Many of the philosophers of major importance arrived at a philosophical system by building upon preceding philosophers and by formulating a set of hypotheses which would dispel weaknesses or flaws in the earlier system. To the philosophy of Descartes, for example, Spinoza adds a mathematical precision that develops the system to a point far beyond its original statement. Berkeley's subjective idealism develops out of his criticism of Locke's method of distinguishing primary and secondary qualities of bodies. Nietzsche takes the philosophy of Schopenhauer and substitutes the "will to power" for the "will to live" to develop his theory of the superman. Thus the basic literature of philosophy is both primary material and critical commentary upon it.

There is a distinction, however, between a major philosophical contribution and a textbook interpretation. The latter concentrates upon an analysis and exposition of a specific philosopher and his school (or group of philosophers and their schools). The former is a critique of a philosopher and his school leading to another formulation. This does not mean that a critical evaluation may not be attempted in the textbook; it means only that the major object of the textbook is to make clear the philosopher's position, whereas the philosophical critique has as its major object the substitution of a "better" statement of the basic questions and a more valid organization of principles. While it may begin as an evaluation of another system of thought, it ends as an exposition of a new one, and the philosopher most clearly explained is not the subject of the discourse, but the immediate writer.

Logic differs slightly from the other subject divisions of philosophy in that it is not a critique of belief, but a technique of reasoning. As such it is an exposition of method which can be applied to all subject fields and not a subject field isolated. In the field of logic too, however, may be found the basic expositions of ideal method, criticisms of these expositions and the presentation of a "superior" alternative, and textbooks explaining the major methodological statements.

Popularization

Popularization — in the sense of simplified presentation of the scholarship — is limited in this field. Hardly a title comes to mind — except for Will Durant's *The Story of Philosophy* — which could qualify in the genre that comprises a large segment of publications in most of the other fields. The explanation may lie in the fact that the "science of the whole" does not readily lend itself to dilution and simplification; philosophical systems are presented in accordance with formal rules of logical presentation, inference from the evidence, and dialectical method implicit in the system itself which cannot be too much simplified without losing their entire meaning.

Consequently, the popularizations tend generally to minimize the philosophical doctrine itself and to concentrate on the philosopher as a man. The Durant volume is essentially a collection of biographical sketches and pays only incidental attention to a presentation of any philosopher's system of thought. Other popularizations frankly appear as biographies: Lewis Browne's *Blessed Spinoza* and Carl Crow's *Master Kung* are typical.

Introductions to philosophical systems and doctrines and simplifications of them do appear frequently but they are generally intended as student texts rather than as popular reading. While these books do essentially what popularizations in other fields do, they lack the popular appeal in style and format which would qualify them for that category. The seriousness of their approach, the lack of dramatic presentation, the character of their publicity and channels of distribution limit their audience almost entirely to students. Even though they exhibit such titles as *Invitation to Philosophy* or *Philosophy for the Millions*, the fact is that they win few readers except serious students of philosophy.

Periodicals

The periodical literature of philosophy reflects the same scholarly emphasis. In 1952 the Library of Congress Reference department published a list of *Philosophical Periodicals*,[3] an excellent basic listing of the periodicals published throughout the world in this field. Over 450 titles are noted, all of them on a high scholarly level, although not all of them are devoted exclusively to philosophical subjects. Of these, very few would be used outside scholarly or research libraries. Ulrich's *Periodical Directory* (8th edition, 1956) listed over 150 titles under the heading "Philosophy," most of them in foreign languages (as are the majority in the Library of Congress list) and again most of them scholarly in nature. Ayer's *Directory of Newspapers and Periodicals* for 1956 listed only twelve magazines under the subject "Philosophical." Of these, seven are university publications; one is a quarterly published by the Cleveland Museum of Art; and one is the proceedings of the American Philosophical Society. The "popular" titles in the philosophical field, as revealed by both Ulrich and Ayer, are of three main types: (1) Organs of particular groups whose writings are of

---

[3] U. S. Library of Congress. Reference Department. *Philosophical Periodicals; An Annotated World List* (Washington, Library of Congress, Card Division, 1952).

little value outside the circle of their own adherents. (2) Writings
on occult "sciences" and similar topics which can only be called
seminecromancy. (3) Publications in the special area of such "ethical" problems as temperance or antivivisection. Few libraries can
justify expenditures for such publications as a charge against their
budget allocations for philosophy.

Popular Philosophy

There is a field of writing, however, defined as philosophy by
the layman, which has a sufficiently heavy popular demand to require some representation on the shelves of the public libraries.
This is the ever-growing area of self-help and consolation books,
which do not so much attempt to interpret the teachings of the great
philosophers, as to present a "philosophy" of practical utility for
those who seek an easy and external solution to perennial problems.
Perhaps the best way to distinguish between a philosophical system
and a popular philosophy is to note the emphasis. In the great philosophers, the important thing is the *question*. The scholar is interested to know: "What are the problems? How can they best be
stated? What are the implications? What approaches to an answer
follow inevitably from them?"

In the popular writers, the stress is upon the *answer*; there is
no logical sequence of thought presented, based upon the correct
statement of the basic problem, but merely a "practical" solution
to everyday problems which may or may not address itself to the
several implications which a complete statement of the question
would entail. Such titles as Robert H. Schauffler's *Enjoy Living;
An Invitation to Happiness;* Alice Hegan Rice's *Happiness Road*
("A prescription book of happiness!"); Vash Young's *Be Kind to
Yourself;* and Walter Pitkin's *Life Begins at Forty* are typical of
the "painless" self-discipline which constitutes "philosophy" for
many patrons of the public library. In the popular field, at least,
the literature of philosophy and psychology properly belong together, for both concern themselves primarily with providing consolation and advice and almost completely ignore the scholar's
emphasis upon method.

Fringe Literature in the Field of Philosophy

It is but a short step from the popular "philosophy" discussed
in the preceding section to the lunatic-fringe "metaphysical topics"
which classifies in the 120's and 130's. "In no other field, save
perhaps religion, is so much twaddle, crank literature, and involved statement produced, as in philosophy," says Francis K. W.

Drury,[4] referring to the psychic and occult revelations and allied charlatanry which issue endlessly from the presses. Such materials would hardly be considered philosophy by a philosopher, but there is a historical reason why they are so classified in the popular mind. The concern of philosophers with the universe, and the eternal and immutable reality of things apart from the observed world of sense, led them often into mystical bypaths. To understand the universe meant that one would be able to control it (note the contemporary interest of philosophers in scientific laws which, when properly understood, will bend a mechanistic world to the will of man) and rational intellection veered off into magic and necromancy. The stone which could turn base metals into gold was known by the alchemists as the "philosopher's stone"; the early cosmological theories of the Milesian philosophers are excellent examples of what we today designate as pseudo science. Contemporary pseudo sciences include numerology, astrology, phrenology, and the like for which a credulous public can always be found and for whom there will probably always be a steady flow of publication. If such publications find their way into the library, they classify as "metaphysical" and take their place beside Plato, Bacon, and Descartes.

BOOK SELECTION IN THE FIELD OF PHILOSOPHY

The major part of any good library collection in the field should consist of the works of the leading philosophers themselves. Since the presentation of the argument is of basic importance in philosophical writing, interpretation of the original text may vitally affect the understanding of the original system. In scholarly and research libraries, therefore, the classic and standard philosophers will have to be represented both in their original language and in translation. The scholars of philosophy will not be content to accept translations in instances where the misinterpretation of a single word may alter the doctrine's basic sense. With the current emphasis upon semantic analysis, this consideration becomes even more important, and authentic texts become as much a scholarly concern in this field as in the field of religion.

For the average layman, typographically readable texts in English will be more needed than those in the original language of the philosopher. Well-selected excerpts from the philosophers are also of value if they represent scholarly judgment and informative annotation. An anthology such as *Landmarks of Philosophy*, edited

---

[4] Francis K. W. Drury, *Book Selection* (Chicago, American Library Assn., 1930), p. 136.

by Irwin Edman and Walter Schneider, for example, gives lengthy and important excerpts from the classics of philosophy, with introductory notes that place each philosopher in his historical context and philosophical sequence. Books of this type often serve to introduce the major philosophers to laymen who would be discouraged by the length and difficulty of their complete works. Care should be taken, however, to check the qualifications of the editor and publisher of such compilations to insure a minimum of distortion, oversimplification, and misinterpretation.

For students and educated laymen, introductions, outlines, and histories of the development of philosophical thought are extremely important. Although such works are, in a sense, a simplification of the basic philosophical systems, they usually are more difficult than the average popularization in other fields and appeal to a limited group of readers. Here again, authority and authenticity are primary requisites and popular appeal is of little realistic consequence. Popularizations, as pointed out before, hardly exist in this field and represent a very minor problem in selection.

The real problems arise in the areas of "popular philosophy" and pseudo philosophy, which do have a large following although they bear little relation to the philosophy recognized by the scholars. The self-help and consolation "philosophies" are in great demand; they are backed by large programs of publisher promotion; they are widely reviewed, often enthusiastically, in reviewing media to which the public has most ready access; and they seem to answer a widely felt need in present-day society. The arguments in defense of this literature are that it releases tensions and assuages fears; that it helps to maintain satisfaction with the status quo; and that it serves a constructive psychological function in helping people with problems to maintain their balance. The arguments against it are that its consolation is false; that it seems to soothe surface ills while failing completely to deal with underlying causes; and that for those addicted to it, it is like a narcotic which is more harmful than the pain it eases. It has been suggested that the adjustments effected by such "philosophies" may be valid only in the unreal world pictured in their pages, and that one who relies upon them may become progressively less able to adjust to the world as it is. If the librarian thinks of his institution as an educational agency he should weigh carefully the arguments cited above and attempt to satisfy himself whether the answers provided by such literature lead to a constructive adjustment, or whether they offer escape from problems by teaching the reader to evade rather than face them.

One difficulty in reaching a decision is that the same book may affect different readers in different ways. A book that would provide one reader with the kind of incentive he needs to help him to adjust to a particular problem might for another reader in another situation lead to further complications rather than to solution. The student may find it instructive to analyze a popular self-help book in terms of its possible effects on readers of several different kinds. He may find the book to be very useful for the aggressive personality but not for the retiring one; excellent for the religious person but meaningless for the agnostic; beneficial to one reader and detrimental to another. To purchase such a book is to do a disservice to some library patrons; to reject it is to deny valuable service to others. The student should attempt to resolve the problem in a manner consistent with his concept of his library's function.

The pseudoscientific materials which classify as "metaphysical" also trouble librarians, although the case here is less complex. Most librarians would agree that one thing that the library should *not* do is promote and extend ignorance and superstition. Yet they often find it difficult to deny to patrons materials for which there is constant demand. How can the librarian, they ask, tell a sincere believer in numerology that such beliefs are false, that literature dealing with it is quackery, and that the library defines as trash that which the patron considers basic truth? The answer is, of course, that the librarian's position gives him the requisite authority in matters of book selection and that he has as much right to brand a dream book as substandard as he has to rule out pornography. The firm believer in crystal gazers may refuse to be convinced that such an attitude is anything more than willful authoritarianism, but the librarian is completely justified in excluding from his shelves materials which will assist charlatans and support falsehood.

The public librarian, dependent upon public support for his library's existence, is often understandably hypersensitive to the temper of his community and the complaints of its more vocal members. Where he must — or thinks he must — assuage every ruffled feeling and satisfy every expressed demand no matter what this does to the character of his book collection, he departs drastically from the ideal of the library as an educational institution. It may be that individual circumstances occasionally force such compromises. This in itself is regrettable, but to justify such compromises in the name of lofty objectives is reprehensible. The librarian should recognize what he is doing when he succumbs to pressures; he should not pretend that these steps are taken as part of his program of public enlightenment; he should not confuse evasion with education.

Once the librarian has decided which fields he will cover within the area designated philosophy he is faced with fewer problems of selection than in other fields in which there is much more prolific

publication on many more levels of excellence and appeal. In the
matter of the basic writings, there is little argument. While contemporary philosophers may disagree with the system of thought
proposed in the writings of Aristotle, or Berkeley, or Kant, there
is little dissension about their importance in the development of
philosophical thinking. Still, the particular system advocated by
the historian of philosophy does color his evaluations to a certain
extent, and it is interesting to note which philosophers are omitted
from each of the several histories of philosophy and which are included and emphasized.

For example, three general histories of philosophy — a standard, conventional, short text, C. C. J. Webb's *A History of Philosophy;* a generally approved history by a Catholic writer, William
Turner's *History of Philosophy;* and Bertrand Russell's highly
personal *A History of Western Philosophy* — were compared for
inclusions and emphases. There is, as would be expected, general
agreement on most of the philosophers to whom major treatment is
given. But there are also some interesting variations, variations
which cannot be explained solely on the grounds of the differences
in length (and presumably corresponding differences in inclusiveness) among the three volumes. The Webb, which aims at a concise summary, contains only 251 pages of text; the Turner, 674
pages; and the Russell, 836 pages. Yet Webb, even in so short a
survey, includes Bruno, Reid, Mansel, Spencer, Herbart, and
Comte, none of whom is mentioned by Russell. Turner is the most
inclusive, noting most of the philosophers in the other volumes
and including besides a large number of the Scholastic philosophers
who are not mentioned in the other two. Russell, on the other hand,
despite his omission of certain of the standard philosophers, includes long discussions of Erasmus and Marx, neither of whom is
more than mentioned in the other volumes, and devotes an entire
chapter to Byron, who understandably is not considered a philosophical figure by the other writers. Emphases also vary. Holding
length constant, one finds a comparatively long treatment of Rousseau in Russell, whereas Webb merely mentions him, and the Turner
volume, which is more than twice as long as Webb, gives no more
space than Webb to its discussion of Rousseau, thereby further
minimizing his importance in the development of philosophic thought.
Gerbert is given extended treatment in Turner, minor treatment in
Russell, and is not mentioned in Webb. Similar variations were
found in a great number of cases of the minor philosophers.

These variations do not necessarily reflect upon the reliability
of the volumes investigated. Rather they may be considered informative of the historian's outlook and as sources of particular strengths
in his handling of the material. Russell's liberal inclusion of men

like More and Byron adds much in the way of cultural background
and general sense of period; Turner's treatment is especially useful for its attention to the Scholastics; and Webb's inclusiveness
shows his book to be surprisingly complete despite the limits placed
upon length. An exercise of this kind in comparative analysis is
suggested here merely to indicate that more than one authority
must be taken as a guide to the master works and that more than
one history must be represented on the library's shelves to insure
a complete coverage of the field.

The question immediately arises: how does the librarian know
which are the most important philosophers if there are disagreements even among the historian-philosophers themselves? If "to
know" is interpreted to mean "to be absolutely and dogmatically
certain," the answer must of course always be he doesn't. But he
can read widely and judiciously; he can be familiar with the consensus of current scholarship; and he can bring his own judgment,
augmented by that of the authorities in the field, to bear upon a final
decision. The librarian has much readier access to the literature
and the guides and interpretations connected with it than does the
average library patron. To be familiar with the "best that is known
and thought" in a subject field is part of the librarian's task. While
he may not rival the subject specialist in substantive knowledge of
the specialist's own discipline, the librarian is supposed to be the
"expert" in the literature and bibliography of any subject field.

The standard guides to book selection are valuable here. Such
tools as the *Standard Catalog for Public Libraries,* the Shaw *List
of Books for College Libraries,* and similar publications will serve
to identify the core works. A greater problem exists in the selection of the most desirable editions of the standard works and the
writings of contemporary philosophers whose position in the development of philosophy has not yet been unequivocally established.
There are certain writers even among the contemporaries — Croce,
Dewey, Joad, Santayana, Russell, to name a few — who have achieved
a position of sufficient authority to make purchase of any new title
virtually mandatory except for the most limited collections. For
lesser known writers, the critical reviews are the main source of
information, although reviews in general media should be used with
caution. The scholarly journals in the field give the most reasoned
and sound evaluations, but as in other disciplines, the learned journals report so long after the publication of the volumes reviewed
that they are of little value for initial purchase. The qualifications
of the author and the reputation of the publisher are helpful, if not
infallible, clues to the worth of those works whose content the librarian feels incompetent to evaluate.

The librarian is not absolved from responsibility because

critical reviews exist. It is not enough that he be able to select those volumes and editions which the majority of reviewers favor; he must also be able to evaluate them in terms of his own patrons and to place them where they can be most constructively used in relation to the other books in his collection and in the mainstream of philosophical literature. As in other subject fields, he can best serve his patrons if he is personally familiar with the history and development of the subject field and the landmark writers and works in which that history is reflected.

A selected list of landmark philosophers and some of their representative writings appears in Table I. Although it is unlikely that many librarians have read completely every title on the list, the patron of the library has the right to expect that the librarian will at least be familiar with all of them and will be able to place

TABLE I

Some Landmark Writers and Works
in the Development of Philosophic Thought

Plato (427?-347 B.C.)	The Dialogues, of which The Republic is one of the most widely known
Aristotle (348-322 B.C.)	The Nicomachean Ethics The Organon
Lucretius (96?-55 B.C.)	On the Nature of Things
Aurelius Antoninus, Marcus (121-180)	Meditations
Plotinus (205?-270)	Ethical Treatises Enneads
St. Augustine (354-430)	The City of God
Aquinas, St. Thomas (1225-1274)	Summa Theologica
Machiavelli, Niccolo (1469-1527)	Discourses The Prince
Bacon, Francis (1561-1626)	Novum Organum The Advancement of Learning
Hobbes, Thomas (1588-1679)	Leviathan
Descartes, René (1596-1650)	Discourse on Method
Spinoza, Benedict (1632-1677)	Ethics
Locke, John (1632-1704)	Essay Concerning the Human Understanding
Leibniz, Gottfried von (1646-1716)	The Monadology
Berkeley, George (1685-1753)	A New Theory of Vision A Treatise Concerning the Principles of Human Knowledge

Hume, David (1711-1776)	Enquiry Concerning Human Understanding A Treatise of Human Nature
Kant, Immanuel (1724-1804)	Critique of Pure Reason
Fichte, Johann (1762-1814)	Critique of All Revelation
Hegel, Georg (1770-1831)	Phenomenology of the Mind The Science of Logic
Schelling, Friedrich von (1775-1854)	System of Transcendental Idealism
Schopenhauer, Arthur (1788-1860)	Pessimism The World as Will and Idea
Comte, Auguste (1798-1857)	Course of Positive Philosophy
Mill, John Stuart (1806-1873)	Utilitarianism System of Logic
Kierkegaard, Soren (1813-1855)	Philosophical Fragments Sickness Unto Death
Spencer, Herbert (1820-1903)	First Principles Synthetic Philosophy
Peirce, Charles S. (1839-1914)	The Destiny of Man
Fiske, John (1842-1901)	Outlines of Cosmic Philosophy
James, William (1842-1910)	Pragmatism
Nietzsche, Friedrich (1844-1900)	Thus Spake Zarathustra
Royce, Josiah (1855-1916)	The World and the Individual
Bergson, Henri (1859-1941)	Creative Evolution Creative Mind
Dewey, John (1859-1952)	Human Nature and Conduct Logic
Whitehead, Alfred North (1861-1947)	Science and the Modern World Process and Reality
Santayana, George (1863-1952)	Realms of Being Skepticism and Animal Faith
Croce, Benedetto (1866-1952)	Philosophy of the Spirit
Russell, Bertrand (1872-)	Problems of Philosophy Introduction to Mathematical Philosophy
Korzybski, Alfred (1879-1950)	Science and Sanity
Sartre, Jean Paul (1905-)	Existentialism

them in chronological time and in the history of philosophic thought. Such a familiarity can be gained, of course, through the use of the surveys which appear in encyclopedias and popular histories. Typical of such summaries is the deliberately oversimplified survey on p. 64, which highlights the identifying characteristics of the successive periods in philosophic history as they are popularly accepted. It is suggested that the student read with care the work of one of the philosophers on the list to test the extent to which his ideas and his orientation are actually reflected in the summary. The exercise will serve to demonstrate whatever advantages such a survey has, but it will also underline the weaknesses of so facile a condensation. In this way the student will learn by his own experience how far he may rely upon the encyclopedic treatment and what values lie in the more intensive study of the major thinkers themselves.

LIBRARY SERVICES IN THE FIELD OF PHILOSOPHY

Special Libraries

The student who majors in philosophy before entering the field of librarianship will find very few special libraries in which he can capitalize upon his speciality. In the three volumes of *Special Library Resources,* compiled by the Special Libraries Association, only three philosophy libraries as such are mentioned: the American Friends Service Committee Library, which houses materials on the religious belief and philosophy of the Quakers; the Supreme Council of the Thirty-Third and Last Degree, Scottish Rite of Freemasonry Library in Washington, D.C., which concentrates on the literature of Freemasonry; and the Pontifical Institute of Medieval Studies in Toronto. A degree in philosophy would be of particular value as background for the librarian in only the third library.

Of the thirty-one special collections in philosophy which are mentioned in the 20th edition of the *American Library Directory* (1954), only six (five university and one college collection) are separately housed under the supervision of a special librarian, and one of these is part of a collection devoted to education and psychology as well as to philosophy. Ten of the colleges which make special note of a philosophy collection are seminaries or religious schools where religious training rather than a background in general philosophy would be the major preparation expected of the librarian. Few public libraries, aside from a unique institution like New York Public Library, have a separate department in the field of philosophy. Whereas large and important collections of books on philosophical subjects may be found in both public and college libraries, they are seldom of sufficient consequence in the library's total operation to require of the administrator a background in philosophy. It can be seen that opportunities are limited for students to utilize philosophy majors in library work.

However, the subject matter of philosophy ranges wide over all knowledge, and few librarians, whatever their special subject interest, will be able to ignore completely the materials of philosophy. As indicated above in the discussion of library classification schemes, each field has its own "philosophy," and librarians in most subject fields will find it necessary to include some of the writings of the philosophers whose inquiries impinge on their subject matter.

Reference Work in Philosophy

While few reference works exist in the field of philosophy, the demand for reference assistance is so limited that librarians have seldom found it necessary to protest the lack. The material of philosophy does not lend itself to terse simplification and quick reference summarization. The students and scholars of philosophy must go directly to the writings of the philosophers themselves and the average layman is not interested in philosophy generally, but in diluted imitations of it.

Five different studies of reference work, for example, found that when reference questions are classified by subject matter, a small percentage of the total number falls in the field of philosophy. The following summary is adapted from a table in the dissertation by Van Hoesen,[5] in which a comparison of the findings in the several studies is made:

Percentage of Reference Questions Falling in the 100 Dewey Class, as Reported in Five Studies of Reference Work

Author of Study	Percentage of Total Reference Questions Classifying in the Dewey 100's
Van Hoesen	2.1
Cole	1.5
Charters	1.5
Rozendal	0.9
Conner	1.0
Average	1.4

[5] Florence R. Van Hoesen, *An Analysis of Adult Reference Work in Public Libraries: An Approach to the Content of a First Year Reference Course* (Ph.D. dissertation, University of Chicago, 1948).

In each study, this number represents the smallest percentage in the entire column of Dewey classes. The limited demand for reference assistance in the field of philosophy is even more evident when one realizes that psychology is included in the 100's.

The studies also report little variety in the kind of questions, with the general information type predominating. The majority of the questions are asked by professional people, students, and housewives who need information for "Use on the Job," "Class Assignment," and "Help in Work with Organizations," reasons clearly reflecting the predominance of teachers among the professional people and of "club paper" use among housewives. Of the 121 questions in the 100 class analyzed by Van Hoesen, only 35 were answered through reference books (not necessarily books classified as 100's); 71 were answered through circulating books (of which 30 were on psychology rather than philosophy); 6 through periodicals and newspapers; and 6 through miscellaneous types of publications (pamphlets, government publications, etc.). It may be hypothesized that reference tools might have been utilized more frequently if they existed, but they apparently were not needed.

Types of reference tools in the field [6]

Only one encyclopedia-type of reference aid exists in the field of philosophy: James Mark Baldwin's three-volume *Dictionary of Philosophy and Psychology,* which was published in 1901. While adequate in its way, it is, of course, very much out of date and of little value except for its historical articles. Its bibliography (volume three of the set, edited by Benjamin Rand) was extremely good in its day but is now half a century behind in its listings.

A good bibliography is probably one of the most needed tools in the field, since guides to reading are much more in demand than the usual quick-reference type of aids. There are three extensive bibliographies available at the moment: the *Bibliographie de la Philosophie,* published by the International Institute of Philosophical Collaboration, arranged by subject and annotated; the quarterly published by the Société Philosophique de Louvain, *Répertoire Bibliographique de la Philosophie,* also arranged by subject matter and universal in scope, although not annotated; and the *Bibliographia Philosophica,* a history of all books, periodicals, and book reviews published from 1934-45 [7] in eleven different languages, arranged chronologically according to the lives of the philosophers of different historical periods and schools. The *Philosophic Abstracts* is

---

[6] See list of Representative Reference Tools, p. 98.
[7] Five year supplements are planned.

of limited usefulness because of its restricted scope and such general tools as the *Standard Catalog* or the general encyclopedias are too highly selective for anything except introductory lists.

It should be remembered that many of the information questions in philosophy can be adequately answered through general reference tools. Although a *Who's Who in Philosophy* exists for Anglo-American philosophers (a second volume is planned for European biography) most of the important living philosophers can be found through *Who's Who* and *Who's Who in America,* or through the biographical dictionaries in the field of education. Encyclopedia articles on the standard philosophers are written by experts and are usually sufficiently detailed for the layman who wants a quick answer to such a question as "What did Berkeley believe?" Most of the standard terms — monad, ontology, solipsism, élan vital, etc. — are defined in an unabridged dictionary, although Runes's *Dictionary of Philosophy* sometimes supplies a few additional details. The average small library need not be too concerned by the limited publication of reference materials in this special field.

Readers' Advisory Work

A more difficult service to perform satisfactorily in philosophy is readers' advisory work. The lack of useful bibliographies has already been noted, but even where they exist — *The Bookman's Manual,* the *Standard Catalog,* and the several selective guides like the Pelican volume prepared by the Committee on College Reading, *Good Reading* — they are not sufficiently detailed as to levels of readability, nor do they define adequately the organization of the individual works. The librarian must be familiar with the various approaches to the material of philosophy taken by the titles on his shelves since the patron often requires information from a particular point of view.

The simplest approach to a study of philosophy is a purely chronological one, which follows the several major philosophers through time and reveals their temporal relation to each other. This is useful because of the dependence of later philosophers upon earlier ones and because of the development of philosophic thought through the elaboration and revision of existing philosophies. A straight chronological history like Russell's *A History of Western Philosophy* or Webb's *A History of Philosophy* is so organized. The national approach, in which the philosophers of a single country are examined, has been mentioned. Another approach is by way of the particular problems to which philosophers have addressed themselves — freedom of the will, the existence of God, etc., taking these problems individually through the several philosophers, ignoring both chronological sequence and national boundaries. A book like S. E. Frost's *The Basic Teachings of the Great Philosophers* is such a treatment, and the *Syntopicon* published by the University of Chicago carries this method of dealing with the material to its extreme.

The student approach to philosophical writings is frequently by way of the *kind* of philosophy about which he wishes to read. The classification of kinds, however, varies with the individual classifier and is so much a matter of interpretation that no one classification of any philosopher's system finds universal agreement. The classification of kinds may be made in the following ways:[8]

1. According to the number of fundamental principles recognized: monistic, dualistic, or pluralistic

2. According to the sort of value attached to the fundamental principle chosen as the basis of organization: materialism, spiritualism, phenomenalism

3. According to the organ or instrument of knowledge emphasized: rationalism, empiricism, sensationalism

4. According to the method pursued,
   a. as regards procedure: skepticism, dogmatism
   b. as regards results reached: agnosticism, transcendentalism

5. According to the relationship assumed between subject and object of knowing: realism, idealism

6. According to the sphere of interest: political philosophy, ethics

The task of the readers' adviser, then, is to become familiar with the organization and special viewpoints of the books on his shelves so that he can select from them the ones best suited to the needs of the individual patron. The recommended exercise in anticipating effects (see p. 88) demonstrates the importance of the readers' adviser in leading patrons to the books which will be "best" in terms of individual needs. He should know the scope of each work, its strengths and weaknesses, the "school" which the writer advocates, and the level of difficulty of its presentation. While these are

---

[8] Adapted from the article "Philosophy" by John Dewey in Baldwin's *Dictionary of Philosophy and Psychology,* II, p. 290-96.

principles of general application in all subject fields, the inadequacy of descriptive bibliographic tools in philosophy makes them doubly important here.

REPRESENTATIVE REFERENCE TOOLS IN THE FIELD OF PHILOSOPHY

Dictionaries and Encyclopedias

Baldwin, James Mark. *Dictionary of Philosophy and Psychology.* 3 vols. in 4. 1901-05. New ed. with corrections, 1925. Reprinted, 1940-49.
Runes, Dagobert D., ed. *The Dictionary of Philosophy.* 1942. (Reissued 1955)

Bibliographies

Bibliographia Philosophica, 1934-45.
   vol. 1. Bibliographia historiae philosophiae. 1950.
   vol. 2. Bibliographia philosophiae. 1954.
Decennial Index to Philosophical Literature, 1939-1950. n.d.
International Institute of Philosophy. *Bibliographie de la philosophie.* vol. 1- 1937-
Philosophic Abstracts. 1939-54. (Discontinued)
Rand, Benjamin. *Bibliography of Philosophy, Psychology and Cognate Subjects.* 1905. Separate edition of vol. 3 of Baldwin (see above).
Répertoire bibliographique de la philosophie. vol. 1- 1949-
Standard Catalog for Public Libraries: Philosophy, Religion and General Works Section. Dorothy E. Cook and Dorothy Herbert West, eds. 1949. (Kept up to date through periodical supplements)
Also useful: *International Index to Periodicals.* vol. 1- 1907/15-

Biographical Tools

Who's Who in Philosophy. Runes, Dagobert D., ed. 1942. Vol. 1 is devoted to Anglo-American philosophers; vol. 2 (projected) is to deal with European and others.
Also useful: *Library of Living Philosophers,* edited by P. A. Schilpp. An annual series of volumes each devoted to a separate philosopher, including a biography, a series of critical essays, the reply of the subject to his critics, and a complete bibliography of his writings.
General biographical dictionaries, like *Who's Who* and *Who's Who in America.*

Reference History

Ueberweg, Friedrich. *Grundriss der Geschichte der Philosophie.*
5 vols. 1923-28. (vols. 2-5 reissued, 1951-54)
Particularly useful for its biographical information and its
full bibliographies.

chapter three

fine arts

INTRODUCTION

The field of the fine arts, however we define the specific types of art which fall into its province, is much broader, even for the librarian, than merely the books about it. The works of art themselves are of primary importance and are the real subject matter of the field. To deal with the books about the arts the librarian should know something about the technical problems connected with the creation of art objects, the qualities which distinguish them as art, and their place in the history of the art's development. In the case of any single field of the arts, like painting for example, the librarian is faced with a task double that of his dealing with an area of the social sciences or the natural sciences, where to be familiar with the content of the books is to be familiar with the content of the field. This double knowledge must be acquired also for each of the several types of art — painting, drawing, architecture, sculpture, design — and whatever other allied creative skills are comprehended in his library's definition of the arts. Furthermore, in the field of art, unlike the field of science, later works do not replace earlier ones; the earliest objects of art are as important, as valid, as "contemporary" as the latest. A cursory knowledge of the past is not enough, and the librarian's knowledge of both the books and the works of art must cover the entire history of artistic creation — a history which begins with the earliest of prehistoric cave paintings.

Obviously, within the confines of a short chapter it is too great a task to cover the field from the standpoint of each of the arts, the books about each of the arts, and the library problems involved in dealing with the books, the objects, and the many other materials which can be used by the library. Students spend an entire academic lifetime in the pursuit of knowledge about art alone; they study extensively the history of art, the elements and techniques employed in each of the several kinds of artistic creation, the basic concepts in the several aesthetic theories, and intensively, many individual works of art themselves. Having achieved this background, they still may be largely ignorant of art bibliography, and certainly they are unaware of the special problems of librarianship. Expert though they may be in art, they still come to the librarian for assistance in using the materials of art which libraries handle.

Since this chapter cannot possibly reach the ideal of making every library student both an art expert and a library expert, the emphasis will be upon the tools and kinds of knowledge required by the latter. The approach to the field of art will be an oblique one: the development of the field, the great creators, the masterworks, the growth of new concepts in the arts, the acceptance of new art forms and techniques and the special terminology will be introduced through the library materials with which the librarian deals. The attempt will be to teach the student what to look for, where to find it, what criteria to apply, and what special problems of handling and interpretation will face him in the library situation. He will not become either an artist or an expert on art. The knowledge which it is hoped he will attain will be the kind of knowledge necessary to make him a valuable assistant to the artists, the art experts, the students, and the laymen in their contacts with the literature and other library materials in the field of the arts.

THE DEFINITION OF THE TERM ART

Merely to define the meaning of the term "art" is in itself a complex problem. In its oldest sense, the term implies any skill or aptitude, acquired or innate, which makes possible superior performance on the part of its possessor. As late as 1946, art was defined as "any intelligent method by which nature is controlled"[1]—a

---

[1] *Encyclopedia of the Arts,* ed. by D. D. Runes and H. G. Schrickel (N. Y., Philosophical Lib., 1946), p. 66.

definition which embraces virtually every activity of man. By extension, a *work* of art is therefore any skillfully executed act and need not even be a tangible object. In certain contexts, this broad meaning still attaches to the term, as in such familiar phrases as "the art of living," "the art of war," and the "art of saying things well."

In general, however, modern usage of the term "art" connotes the skillful production of the beautiful in visible forms; the application of skill to the arts of imitation and design, and most specifically, to the arts of painting and drawing, sculpture, and architecture. While this sense of the term does not appear in any English dictionary until after 1880, it is now its most usual modern meaning, and arts which are nonvisual are generally specifically indicated by a qualifying adjective — the *literary* arts or the *musical* arts. When the term is used without qualification of any sort, its most frequent sense is that of the visual arts, or even of painting only, and it is not unusual in modern English to speak of someone who prefers art to music, or to use the term "artist" to refer specifically to a painter.

Yet painting, sculpture, and architecture did not always dominate the list of the arts; historically, they were more often omitted from the select company of the fine arts in favor of poetry and music. In Greece the arts of the Muses included poetry, music, drama, history, astronomy and the dance, but not any of the visual arts, although today a museum (a temple of the Muses) is more likely to contain paintings and statues than poems and plays. In the Middle Ages, the value of the visual arts was thought to lie primarily in their utility: figurative art was valuable in illustrating moral doctrine and sacred history; architecture was important in providing shelter and commemorating events and persons; and the painter or sculptor was essentially a mechanic or artisan. Only the liberal arts were deemed genteel and elegant enough to befit a freeborn gentleman, and the liberal arts were what today would be thought of as the science of the time rather than its art. These were the trivium — grammar, dialectic, and rhetoric; and the quadrivium — arithmetic, geometry, music, and astronomy, with music having as its object the proportion of numbers rather than the creation of beauty addressed to the sense of hearing. Although certain changes have occurred, the modern liberal arts curriculum and the bachelor of arts degree stem from this medieval concept of the nonservile arts suitable to the gentleman, and the "arts" of which a modern college graduate is master are anachronistically those of the thirteenth century rather than those of the twentieth.

Despite the predominance of painting, sculpture, and decorative art in the creative production of the Renaissance, the word art continued to connote, for many, scientific knowledge rather than creation of beautiful objects, and vestiges of this concept of the arts remain in such contemporary terms as industrial or medical arts. Masters like Cellini and Leonardo found it necessary in their writings to defend the dignity of the art they practised on the grounds that a knowledge of mathematics and other sciences was necessary to the good painter or sculptor and that he therefore deserved elevation above the level of the mechanic and the manual worker.

By the end of the fifteenth century, the arts of design had risen in public and critical esteem sufficiently to warrant their inclusion among the nonservile arts. The establishment of academies as institutions for training young painters, sculptors, and designers gave status to these disciplines, and seventeenth-century France saw the creation of the Académie Royale des Beaux-Arts and other similar academies which firmly established these arts and music as fine arts. The term "fine arts," however, does not appear in general use in English until the eighteenth century, entering the language as a translation of the French *beaux-arts* and following the lead of the French academies in the kind of arts the term embraces. The establishment of separate academies for music and the dance and the elimination of the literary arts from the *beaux-arts* academies undoubtedly did much to shape our contemporary conception of art as essentially visual.

The development of the concept of art through time shows an almost complete reversal in thinking: the visual arts which were considered too manual to be included with the fine arts have grown to be the dominant arts; the leading arts of earlier times — poetry and music — are now frequently omitted from the list; and science, which was once synonymous with art, is now often placed in diametric opposition to it.

Practical Definition of the Term

Such a complex and constantly changing situation presents difficult problems for the librarian or any other worker with art materials (the curator of a museum, the administrator of an art curriculum, and others). What materials are properly classified in the field of art? What should be included or omitted? How far may the limits of the field be extended? The answers to such questions are not merely academic; they shape practice in the classification of books, the selection of materials, and the establishment of educational requirements. The adequate definition and delimitation of the term, "art," is therefore a practical as well as an academic problem and in its practical aspects it is of great importance to the librarian.

The practical approach to a definition cannot be completely divorced from the theoretical, however. Despite the popular stereotype which pictures the philosophers as abstract thinkers out of touch with reality, their analyses of the nature of beauty and aesthetic experiences have provided the criteria upon which they have based their classification of the arts, and librarians have adapted the philosophical classifications to their own needs in the identification and classification of books.

Philosophical Classification of the Arts

The classification of knowledge has been a concern of philosophers from earliest times, and the classification of the arts has naturally been an incidental part of that total activity. Aristotle's *Poetics* is a full-scale treatment of one of the arts and may indicate, many believe, that he intended a similar classification of all the arts which was never completed or has not survived. Bacon's classification treats broadly of all knowledge and so includes the arts in a general way in terms of an all-inclusive theory of the nature of art. It was not until Alexander Gottlieb Baumgarten in the early eighteenth century introduced the term "aesthetics" to be used as the name for "the criticism of taste" and called for the recognition of aesthetics as a branch of philosophy equal in importance to ethics, that the systematic classification of the arts became recognized as a distinctive branch of philosophic investigation. Aesthetics, in its original Greek meaning, refers to all sensuous perception, and Kant and others attempted to reserve the term for this wider concept. But Baumgarten's use of the term to apply to the philosophy or theory of taste, or of the perception of the beautiful in nature and in art, gradually gained acceptance in both German and English, and today is recognized as the common sense of the term. Since the establishment of aesthetics as a valid philosophical concern, a great many classifications of art have appeared, seeking not only to show the place of art in the total scheme of world history and culture, but also to explain the basic similarities and differences among the several arts themselves.

A variety of bases are introduced in the several systems for the differentiation of the arts. In Bacon, the fine arts are defined in terms of "sensual pleasure," and divided on the basis of the sense addressed: the pleasure of the eyes (like painting) and the pleasure of the ears (like music), while poesy (which includes all imaginative writing) is separated from the fine arts as a distinct category. In Lessing's *Laokoön* the arts are differentiated, in terms of the nature of the medium, into the arts of space (painting, sculpture) which use figures and colors, and the arts of time (literature, music) which use tones and articulated sounds. Herder divides the arts on the basis of the sense addressed: vision, hearing, and touch. Kant's classification is more elaborate: the arts are separated into the mechanical and the aesthetic. Within the latter, they are divided into beautiful and agreeable arts, based upon the kind of demand made upon the spectator; and within the beautiful arts, the division is based on the mode of expression: arts of speech, plastic or shaping arts, and the arts of the beautiful play of sensation.

The attempts of the painters and sculptors to improve the status of their own specialty is also a part of the history of art classification in a way, since skills were divided on the basis of principles of differentiation similar to those employed by the philosophers (the kind of process involved, the demands made upon the artist, the tools employed, etc.). Similarly, the reformers and moralists who attacked the arts, or set up guides to subject matter, or established acceptable and nonacceptable art forms were also classifying the arts in terms of their effects upon the beholder, or their correspondence to a particular version of truth.

It is not difficult to see how the pragmatic distinction between manual and nonmanual arts which concerned the Renaissance writers; the moralistic distinction between arts which instruct and arts that merely please which concerned the reformers; the distinctions tween arts suitable for a gentleman and those which are servile which characterized the curricula of the medieval universities; and the philosophical distinction between mechanical and aesthetic arts by Kant were transformed into the familiar division of useful and fine arts. This distinction, between arts which serve some utilitarian purpose lying beyond the specific artifacts and those whose products serve no ulterior purpose but are valued for themselves, is one which continues today in the most "practical" classifications. It is not a dichotomy of strictly antithetical subdivisions, however. There is much overlapping between the fine and the useful arts, since many of the so-called fine arts are useful and many useful arts display aesthetic qualities. As a classification scheme which will comprehend the entire field in discrete and meaningful categories, such a distinction leaves much to be desired. At best, the terminology reflects merely differences in degree or emphasis; at worst, it implies a claim to superior quality for fine arts with which many aestheticians disagree.

Library Classification Schemes and the Arts

Although few philosophers are convinced of the validity of the distinction between useful and fine arts, the concept is accepted by

the two library classification systems most widely used in the
United States -- the Dewey Decimal system and the Library of Congress classification. In Dewey, this separation is made specific,
with the 600's devoted to the "Useful Arts" and the 700's to the
"Fine Arts." In Library of Congress, the fine arts are covered by
the N classification, with the T classification — technology — covering most of the materials comprehended in the term "useful arts."

But even in practical systems like these, there is no absolute
agreement on what constitutes the fine arts. In Dewey, the 700's
are divided into main subdivisions for landscape and civic art,
architecture, sculpture and plastic arts, drawing and decoration,
painting, engraving, photography, music, and amusements. The
subdivision amusements includes subjects like dancing and stage
design which are defensible as arts and others like party planning,
card games, and sports which can be called arts only in the sense
of "skill." The Library of Congress classification agrees with
Dewey on the inclusion of architecture, sculpture and related arts,
graphic arts in general, painting, and engraving, but decoration and
ornament are included under a catchall heading, "Art Applied to
Industry"; photography is classified with technological works; landscape gardening with agricultural subjects; and music has a main
category of its own which separates it completely from the field of
the fine arts. Both classification systems, like that of Bacon, omit
literature from the fine arts field, and both list many subjects (like
ceramics, metal work, textiles, etc.) in more than one place, counting them as useful arts when the treatment accorded them in the
individual book under consideration is technological and as fine
arts when the treatment emphasizes the aesthetic.

Here again we find illustrated the basic difference, which has
been mentioned before, between a classification of knowledge and a
classification of books (see p. 76). While it is desirable and usually
useful to base a classification scheme upon some overarching concept of the interrelations between the many areas of human knowledge, the progression from one discipline to another is often, in a
library classification, not based upon a single, logical, integrated,
comprehensive outline of human knowledge. Inconsistencies, conflicts, and dissimilar bases of organization for different disciplines
are acceptable if they reflect the state of the literature. To serve
the purpose for which they were devised, it is more important that
library classification schemes correspond to authoritative current
usage as it appears in the books in the field and to the concepts with
which readers are familiar than that they illustrate a special (usually controversial) conceptual organization which theoretically mir-
rors the true and essential order inherent in the fields of knowledge. The theoretical relationship of subject matters, while neater

and more logical, may bear very little resemblance to the way that books are actually written and asked for by readers. Since the public library's primary purpose is to bring the existing literature and the general reader together, a consistent and comprehensive theory which confuses the layman is less useful than an imperfect scheme that works.

In the classification of books in the field of art, some of the general problems of aesthetic theory are encountered when the books are grouped according to arts and the kinds of arts, but many other groupings are also used, and different arts are sub-divided on different bases. Grouping by nationality and period is a common concept in art writing and is reflected in classification schemes; grouping by the approach of individual writers — histori-cal, theoretical, analytical, etc. — is another that is employed. In both Dewey and Library of Congress, the major subdivisions of the field (painting, architecture, sculpture, etc.) are further subdivided in several different ways according to several different kinds of classification. Painting is divided mainly on the basis of the sub-ject represented (religious, portrait, landscape) with additional groupings in Library of Congress for techniques (watercolor, gou-ache, etc.) and history (medieval, old masters, modern). Archi-tecture is subdivided by historical period (ancient, medieval, mod-ern) and by function (public buildings, ecclesiastical, sepulchral monuments, factories, etc.). Sculpture is broken down into groups for periods, for methods, and for subjects. In such a series of breakdowns, there is obviously much overlap. Roman equestrian statues in bronze may be placed in any one of three different cate-gories within the larger group, sculpture; water color marine studies done in nineteenth-century England may be classified as water colors, as marine studies, as English painting, or as ex-amples of the particular style they represent. From the stand-point of a systematic theory of aesthetics, such a classification is badly conceived and poorly organized. As a classification of books in the library, however, its criticism must be based on the extent to which it interprets the patron's approach to the literature. For in the main, it is the way the patron uses the literature of art which concerns the librarian and shapes the classification scheme he will use.

Departmentation

Allied to the problems of classification is the administrative problem of departmentation which must answer the same kinds of questions. For whom and for what purpose will certain subjects and certain treatments be most useful? What groupings of subject

materials will reflect the kind of use made of the library by its
patrons? How are fields of interest allied in practice, and what
lines are crossed from one field to another in research?

As in classification, decisions must sometimes be arbitrary,
based on the librarian's knowledge of past practice and his conjectures as to the future. Some research has been done in the
fields of the sciences to determine the extent to which physicists
consult the literature on chemistry, for example,[2] but little has yet
been done to provide facts on which to base a logical departmentation in the fields of the arts. Should books on architecture be kept
with books on engineering, or with books on painting and sculpture?
Should books on home decoration be within easy reach of the house-
wife or the designer? How far should the materials on iconography
be from books on ecclesiastical history? Is music logically kept
with the other arts materials, or should it be housed separately?
A wide range of remotely connected materials covering several
subject fields can broaden and vary the knowledge of the layman;
on the other hand, a welter of unrelated materials merely impedes
the research of the specialist.

Many libraries attempt to achieve the advantages of both systems by providing a part of both. Special departments are established for the subject fields, but a general department which contains the popular materials in those fields is also maintained for
the nonspecialists. The cost of extensive duplication is one flaw in
such an arrangement; another is that it solves only part of the
problem, since there is still the necessity for arbitrary decision
concerning which subjects belong in which departments, and which
ones should be grouped together.

College and university libraries reflect the school's departmentation scheme: the subjects comprehended in the departmental
curricula will form the basis of the division of the book collection.
Public libraries do not have such a ready-made plan available to
them, although they have a knowledge of their communities' interests and of the use of the collection to guide them. No departmental
plan can be absolutely foolproof in any case. It will always be necessary for the cataloger, the reference librarian, and all those involved in interpreting the collection to the patrons to provide the
necessary cross references which will lead the architect to the
engineering department, or the homemaker to the art department,
when their needs can be better answered there. In smaller libraries

---

[2] Herman Howe Fussler, *Characteristics of the Research Literature Used by
Chemists and Physicists in the United States* (unpublished Ph.D. dissertation,
University of Chicago, 1948). Also in *Library Quarterly* XIX (January, 1949),
p. 19-35; (April, 1949), p. 119-43.

such problems are less acute, since the patron need only step from one shelf to another to find the books in both fields. In larger public libraries, and in university and college libraries, the departmentation of the collection often causes dissatisfaction on the part of the patron who sees only the aspect of the field in which he is concerned and who cannot understand the necessity of traveling from floor to floor, or from building to building, in order to consult two or three books which appear, from his standpoint, to be on the same subject. The duplication of titles necessary to remove such inconveniences would be financially prohibitive, of course, and would end — if carried to its logical extreme — in destroying completely the kind of specialization which departmentation is set up to provide. The best that can be done is to classify books in terms of the most likely use to which they will be put; to make the necessary cross references in the language used by the patrons; and to educate the library's users to recognize the allied fields which may contain materials pertinent to their major field of interest.

FUNCTIONS OF THE ART LIBRARY

Art, in one form or another, is experienced by everyone. Practically every moment of his waking day, the average human being is exposed to art in some one of its forms: as architecture, as interior decoration, as landscape gardening, as costume design, as advertising art, and so forth. He learns to accept or reject certain combinations of colors, certain symbolic representations of the world he knows. He is constantly brought into contact with the application of artistic principles in the design of his magazine covers, the format of his books, the composition of the moving pictures he sees, the pictures on the billboards, the arrangement of window displays, the wall paper in his room, the comic strips, the pictorial supplements, and even the arrangement of headlines in his newspapers. Almost everyone unconsciously forms attitudes towards art every day, even though he may not visit museums or deliberately seek enlightenment.

While this condition has certain advantages in establishing a potential clientele for the art library, the very fact that much of the art with which the average man comes in contact is mediocre or worse and that much of his art education is unconscious creates a problem of a different sort. It is not only that many library patrons are not interested in art as such (although this is certainly true of a large proportion of the library public) but that those who are interested often will accept only those approaches or types of art with which they are familiar, thus limiting themselves in growth beyond a certain point. Many groups — study clubs, women's clubs, and others — maintain formal programs of art study and use the library for pictures of the art objects and books about them. While on the surface it would seem that a group so motivated would most readily respond to a program of planned progress in understanding and appreciation, its members are frequently either not interested or not sufficiently prepared to go beyond a certain popular level, and their responses to anything mildly unconventional or untraditional, despite their organized profession of interest in the arts, are no more open-minded than are those of the average layman.

This raises the problem for the librarian of where he should place his greatest emphasis in interpreting the arts to his patrons. In view of the general low level of popular art experience, should the library make a deliberate effort to elevate public taste? Or, since it is publicly supported, does the library have a prior obligation to provide the kind of art which the public has already learned to like, even if this means duplicating the lowest common denominator and contributing to its perpetuation? If the educational function seems appropriate, how should the library serve it: by having the high-level materials on hand for those who ask for them, allowing the uninterested to remain uninterested, or by initiating a program of education which will attempt to recruit a wider audience from those who are not now self-motivated? And if the "missionary" function is approved, how far should the librarian go to combat public indifference, resistance, or outright opposition to the library's program of "improvement"?

No absolute answer can be given for all libraries and all library situations. The nature of the community served is an important factor in shaping the aims of the library and defining its scope and function. A large city which also supports art museums, art schools, and practicing artists of many kinds will make different kinds of demands upon the art department of its public library than will a small town with no museum or gallery and little professional need of art materials. A library in a museum serves a function different from that served by a library in an art school, and both differ from the art department in a public library serving a general, nonstudent clientele. The more specialized the library, the simpler is the solution of this problem, but as the public which the library serves becomes wider and more general, varied needs arise and many more functions might logically be assumed by the art library.

The Museum Library [3]

The museum library affords a good example of the specialized

---

[3] Museum as used in this section refers, of course, to museums which include art in their field, and not those which collect the materials of history, science, or technology.

library which assumes a readily defined function. In many cases, the museum library is meant solely for the use of the staff and only in exceptional instances for members of the general public. Where this is the policy, the librarian need not concern himself with reaching a wider public, with providing popularizations, or with elevating the taste of his clients. His subject fields are prescribed by the specialty of the museum, his clientele is made up of experts, and his role in the provision of materials is generally meant to be a passive one, meeting demands made upon him but not reaching out to win more readers or create new interests. Other museums maintain an art school under the general administration of the museum and expect the library to supply the necessary reading and pictorial materials to supplement the school's curriculum. Still others broaden the role of the library, opening it to the public and even providing some materials for circulation. In any of these cases, or in any combination of these types, the museum library is an arm of the parent institution and exists to further its aims. Its collection is expected to maintain the same high standards as those set for the collection of art objects in the museum proper, and its subject fields will be those which are represented in the museum itself. Broad policy is established by the museum administrators, and the librarian then executes that policy in his own field through his special knowledge. But he does not attempt to carry on all the functions of a traditional public library, nor does he initiate programs of his own which are not consonant with the programs set for the institution of which he is a part.

The specialized research demanded of the special librarian in the arts requires intensive training, broad background, and an ability to deal both with art and the producers of art. The patrons of a research library assume expert knowledge on the part of the librarian; they wish to be able to employ the technical idiom of the field and to receive responses in their own terms. The librarian should have a minimum of a college major in the field of art, covering the history of art intensively and ranging broadly over the several fields of art: painting, sculpture, architecture, graphic arts, and photography. He should also have a strong supplementary background in the fields of ancient and medieval history and of classical literature and mythology. Finally, he should possess a functional knowledge of many foreign languages; French and German are a minimum requirement, Italian and Spanish are almost equally essential, and as many others as possible are desirable.

In addition to the basic library techniques, the research librarian in the arts has special need of a wide acquaintance with authorities and organizations in the field from whom information can be had and materials secured, a mastery of the techniques of indexing and abstracting, and the ability to handle special materials like slides, photographs, and vertical file materials of all kinds. Most especially a knowledge of trade bibliography, particularly of the old, rare, and secondhand book fields, is essential. In the field of the arts, unlike that of the sciences, the older books are often more important than the new. Works on a subject in different periods and different countries and works on an artist at different stages of his development are especially valuable. The kinds of materials that interest the historian are also of importance. Wills, inventories, statutes, and other materials of archival and documentary research have a bearing on the history of art as they do on any history. In libraries which attempt to provide the materials of research there would be a need to collect such materials and books about them which would not be felt in the general public library. Finally, it should be recognized that English language texts comprise a relatively small portion of the literature of the field. The German, Italian, and French publications still dominate the field both historically and contemporaneously, and particularly in the field of serial publication, most of the leading scholarly works are in foreign languages. To procure such works, to keep abreast of new publications, and to be able to organize them most efficiently for the use of the library's patrons requires not only a reading knowledge of the several languages, but also a familiarity with the characteristics of large and small publishers and dealers, both here and abroad. Since this aspect of the librarian's task is in itself a full-time occupation, it can be seen that the research librarian is not less active merely because his public is more limited.

The Art School Library

Libraries connected with educational institutions, whether independent schools of art or departments within a larger university, also shape their programs to fit the policy set down by the parent organization. The demands of curriculum must first be met, and subject fields which lie outside its scope are not represented in the library unless they bear some relation to the broad educational aims of the school. Where school policy permits or fosters a program of extracurricular education and recreational reading, the library may take on some of the aspects of a public library, but in general the library of an art school keeps its collection within the subject limits and scholastic levels of the school curriculum.

The librarian of an art school, or of an art department in a larger educational institution, works less frequently with technical research, but has a different responsibility in his dealings with students. Here, too, an intensive knowledge of the field of art and

the allied fields of history, literature, and mythology which bear
upon it is important. While the students are, on the whole, not yet
experts in the field, they are exposed to the writings and lectures
of the experts and are familiar with the technical language and
concepts of the subjects. Although their work will not often demand
such intensive technical skills as are required in assisting researchers, they will have greater need of guidance and assistance
in the selection and use of the tools and general introductory materials of their field. The level on which the school itself operates
will dictate to a certain extent how much of the serious scholarly
materials will need to be represented in the collection and how
much of the advanced type of research is likely to be carried on
by students and faculty. The librarian will have to work closely
with both students and faculty, keeping in touch with class assignments, assigned readings, and reference problems which will
make demands upon the library collection. He will be expected to
keep the faculty informed of new publications and materials in
their several fields, to fill in gaps in the collection, and to supplement the school's program with whatever devices lie within the
library's province. Many libraries, for example, are responsible
for the making of exhibits, slides, and other informational and
educational aids which benefit the school as a whole.

The Art Department in a General Library

The art department in a general public library serves a much
more varied public than does either of the other types of art library.
In many large urban centers, practicing artists both professional
and amateur and serious students of art from art schools and general schools are library patrons. For such users, the library must
supplement the kind of service that is provided by the more specialized libraries, and in communities where no museum or art
school library exists, the public library has no alternative but to
try to provide the services which these specialized agencies usually
furnish. In addition, its patrons will include enlightened laymen who
are interested in the arts and bring some background to their reading and other laymen who have little or no training to equip them to
understand the materials of art. For these patrons, the library
must provide general reading on all levels of profundity, covering
a wide variety of topics within the most broadly defined field of art,
and serve as a guide for those who cannot be expected, on their own,
to find their way. The librarian's duties range from technical and
extended research to low-level spoon-feeding. If, in addition, he
assumes the task of fostering exhibits, displays, lectures, and
forums his duties are complicated indeed.

In the smaller public libraries, little serious research or
scholarly reading in the field of art is pursued. The average small
community will find a limited demand for foreign language publications, for example, even when these publications represent the best
of current and past scholarship. The expense of the definitive classics in the field will often be prohibitive in view of the small demand for them. The heaviest demand will be for popularization
and introduction; and the librarian will be sufficiently occupied attempting to keep a well-selected and current collection of the how-
to-do-it and "appreciation" titles on hand. While it might be expected that the library in communities without museums or special
schools would take over the functions usually assumed by these
agencies, the truth is that these functions are more often assumed by
libraries where other agencies do exist. Communities without the
special agencies generally are deprived of such special services
from the library as well. This is understandable; the larger the
community and the wider the interested public, the more need there
will be for such services — and the more financial provision will be
made to make them available. In communities which do not have
sufficient public support for a museum there is often insufficient
support for an art program of any kind, and the library finds itself
without the facilities or the public to make such programs possible.

THE LITERATURE OF ART

The literature of art reflects the needs of specialists and nonspecialists, of professional artists and interested amateurs, of
those who create and those who enjoy the creations of others. Since
books exist to fit a variety of interests and many levels of intensity,
the librarian — no matter what kind of library he administers —
should be familiar with the several ways in which the arts are classified, or studied, or grouped in the minds of the readers who use
his collection. Such approaches to the material are likely to reflect
the traditional organization of art curricula and the conventional
historical concepts of tradition and style, and most of the literature
will be based on similar concepts. The distinctive task of the librarian is to understand and analyze the literature in such a way
as to be able to match the need of the reader with the book which
answers it and which answers it in terms most satisfactory to the
patron.

One of the simplest ways to carry on such an analysis is to
establish the characteristics of the reader's major approaches and
then to see the extent to which a work exhibits these characteristics.
It is possible, thereby, not only to note the logical sources of information (dates should logically be verifiable in a book which purports

to give the history of a subject) but also the less logical sources —
the books supplying information which their title does not reveal; or
promising a kind of information which they do not supply; or illustrating approaches which their avowed subject would not lead one
to expect. Much readers' advisory and reference work succeeds
because the librarian remembers, or discovers by accident, just
such illogical sources of information. Since no pattern for illogic
can be established, a technique cannot be learned beyond the one
here described: the systematic analysis of materials as they come
into the librarian's hands, with a view to noting the type of information and kinds of approaches they contain quite apart from their
titles or the general classification into which they fall.

In the books about art four main approaches to presentation
can be distinguished. These may arbitrarily be described as the
historical-critical approach, the technical and practical approach,
the theoretical approach, and the purely factual, or reference approach. These categories are not wholly distinct, and do not restrict a book to one literature-type. But the librarian can use them
as general guides to the kind of content for which the patron of an
art library is likely to ask, and his recognition of the sources in
which they exist can be of great value in his work with patrons as
readers' adviser, reference assistant, or bibliographer.

The Historical-Critical Literature

By far the largest category of books about art is that which includes the historical presentations of the subject; that is, the systematic narratives which place events in time. Such a category is
extremely broad: it embraces any accounts which present, in a
connected fashion, factual events either past or present. In addition to traditional history whose major purpose is the sequential
account of events, it includes biographical studies, studies of influences in either a historical or contemporary art form or movement, and even lists of artistic works, where such lists serve to
present a systematic view of the development or the pattern of the
work of an artist or artists.

In its narrowest sense, a historical work presents merely a
chronological sequence, objectively presented. Actually, every
historical account is based, implicitly or explicitly and to some
degree, on some kind of critical principles. The writer selects a
period, or a type of art, or a school of artists, or a single artist
as his subject, and in the act of selection implicitly indicates his
judgment concerning the importance of the subject which he has
chosen to treat. Even where the presentation is purely chronological or objective — as in such a volume as Bernard Berenson's

Italian Pictures of the Renaissance, which purports to be nothing more than a list of artists and their works with an index of the places where they may be found — the critical principle is apparent in the matter of selection, the inclusion or omission of artists, and the relative emphasis given to one artist or another. In most cases, however, the chronological presentation of the development of an art or arts includes critical judgments explicitly stated. The notable eight-volume *Histoire de l'art depuis les premiers temps chrétiens jusqu'à nos jours*, edited by André Michel, for example, while arranged chronologically and related to the historical development of the countries and races studied, is also a critical and interpretative analysis of the arts under discussion. The reader learns not only the sequence of events, but something of the writer's evaluation of the particular artists and their works selected for inclusion. Such a work then may be of interest to one reader because of the historical narrative and to another for the critical judgments expressed.

Whether a book is classified as historical or critical is, then, often merely a matter of comparative emphasis; many critical works are historical in their approach, many histories are critical in their presentation. But in classification, selection, and interpretation by the librarian, the decision to bring out the historical or the critical aspect of the work may be more a matter of patron interest than of actual objective measurement of the emphasis within the book itself. Both facets of the same book may be of value, and both should be recognized by the librarian and so noted that the book can be produced to fill either of the needs.

Within the broad category of the historical-critical treatment, a great variety of limitations may be placed upon the scope of the individual work. Certain volumes attempt a universal history of art which will cover not only a time span from ancient times to the present, but also the several arts and the several national manifestations of them (Helen Gardner's *Art Through the Ages* or Upjohn, Wingert, and Mahler's *History of World Art*). More specialized histories are more frequent, however, and limitations may be set on time, on form, on country, or on any combination of the three aspects. A book may be comprehensive in time but limited to the type of art with which it will deal, as Sir Banister Fletcher's *History of Architecture on the Comparative Method* (which is devoted to architecture only, but places no limits on time or place or kind). Time as well as form may be limited (Ernest Arthur Gardner, *Handbook of Greek Sculpture*); place and form may be restricted but not time (John Gloag's *English Furniture*); place, form, and time may all be held within limits (Oskar Hagen's *The Birth of the American Tradition in Art*), yet all may still be primarily historical, in terms of their emphasis upon chronological sequence.

Certain time periods and certain similarities of style have gained general acceptance as useful divisions for historical treatment. Although such divisions are arbitrary and a trifle too facile, and although there is no universal agreement on all of their details, they have been found sufficiently useful to gain general popular acceptance. In the public library it is often necessary to follow such popular terminology and concepts if book and reader are to be brought together, because they are used so frequently in historical writing in the field and because they are well-known to the general patron and shape his interests and requests. They should be familiar to the librarian even though he recognizes their weaknesses and the scholarly objections to them.

The following list gives the more familiar and broadest of these divisions as applied to European art and indicates the approximate time period comprehended by them:

Prehistoric (Paleolithic, Mesolithic, Neolithic)	(to about 2000 B.C.)
Aegean	(3000-1100 B.C.)
Early Greek	(1100-400 B.C.)
Hellenic	(4th century)
Hellenistic	(323-1st century, B.C.)
Etruscan and Roman	(1000 B.C.-500 A.D.)
Early Christian	(300-500 A.D.)
(in Rome)	(to 1500)
Byzantine (in the East)	(to 1500)
Dark Ages	(500-1000)
Romanesque	(1000-1150)
Gothic	(1150-1500)
Renaissance	(1400-1600)
Baroque-Rococo	(1600-1800)
Eclectic and Modern	(1800-to date)

Within these broader groupings, much more specific subdivisions are made; the arts of particular countries are differentiated from each other (Dutch art, Italian art, or even Venetian or Sienese art), and within these national groupings, the same kind of period series may exist. Chinese art, for example, is broken down by the several ruling dynasties (T'ang, Sung); Japanese art by the several Shogunates (Jogan, Fujiwara); Egyptian art by the political periods (Old Kingdom, Middle Kingdom, New Empire); etc.

The student will have noted certain characteristics of the list. One is that the periods are not distinct; they overlap and even contradict (Dark Ages with Byzantine Art, for example). Another is that the series of designations is not consistent; periods are

characterized in chronological terms (prehistoric), political terms
(Roman), stylistic terms (Romanesque), and general, all-embracing
terms descriptive of the "spirit" of the period (Dark Ages, Renaissance). The more detailed such breakdowns become, the more disagreement among the scholars and the greater margin for error.
An all-inclusive designation like Gothic can cover a wide period
without committing itself to too much precision on specifics. When
the breakdown attempts to date more precisely the appearance of
variations in Gothic styles in each of the several countries, the
opportunities for disagreement multiply, and the individual differences between specific art works demand a recognition that the
broader generalizations can pass over. Certain movements are
later in some countries than in others: the Renaissance, for example, reached France and England about a century after its appearance in Italy. The particular manifestations that the style
takes also differ from one country to another: the period of flam-
boyant Gothic in France occurred at the time of the perpendicular
Gothic style in England. And within such broad classifications,
there are obviously many variations and subclasses which are important. Such a division as "Eclecticism" is meaningless except
as the broadest kind of inclusive category. It becomes important
to know what the several styles are which made up this eclecticism,
and these too will differ in different countries. In France, the neoclassic, romantic, impressionistic, and postimpressionistic styles
were in the ascendancy in succeeding periods throughout the nineteenth century; in England, the neoclassic, romantic and Victorian
styles have been differentiated; in America, these movements found
their parallels in styles known as federal, Greek revival, and Victorian eclectic. Each of these groupings has also been broken down
by critics and historians into smaller segments, and as the number
of subdivisions increases, so too do the number of disagreements.

For the librarian, it is extremely useful to know the broader
classifications and to have some sense of the major movements and
styles with their approximate periods. But he should always be
alert to the variations which can occur within each grouping, and
he should be careful to note the particular interpretations which
individual writers put upon the conventional concepts. It is not
enough to assume that a book entitled "Renaissance Art" will cover
the dates which have arbitrarily been set by popular tradition; the
writer of the particular work may limit himself to a specific period
within the broader one, or may even have a new interpretation of
"Renaissance" in art. For that matter, of course, the librarian
cannot be sure what "Art" means in this connection until he looks
at the book — it may mean all arts, visual and nonvisual; it may
mean only painting; it may mean only painting in Italy, or it may

mean only the Sienese school of Italian painting during a part of the
Renaissance period. Thus the categories have value to the librarian not because they cover comprehensively and precisely the subject matter of all books, but because they help to identify the variations, the innovations, and the unusual as well as the conventional,
the traditional, and the expected.

The biographical literature

An extremely important form of historical text in the arts is
that which emphasizes the biographical approach. In the humanities, where the subject matter is so frequently related to the creations of individual genius, the biographical approach has been found
to be particularly fruitful and popular. Despite the emphasis upon
the influence of historical period and environment upon artistic
techniques and subject matter, a work of art can seldom be considered as a product of environment or *Zeitgeist* alone. The immediate creator of the individual work is a factor which cannot be
ignored. Many of the treatments of the arts in terms of a school
or a group are in reality studies of the men who comprise it, and
many studies center around the works of a single individual even
though the straight biographical data are less emphasized than are
critical evaluations of the man's work. Hence the great popularity
in the literature of the arts of the kind of study so frequently sub-
titled "The Man and His Work." In such a book as Alfred H. Barr,
Jr.'s *Picasso: Fifty Years of His Art,* the emphasis is upon interpretation and criticism of the painter's works, and although it traces
the artist's career from his earliest paintings in Spain to his recent works, the book is not a biography in the ordinary sense.
Straight biographies do exist, of course, and studies which combine
biography and criticism in varying degrees of relative emphasis.
One of the great classics in the field of art biography, for example —
Vasari's *Lives of the Artists* — combines anecdote and even invention with critical evaluation, biographical information, aesthetic
theory, and extensive description of technical processes. The librarian who serves his public most effectively would take note of
these many aspects of Vasari so that its title, or its arbitrary classification with biographical studies, would not conceal its value in
these many other spheres of interest.
The several kinds of autobiographical writing are also important in this field because of the insight they provide, consciously or
unconsciously, into the thoughts, attitudes, and aesthetic theories
of the artists. Such an autobiography as that of Cellini, which can
hardly be omitted from any comprehensive collection of books by
and about artists, is much more a revelation of character and of

the period in which it was written than it is a study of art. Other
writings by artists include dissertations on art in general, as in
Sir Joshua Reynolds' *Discourses on Painting*; deliberate defenses
of the artist's own aesthetic theory and art, for example, Whistler's
Ten O'Clock; journals (Delacroix), letters (Van Gogh), and notebooks (Da Vinci) which were not necessarily meant for publication
but which provide understanding of the lives and works of the artists; and traditional autobiographies in which the artist sets out to
present a straight account of his life and artistic development, as
in Thomas Benton's *An Artist in America*.

Fictional Accounts. Allied to these biographical studies are the
fictional accounts based on the lives of artists. Such works may
range from those, like Irving Stone's *Lust for Life*, which attempt
to recreate imaginatively the life of the artist, through those like
Merezhkovskii's *Romance of Leonardo Da Vinci*, which use a real
artist as an actor in an imaginative work, to those, like Zola's *The
Masterpiece* or Maugham's *The Moon and Sixpence*, which take
their inspiration from the life of a real artist but create a fictional
character to represent him. Such fictional treatments need not
necessarily be represented in the art department of a general library, since the patron may be referred to the general book collection for them, but in special libraries in the arts it is often part
of the librarian's responsibility to keep his patrons in contact with
all forms of writing which touch upon the field of their special interests. Most architecture libraries, for example, unless they are
limited absolutely to technical and practical works, might find it
necessary to stock such a book as Rand's *The Fountainhead* which,
weak as it is in literary value and faulty as it may be in the architectural theories it upholds, is of interest to architects because of
its possible resemblance to certain events in the lives of Louis
Sullivan and Frank Lloyd Wright.

Popularization. The fictional account may also be taken as a
form of popularization in the field of the arts. By emphasizing the
"dramatic" incidents in the life of the artist or the "story behind"
the creation of certain works, fictional treatments often appeal to
readers who are not interested enough in art per se to read straight
historical or critical accounts. Much of the popular writing in the
field is based on the assumption that interest must be stimulated
or even created; they frankly announce their purpose to be that of
promoting "appreciation." More serious criticism is based on the
assumption that the reader has either already seen the object under
discussion or can be counted upon to do so, but popular writing
must frequently assume that the reader not only has not seen the

work of art, but is not likely to make any effort to do so unless motivated by some outside stimulus. Therefore appeals on another level are introduced: the biographical (the work illustrates an interesting life history); the literary (the work tells an interesting story); or the social pressure (everybody agrees that this is a great work). All of these approaches are legitimate ways of stimulating interest in the arts, but their emphasis upon nonaesthetic criteria places certain limits on their value. They tend to be overenthusiastic, eliminating almost all critical analysis in favor of stimulating interest in the entertainment or prestige value of certain works of art. Since they are concerned almost exclusively with dramatic biography, literary effects, and general consensus, they do not teach the reader enough about materials, methods, and the creative process to help in the understanding and appreciation of other works. They perpetuate the demand for the familiar and the traditional and may even inhibit independent judgments and the establishment of personal critical standards.

Theoretical Works

It has been indicated above that the critical studies in the field of art are generally combined with the historical studies and that critical principles underlie selection and organization of the historical treatment but do not necessarily appear as explicit expressions of normative judgments. There is not, in the field of the arts, a vast literature of praise and blame such as exists around the works of the literary artists; in the writing on art, criticism is generally implied on a relativistic basis, with the comparative importance given to certain works or artists, or the selection and rejection of materials for discussion, providing the clue to the writer's critical position. Where definite stands are taken, they are generally defenses or explanations of a particular point of view rather than an attack upon others; the polemical literature which allegedly accompanies the founding of new schools and the revolutionary statements of the innovators are usually limited to the newspapers and ephemeral critical journals of the time and remain in libraries mainly as curiosities for a later age rather than as critical milestones in the literature of art.

There is, however, a small body of works on aesthetic theory the aim of which is to establish the principles on which art and beauty can be evaluated. Some philosophers have attempted to abstract the characteristics of the several kinds of art object — the poem, the painting, the statue, the symphony — in order to isolate those which are common to all art, above and beyond the individual work or medium. Others have attempted to analyze the aesthetic experience either for the artist or the viewer of art, to see in what it consists and what the sources of aesthetic pleasure are. Typical of the many aspects of the creative process, of the form of the object, and of audience reaction which have been discussed are: the internal organization of art objects (what is the relation of the several elements to each other?); the technique of the creator (how are the materials handled and how are all the special problems of the medium solved?); the purpose that a work of art serves, both for the creator and the user of the work (is art a form of play, a release from emotional tension, a method for achieving vicarious wish fulfillment?); the subject matter of art (is art a copy of nature, an imitation of the ideal, or an objectification of moral principles?).

Certain philosophers place greater emphasis on some of these factors than they do on others, but in most aesthetic systems, the aesthetic experience is seen as a complex of many factors in combination, and almost all aestheticians concern themselves to some extent with all of these problems. Thus, in Plato, the artist is seen as an imitator (method) whose mastery of his technique (skill) may convince the beholder of the truth of his presentation (effect), and this conviction of truth is adjudged good or bad depending upon the fidelity of the work of art to essential truth (subject). The statement of aesthetic principles cannot be much more specific or less abstract than this since the object of the aesthetician is to find the characteristics common to all the arts. Occasionally a single type of art (painting, literature) is discussed, but such specific discussions would generally classify as critical rather than as theoretical works. The distinction between critical and theoretical as made here is mainly a matter of the generality with which the writer deals with his subject. If his subject is the function, value and place of art (or some one art) in general, the work may be said to be theoretical; if his subject is the evaluation of a specific object or artist, involving the application of the general principles to an individual instance, the work may be described as critical. And in such a work as Élie Faure's five-volume *History of Art,* all three of the approaches so far discussed are present. The work can be considered a straight chronological history, but it also contains critical judgments of the writer, and — in volume V under the title, "The Spirit of the Forms" — there is a statement of the author's philosophy of art which forms the groundwork of his specific critical opinions.

The difficulty in keeping the distinction clear between critical and theoretical writing often arises when the aesthetician illustrates his principles with specific examples; or when the critic, in discussing a particular work of art, analyzes the aesthetic principles which it exhibits. In such a book as *Artists on Art,* compiled by

Robert Goldwater and Marco Treves, one can see the entire range
from purely critical to purely theoretical writing. Consisting as it
does of excerpts from the journals, diaries, letters, and formal
publications of practicing artists, the book contains examples of
aesthetic theory unrelated to any specific art form, evaluations of
a particular medium as an expression of aesthetic principles, general criticism of artists and schools, and evaluations of individual
works, or even parts of works, in technical, philosophical, and/or
psychological terms. An analysis of a few of the excerpts from
such a book by the student will provide him with an illuminating
demonstration of the varying degrees of emphasis upon critical and
theoretical principles which can characterize publication in the
field. Such an exercise will show how inadequate a single call
number (701) or a single subject heading (aesthetics) is to describe
the rich variety of appeals represented in the literature of the field.

The classification of theoretical works

Makers of library classification systems have consequently
been confronted with difficulties in their attempts to fit the works
on aesthetic theory into their over-all scheme. While the Library
of Congress system recognizes the place of aesthetics as a branch
of philosophy and provides a number for it in the philosophy section
(BH), it also finds it necessary to leave room for studies of aesthetics among the works on art (N). Theoretical works on the visual
arts would classify in the latter group, but general theoretical works
which embrace all the arts including literature and music would
fall in the BH section. Works on the aesthetics of literature or
music as individual arts would classify with other works in the field
of literature and music. The Dewey Decimal system, on the other
hand, does not recognize aesthetics as a branch of philosophy, but
places it among the theoretical works on the fine arts, with the number 701 to keep it consistent with the general "philosophy of a subject" designation: 501 - the philosophy of science; 901 - the philosophy of history; etc. This means that general aesthetic studies
which cover other arts besides the visual (like Lessing's *Laokoön*,
for example) are filed with the books devoted exclusively to the
visual arts, and the student of literature, music, or philosophy who
is interested in aesthetic theory which involves his discipline will
find many of the most important works in the field among the books
on painting and sculpture. Works devoted exclusively to one art or
another will be filed with the works on that individual art. In both
systems, works which are theoretical in nature may appear in any
number of places, depending on the cataloger's definition of their
scope. This flexibility in classification is necessary; a work on

general aesthetics is of interest to the philosopher, the artist, the writer, and the musician, and where special libraries or collections exist for each field, such a work will probably have to be represented on the shelf.

The list which follows contains some of the titles which have become classics in the field of aesthetic theory, with a comparison of the recommended subject classes for each given on the Library of Congress card and the class group actually used in the University of Chicago Library. Each book on the list could be justified as philosophy, art, or literature, and the results of the logical difficulties that arise in attempting to use a single subject designation for works which are pertinent to more than one subject field are graphically demonstrated. The particular classifications used by the University of Chicago reflect the subject emphasis of the curricula of that school and are neither more nor less logical than the ones suggested by Library of Congress. Neither should be taken as mandatory by other libraries in which other emphases may more realistically reflect patron needs. But any special library of philosophy, art or literature, which does not have access to a general collection, would undoubtedly expect to represent these titles on its shelves.

		LC	UC
Croce, Benedetto	Aesthetic as Science of Expression and General Linguistic	BH	BH
Dewey, John	Art as Experience	N	N
Hegel, G.W.F.	The Philosophy of Fine Art	N	B
Hulme, T.E.	Speculations: Essays on Humanism and the Philosophy of Art	B	PR
Kant, Immanuel	Critique of Aesthetic Judgment	B	B
Lessing, G.E.	Laokoön	N	PT
Santayana, George	The Sense of Beauty	N	BH
Tolstoi, Leo	What is Art? and Essays on Art	N	PG

Popularization

Popular writing in the field of aesthetic theory is limited, like popular writing in any philosophical field. There are a few attempts to present aesthetic principles abstractly but in simplified form for the layman (Irwin Edman's *Arts and the Man*, for example) but such efforts are usually simple only in comparison with philosophical scholarship; they are still difficult and high level as compared to the "popularization" which is really popular (i.e., easily read by a large number of average readers). The other kind of simplification of the subject matter of aesthetics follows the textbook pattern — and so is also limited in its appeal. In this kind of treatment, the purpose is to summarize the aesthetic theories of other philosophers, with some critical evaluation perhaps, but with no intent on the part of the writer or compiler to establish an aesthetic of his own. This kind of book (*Philosophies of Beauty from Socrates to Robert Bridges*, edited by Edgar Frederick Carritt, for example) is designed as an introduction to the works of the philosophers themselves, or as a substitute for the reading of the philosophers for those who would not, or could not, attempt to comprehend the special language of the scholarly aesthetician. Often, however, when such a work is a reliable and accurate reflection of the philosophical theories it treats, it becomes in itself comparatively learned and difficult for the average reader, and such a study as Bernard Bosanquet's *History of Aesthetic* appeals to the scholar rather than to the layman.

Practical and Technical Works

As in other fields, a highly important segment of the literature is made up of the how-to-do-it books. Since the field of the arts may be broken down into very minute fields of performance, the number of these books is extremely large. Not only are there the several subdivisions of the major arts — in painting: water color, oil, distemper, gouache, etc.; in sculpture: wood carving, stone carving, work in metal, intaglio, etc. — but there are also many minor arts and crafts which classify with the arts in most libraries — ceramics, furniture making, weaving, mosaic, etc. In the minutely detailed Contents of Robert Kingery's *Guide to How-To-Do-It Books*,[4] for example, there are 105 major entries which fall into areas which would classify in the Dewey 700's (exclusive of music). Yet this is an extremely conservative indicator of the number of how-to-do-it titles in the volume which would be suitable for inclusion in a library's art department, since only the subject heading "Sports" was counted but not individual sports and only the heading "Games" was counted, not individual games.

Another gauge of the numerical importance of the how-to-do-it books in this field can be found in the lists of new books in the *Library Journal*. Of 133 titles in all the fields and phases of the arts

---

[4] Robert E. Kingery, *How-to-do-it Books: A selected guide.* 2nd. ed. rev. (N. Y., Bowker, 1954).

as listed in the *Journal* for September 15, 1950, 20 were how-to-do-
it books, covering such varied subjects as painting, sketching, lith-
ographing, interior decoration, scene painting, and lettering. In
addition many titles like Geoffrey Bemrose's *Nineteenth Century
English Pottery and Porcelain*, which illustrates authentic work
by identifying characteristics, are used as how-to books by collectors and antique dealers. Recently the *Library Journal* has
made a separate category of "How-To" in its "New Books Ap-
praised" department, and of the 50 titles listed under that heading
from January to June, 1955, 13 were in the field which the library
classifies as the arts.

Another type of technical book in the field of the arts is that
which analyzes the technique of particular artists and works, less
as a guide to practice than as an aid to appreciation. These titles
may range from highly technical works meant for the reader familiar with art terminology and art techniques to simple introductory
works which are designed to introduce the beginner to the basic
concepts of composition, balance, and design. In a sense these
books may be considered to be critical works similar to those mentioned above which are written to foster appreciation of specific
art works. As such, they approach more nearly the kind of introduction to art for the layman which is acceptable to the artist and
the art critic than do the biographical and storytelling approaches.
In the technical approach the reader is given an insight into the
problems of the creator of the art object; he learns something of
the use of materials, the limitations of media, the elements of
composition and design which he can transfer from his study of the
individual work to many other works in the field and to an appreciation of arts of many kinds. Harriet and Vetta Goldstein's *Art in
Everyday Life*, for example, attempts to show how the basic elements of good design, balance, unity, and composition can be applied to familiar objects and activities in everyday life like dress-
making, interior decoration, flower arrangement, etc.

This kind of "practical" approach to the arts, while it hardly
qualifies as fine art in the usual philosophical terms, is an important part of any public library's 700 collection. Books on home
arts and handicrafts, of little appeal to the professional painter or
sculptor, have a much wider audience among laymen, whose creative talents find an outlet in such minor crafts. Many examples of
domestic art have a legitimate place in the history of art, as in the
pottery of the ancient and Greek artisans, the tapestries of the
Middle Ages and the Renaissance, and the fine embroidery, weaving,
and needlework of many periods. Books which deal with such arts
naturally fall into the 700 classification; by extension, then, the
practical books on needlework, ceramics, and similar domestic

arts also classify there. The extension sometimes strains the
definition of art, and while library practice does not suffer from it,
the use of generalized statistics based upon circulation in certain
classifications sometimes may misrepresent the library's particular contribution to society. To use the number of books circulated
in the 700's as an evidence of wide interest in the fine arts is to
ignore the fact that a large part of that circulation is limited to the
practical books on knitting and flower arrangement.

Reference Works

The categorization of books on art as historical-critical, theoretical, and practical is a classification dependent on the approach
of the writer. The reference category, however, is of a slightly
different order and relates more closely to a classification by format than by content. For reference work is not limited to the use
of any single group of books or types of books; its materials may
be found everywhere, in books which circulate as well as those
which remain inside the library. Yet there are certain types of
books — dictionaries, encyclopedias, and others — which do not limit
themselves to any single approach to the arts but which attempt to
provide quick, factual answers to questions. These are the true
reference books; the intent of the compiler or editor or writer is
not to provide a historical overview, a critical analysis, a theoretical dissertation, or a technical manual, but to make readily available
in easily used form a wealth of miscellaneous factual information.
Since these can classify under no single subject heading, the arbitrary designation "Reference" has been set up to take care of them:
a designation which is justified by the heavy use to which such
works are put by the librarian.

The standard types of reference books can be found in the field
of the arts. Encyclopedias and dictionaries exist for art in general
and for specific arts and are extremely useful for the definition of
terms and concepts, the identification of artists and works, and
generalized summary treatments of different aspects of the field.
Biographical dictionaries also exist for artists in general and for
workers in specific fields of the arts. Bibliographies, as in every
discipline, are of great value to the scholar, the student, and the
general reader. Yearbooks, which summarize the events in the
field of art for the preceding year and include a wealth of miscellaneous and difficult to find information, are also important.

In addition, there are special types of reference tools which
are designed for use with art materials; indexes in the field of art
often serve a specialized purpose. The traditional periodical index
is paralleled in the field of art by the *Art Index*, which is organized

in the usual H. W. Wilson form for periodical indexes, and covers
magazines and museum bulletins in the field. But equally important to the worker with art materials are the indexes to illustrations
and reproductions. Patron requests for pictures of objects, persons, designs, and works of art form a major part of the reference
questions in an art library or art department. Despite the existence of several indexes to illustrations this is still frequently a
difficult request to fill, and the librarian should be aware of illustrations in any book examined for future reference. Closely allied
to the indexes to pictures are the collections of pictures themselves (see p. 129), which are also an important reference source
in the art library.

Directories in the fields of the art also serve a special function. These are directories of museums and special art collections,
of art and antique dealers, of publishers and distributors of prints
and other reproductions, and of auctions, sales and prices. Other
specialized tools of reference are sales catalogs which often contain much descriptive material of value to the art librarian; catalogs and announcements of art exhibits and galleries; dictionaries
of colors; and historical treatises on the arts or special aspects
of them which provide concise or readily available data on periods,
persons, and works, or illustrative materials of value.

Homemade files

In many libraries, the printed and published works of reference
must be supplemented by a homemade index. Because published
indexes in the field of art do not yet sufficiently cover the field,
most libraries keep a file of references to pictorial and textual
materials for which a need might arise but to which no regular indexing services will lead. Exceptionally well reproduced or hard-
to-find pictures, biographical notes, news items, and materials on
local artists or art activities are most frequently represented in
such homemade files. To build a file that will be comprehensive
but not unwieldy and useful but not time-consuming in its construction, requires the application of most of the professional skills of
librarianship. On the administrative level, it calls for the ability
to analyze the needs of patrons, to anticipate future demands, and
to weigh comparative values of one item or one need against others
in order to organize both staff time and storage space. On the
technical level, it requires a sound knowledge of the principles of
cataloging, classification, selection of materials, reader guidance,
and reference work. On both levels, the skills of librarianship
must be supported by a sufficient knowledge of the subject field of
art to give specific direction and meaning to the general principles,

and both library principles and principles of art are further modified by the librarian's concept of the library's proper function in
the field of art.

Collections of Pictures

It has been pointed out that the primary works in the field of
art are art objects, not books about art. The books are of greatest
value to both the amateur and the expert when they are used to
supplement the study of the works of art themselves. The library,
however, is primarily a book agency which cannot in most cases
take on the task of accumulating a museum-type collection of art
objects, and the logical substitute for the object proper is a comparatively inexpensive copy or picture of it which can be bound and
handled like other books. The illustrated books, the books which
separate into individual volumes the text and the plates which illustrate it, and the books or folios of prints which are exclusively
collections of illustrations are, therefore, usually considered an
important part of any art library collection. While they serve the
same purposes as traditional books and are classified, usually,
alongside the texts which cover similar material, they are mentioned separately here because their distinctive format sometimes
leads to special problems of handling.

The organization of these collections may follow any of the
major subdivisions of art publication already mentioned. The historical arrangement is possibly the most popular because it answers the same needs as the historical textual treatment, and the
variety of types of collections is as great as the variety of historical texts. There are universal collections which attempt to cover
many centuries and countries, collections which cover the historical development of some one art in a particular country, collections
which trace the chronological development of the work of a single
artist, or of a single school or of a single period. There are also
nonchronological collections which illustrate many different styles
or many different media, and works which deal with a single subject
matter, or with the art treasures of a single collection or gallery.

In the selection of such collections by types, the same criteria
apply as in the selection of the textual approaches to art: the needs
of the library's patrons, the levels of interest and ability at which
they are directed, the kinds of problems to which they provide answers. But the type of collection is not in itself a guarantee that
the book will be valuable even though it seems to answer a need for
the type of material covered. The quality of the pictures is an important additional factor. Are they in color or in black and white?
If in color, is the color faithful to the original? If in black and

white, is the absence of color a handicap to any real appreciation of the work reproduced (as it may well be in reproductions of many of the Romantic painters, for example, in whose work color is of great importance)? Is the object clearly and faithfully reproduced (in photographs of sculpture, for example, does the lighting distort or obscure features of the original work)? Is the object completely shown, or only fragments of it? If completely shown, is the object too large to allow any sense of detail (as in pictures of cathedrals, murals, etc.)? If only parts are shown, is an adequate sense of the whole conveyed? Such evaluations of the quality of the pictures are extremely important, and can usually be made only upon examination of the books themselves; they cannot be deduced from the title or alleged aim of the collection.

For the librarian, collections of pictures exhibit the same advantages and disadvantages as anthologies of any kind. They gather many works into a single handy and readily available source, thus providing many pictures for the price of a few. They are often organized around a principle which clarifies and enriches the study of the works collected. They often provide explanatory material and factual data about the pictures which cannot be easily found, to accompany individual reproductions and prints. On the other hand, certain familiar works (Botticelli's "Birth of Venus," Van Gogh's "Sunflowers," Grant Wood's "American Gothic") are selected for inclusion in collection after collection so that certain works must be duplicated to an unnecessary degree in order that the other pictures in the collection may be acquired. The unifying principle around which some collections are organized is of dubious value, pulling together unlike materials on the grounds of some farfetched basis of comparison which adds little to understanding or appreciation. If the books circulate, a single borrower monopolizes many pictures even if he is interested in only one of them, thereby depriving others of access to the pictures. Often the heavy cost of plates and reproductions adds to the cost of explanatory material which is available much more cheaply in another format. All these factors, pro and con, should be taken into account whenever a new collection of pictures is being considered for purchase.

In recent years there has been an increase in the number of books with colored plates and well-done reproductions of art masterpieces. Several general trade publishers, as well as publishers exclusively in the field of art, have brought out collections of reproductions at comparatively reasonable prices, and many publishers issue special series publications which are valuable additions to the library collection. A few notable series are listed below. The list is not exhaustive; it is meant merely to indicate the range and variety which such series represent.

"The American Arts Library" (World Pub.). Short, authoritative
    monographs with both black and white color illustrations. Each
    volume devoted to a single subject, like Pennsylvania Dutch
    Art, American Glass, American Silver, etc.
"Gallery of Masterpieces Series" (Scribner). Folio size volumes
    including about 30 reproductions using a new process embody-
    ing not only Kodachrome photography and ordinary four-color
    printing but a method of applying additional corrective touches
    to the plates to reproduce fidelity to the original.
"The Library of Great Painters" (Abrams). Each volume is de-
    voted to a single artist, with fifty large full color reproduc-
    tions and commentary on each.
"The Master Drawings Series" (Harper). Good reproductions,
    with descriptive notes.
"Masterpieces of French Painting" (Skira-World). Each volume
    devoted to a short biographical note on some one painter with
    full color plates.
"Masters of Painting Series" (Harper). Studies of the life and art
    of individual painters, with accompanying full color and half
    tone reproductions.
"Phaidon Press Books." Series on individual artists, or group of
    artists, with excellent color reproductions.

To the art librarian, the illustrated book is also of value as a
source of pictures even though its primary purpose is not the collection of pictures but the presentation of text. The same questions
can be raised about the quality of illustrations as were suggested
above for the evaluation of reproductions, and where the answers
are satisfactory, the illustrations may often be used in place of
more expensive pictures published in other ways. It is especially
important that the librarian remember that illustrations have a
value for the art library quite apart from the subject matter of the
book in which they are included and that many books which do not
classify in the 700's may well be represented in an art collection
because of the illustrative material they contain. Obviously, the
edition of *Moby Dick* with the Rockwell Kent illustrations is a valuable addition to the Rockwell Kent materials in an art library even
though the text would place the book in the literature collection.
Similarly, many books of travel contain illustrations of cathedrals
and other buildings, or of art objects of many kinds, which have
value to the student of art as much as they do to the student of the
particul. r country with which the book deals. Books dealing with
religious and historical subject matter also often contain illustrative material which is useful to the art department's collection of
materials on costume, architecture, painting, and other arts. And

many general reference tools — like the *Enciclopedia Italiana* and others — contain plates in color and black and white which rival the quality of the reproductions contained in books specifically in the fields of the arts.

NONBOOK MATERIALS IN THE ART LIBRARY

In the preceding pages it was suggested that even in the library, the book plays a secondary and ancillary role in the art collection. Recognizing this, art librarians pioneered the acquisition of nonbook materials far beyond the pamphlet and periodical stage which so long set the limit of materials in other departments of the library. Slides, mounted pictures, clippings, and post cards have long been standard library material for the art library; the stereopticon was well established in the art department when the film projector was being bitterly opposed by other administrators as outside the library's proper province. Today, with all departments of the library expanding the kinds of materials they will make available, the art library is still in the vanguard, providing new services and new devices for going beyond the book to a more direct study of art.

The selection and administration of nonbook materials multiplies the problems which the librarian must solve, since he is not in any way absolved through his provision of prints and slides from the construction of a collection of the needed *books* in the field. An entirely different group of reference aids, a completely new set of criteria, and talent and knowledge of another sort must be utilized in building up the collection of nonbook materials, and as yet the reference materials and the special training fall far behind the need.

Pictures

The constant demand for pictures is answered in part by illustrated books and collections of pictures; but some of the problems which are introduced by the book-bound picture must be considered. Size is one of these; to limit the size of a picture to that which can be conveniently bound in an average-sized book often reduces it too much, whereas to increase the size of the book to accommodate the picture creates problems of handling and expense. Monopoly on use is another; as has been mentioned before, when a collection of pictures is bound together, the entire collection is made unavailable by a single borrower whose interest may be in seeing only one or two of the pictures in the group. Inconvenience is still another; pictures bound in volumes are difficult to display for study, even more difficult to hold before a group for examination, and impossible to place against a wall so that they can be seen as a picture is normally seen.

For adequate reproduction of detail, for individual or group study, and for lengthy examination, prints, slides, and mounted pictures are more satisfactory. Two problems, however, complicate the selection and acquisition of these materials by the library. One is the absence of sufficient guides to their sources. Since photographs and reproductions are generally distributed by an entirely different group of agencies from that which distributes books, the usual bibliographical aids upon which the librarian relies are of little value. A few special directories have been compiled, but they rapidly go out of date, and they do not contain the kinds of information that the novice needs to know: In what materials is a particular dealer strong or weak? What special services are rendered by individual firms? What quirks and problems should be taken into account in dealing with certain agencies? It is true that similar facts must be learned about book publishers also and that they can be learned best through experience and continual contact with the firms involved, but the bibliographical aids to the process are less complete and less readily available for art materials.

A second problem concerns evaluation of the materials' quality. Mention has already been made of the importance in reproductions of clearness, accuracy, and fidelity to the original. The analysis of these characteristics, however, demands special knowledge which many librarians do not possess. First, a knowledge of modern print processes, techniques, and materials is necessary if the librarian is to judge the quality and cost of prints and the comparative desirability of one process over another. Secondly, some familiarity with the originals is required if a responsible judgment is to be made as to fidelity and accuracy. Thirdly, a technical knowledge of the creative art process itself is helpful in recognizing details of technique, organization, and construction. Obviously, few librarians have such a background, which means that often they must rely on the judgments of experts, in the same way that general library selection relies on critical reviews. But in the field of the arts, critical analysis of prints and reproductions is extremely limited. Perhaps the most useful sources of information about prints are the UNESCO catalogs (see list p.148) which combine directory information with evaluation. Inclusion of a reproduction in the selected UNESCO list is an indicator of the quality of its reproduction of color and values, and the descriptive notes specify the scale of the print and the form of reproduction. If the librarian must rely on expert assistance to compensate for his own limitations in the evaluation of reproductions, the UNESCO catalogs are a reliable source.

Films

The lack of guides and the problem of evaluation are difficulties
that also arise, but to a more limited extent, in the selection of
films and filmstrips for the library. Again, few guides exist to
sources of films on art alone, but other guides to documentary,
educational, and commercial films in general include notices of art
films, and a sufficient number of bibliographies and lists of this
type are available to make the task of finding films simpler than is
that of finding good reproductions. Other problems of evaluation
arise, however, because films cover a wider range of materials
than the mere reproduction of a single art object. There are films
to be used as guides to appreciation *(What is Modern Art?)*, technical and instructional films *(Brush Techniques)*, biographical and
storytelling films *(Rubens, Van Gogh)*, and films devoted to the detailed and technical study of individual works *(St. Paul's Cathedral)*.
Each film must be evaluated in terms of the purpose it seeks to
serve, the audience to whom it is directed, and the degree to which
it accomplishes those ends for that audience. In addition, technical
criteria should also be applied. The clarity of sound reproduction,
the literary excellence of the script, the appropriateness of the
musical score, the use or absence of color, the quality of the lighting, camera work, visual continuity are all aspects of a film which
should be weighed as carefully as the technical literary qualities
of a novel or a play. Such analysis is especially applicable to the
experimental films which attempt to create original art effects on
celluloid, like the work of Norman Maclaren, who paints interpretations of music directly on film *(Begone Dull Care, Fiddle Dee
Dee)*. Although reviews of art films are becoming more readily
available as the documentary film gains status, a knowledge of
film technique and construction is a valuable asset to the librarian
who is charged with film selection.

Some Reference Aids in the Location and Selection of Films
For Art Films Exclusively

Films on Art; Panorama 1953, in collaboration with the International Art Film Federation and Denis Forman (UNESCO
 publication) Columbia, 1954.

Gilbert, D. B. *Guide to Art Films.* (Magazine of Art). 2d ed., 1950.

Miller, Harry L. "Art is for Everybody," *Audio Visual Guide*
 XVII (Dec. 1950), p. 22-24.

For Films and Fimstrips in General

Educational Film Guide. v. 1, 1936 -

Educators Guide to Free Films. 1940 -

Films for Public Libraries. Selected by a Committee of the A.L.A. Audio-Visual Board. 1955.

The Filmstrip Guide. 1948 -

Current Reviews

"Ideas on Film," department conducted by Cecile Starr in *Saturday Review.*

"The Film Press" department in *Film News.*

"New Audio Visual Material" department in *Business Screen Magazine.*

Slides

Another important device for making reproductions of art works available is the slide. The old-fashioned lantern slide and the currently popular 2" x 2" slide are widely used, particularly in college and university art departments. In many colleges and universities, these are handled by the academic department rather than by the library, but in the smaller collections responsibility for obtaining, housing, and making slides available for use is given to the library or the art department's branch of the library. As always when nonbook materials are involved, special handling and purchasing problems are encountered, and no single solution is equally applicable to all library situations. The particular uses to which the slides are put will dictate the best arrangement for them; and the particular agencies and facilities available to the librarian will determine where the materials will be obtained.

No really good sources for evaluating the quality of available slides exists. A directory of sources from which slides can be purchased was issued by Enoch Pratt Free Library in 1953 *(Where to Buy 2" x 2" Slides: A Subject Directory)*, but like most directories of this kind, it must constantly be brought up to date to be currently useful. It is typical in colleges and universities, in any case, for the art department's faculty members to contribute their own photographic slides to serve their classroom needs, or to suggest the

particular book illustrations, prints, or other pictorial materials
of which they wish to have slides made. Purchasing directly from
slide distributors is less frequently the way that slide collections
are built for academic purposes. The task of the librarian in such
situations is mainly that of organizing the collection of slides rather
than of selecting slides for it and of negotiating with slide makers
to have the desired items made. The local telephone book is the
reference tool needed here.

Libraries that are just beginning slide collections will find the
Enoch Pratt directory mentioned above useful, but they may also
wish to write to museums and art galleries, both here and abroad,
for information concerning slides which are needed to build a core
collection. Public libraries will be called upon more frequently to
build up collections of a general nature in this way than will academic libraries where the art faculty will take major responsibility,
and the art curriculum will dictate the nature of the collection.

Printed Catalogs

Still another important tool in the art library collection is the
printed catalog related to the general field. The catalogs which list
the materials that make up museum and gallery collections — like
the catalog of the National Gallery of Washington, D.C., for example —
often contain good illustrations and rather full comment on the pictures represented. More specialized are the catalogs of private
collections. These are often issued as "deluxe" publications, but
vary greatly in value. While they may represent the full listing of
a particular group of art works, the collections may no longer be
in existence as such, and the catalogs, although of historical interest, may be valueless as an inventory or guide to present location
and ownership. Catalogs of specific exhibits and shows also often
include a wealth of descriptive and illustrative material which is
especially compiled for the particular exhibition, but these too may
have limited value as guides to collections, since the works listed
are usually gathered from a variety of sources and are only tem-
porarily assembled together. The standard information furnished
by most of these catalogs includes data on the size of a particular
work of art, the medium in which it was executed, the artist, the
present owner, the current location of the original, and the date of
creation. In addition, many such catalogs provide information on
prices, which is frequently wanted by patrons and often difficult to
obtain from other sources.

Related to these catalogs, and also very useful, are many of
the guidebooks and other tourist aids published in Europe. Many
of these provide detailed and accurate information about art museums

and collections as well as useful descriptive matter about architectural and historical monuments of the countries to which they relate. While these are usually thought of by the librarian as "geographical" tools, they should not be overlooked as aids in the art department as well.

The catalog can be as valuable as the traditional book in its contribution to the historical, critical, theoretical, practical, or reference collection. Many of them are important sources of substantive information and one looks in them for discussion of a work just as one goes to the great standard histories. Loÿs Deteil's catalog of Daumier is a standard reference work on that artist, and Adam Bartsch's 21-volume *Le peintre graveur* (Leipzig: 1854-76) provides the "Bartsch number" which is the standard identification on prints. For maximum usefulness, then, catalogs should be treated like any other book, be placed alongside conventional books in the fields they touch, and be as completely indexed as any addition to the book collection.

However, many librarians attempt to simplify technical processes by dealing with their materials by form, and place catalogs in a separate file separately classified and cataloged and treated separately from books. From the standpoint of patron use, such handling is not satisfactory. Catalogs of museums and galleries would probably more logically be placed with the annual reports, bulletins, and other publications of the respective museums; catalogs of exhibitions, with the subject matter of the particular exhibitions. Since catalogs provide lists of works, bibliographies, essays on art and artists, biographical information, critical evaluations of the works listed, and the like, to put all such material into a form-group called catalogs is to deprive many users of access to important information.

Commercial catalogs are also valuable for their information concerning art materials and the sources of purchase for tools, prints, publications and other paraphernalia of the artist. These catalogs, like bibliographical tools in the field of general books, are used not only by the librarian but also by many patrons and should be recognized and made available as reference materials for public as well as staff use.

Some Reference Aids in the Location and Selection of Catalogs

Lancour, A. H. *American Art Auction Catalogues, 1785-1942; A union list.* 1944.
"The Weekly Record," *Publishers' Weekly.* Note especially items on lower part of the divided page in "The Weekly Record."

Ephemeral Materials

Post cards, stereopticon slides, and like materials can supplement the collection of pictures needed by the art library. They should be selected on the same basis as more expensive materials, for the cost of handling, preserving, storing, and circulation often makes them a more expensive luxury than would appear from their low initial cost. Needs of the patron and quality of the material should always be primary considerations rather than low cost per se.

This rule applies even in the addition of clippings to the library collection. In the art library clippings can be of great value. Many magazines and periodical publications that are not indexed print news items in the field of art which cannot be found readily elsewhere. These include house organs, local and regional publications, publications dealing with highly specialized subjects (stained glass, ecclesiastical art, typography), and — most important — a great many foreign publications. In addition, clippings from magazines, pamphlets, brochures, and other sources are often used to supplement the picture file, either in a miscellaneous vertical file or even as mounted pictures. The series of art reproductions published in *Life* magazine, for example, has provided many an art library with inexpensive reproductions for its picture files. But again, the low cost of the source materials does not represent their total cost to the library. The time spent in selecting, marking, cutting, labeling, filing, and eventually weeding the clipping file materials, and the provision of space, folders, and cabinets for their storage should all be added to the total expense which they represent. The very fact that clipping files are of such usefulness in the library (the reason usually put forward to combat criticism of the time spent in their compilation) argues for greater care in the selection of materials so that the good materials will not be lost in a welter of useless items.

The quality of such reproductions must also be considered. Where the reproduced picture gives a false impression of the colors of the original, or alters the scale or proportions of the original work, or loses any real sense of the texture and technique of the original, the librarian may well ask whether his provision of the picture is performing a useful service. In a sense, such a reproduction disseminates false information, and should be as ruthlessly denied library space as a book which is false or incorrect. Yet librarians, in general, have tended to be extremely lax about checking the accuracy of a reproduction, justifying their provision of poor prints on the grounds that some idea of the original - however incorrect - is better than no idea at all. The student should attempt to define his own view of the library's role in the provision of art reproductions. Different materials and different audiences may require corresponding differences in procedures, but some set of principles related to the library's objectives should be discernible in all its practice.

Problems of Handling Nonbook Materials

Whenever library materials take a form outside that of the book or periodical, they create certain problems of handling for the library. So simple an operation as the shelving or storage of materials becomes complicated when the usual book shelves cannot be used. In the art collection the handling of prints and pictures presents one of the biggest problems of this kind for several reasons. First, there is the question of space. In most cases, reproductions are mounted for protection and filed in large file cabinets which, if the collection is of any size, soon fill up much more floor space than many libraries can conveniently spare. Nor can the size of the collection be kept within limits through a process of weeding such as is applied to a clipping file. Works of art are not superseded; the addition of new works does not result in the removal of older ones. The collection of pictures must and should be a constantly growing one and must inevitably absorb whatever space and storage facilities are available.

Secondly, there is the question of classification. Subject classifications are useful because even the works of noted artists are sometimes wanted in terms of their subject — portraits, seascapes, nativities — and because picture files contain photographs and pictures which are not identified by artist but which are needed because of the subject they present. National and school breakdowns are also often useful; patrons seek reproductions of the works of Flemish painters, or of Impressionist art, or of examples of the British landscape school. There is no single "best" system; libraries devise their classifications for such materials out of their knowledge of the kind of use most frequently encountered in their own libraries, but since no single kind of use ever exists, the conflict between one kind of arrangement and another is always present. Whatever is finally accepted, the problem of adequate cross reference remains, and the skill of the librarian in translating his library techniques and his knowledge of the subject field into a system for the guidance of his patrons becomes the cornerstone of a well-interpreted collection.

Films, like still pictures, represent another form of material which is frequently handled differently from the traditional book and periodical. In some cases, a film department is established which handles all films whatever their subject matter, thus placing the important and growing collection of art films with historical, sociological, and technical films; in other cases, films are handled by the individual subject departments most concerned with the specific film content. Obviously a film like *Three Paintings by Hieronymus Bosch*, which is a detailed study of the painter's work, will be most useful if it is made readily available to the students of the painter, although administrative efficiency often seems to dictate the separation of materials by form, to conserve space, to speed up processes, or to adjust the work to fit a small staff. The cost in curtailed service should also be considered, however, and if all the necessary cross references and adjusted processes were made to assure the best use of such materials, it is doubtful whether, in the long run, this kind of organization would really represent an increase in efficiency.

Such problems raise the question of the classification and cataloging of nonbook materials. To what extent, for example, should such materials as pictures, catalogs, films, pamphlets, slides, etc., be listed in the general card catalog, complete with subject headings, cross references, location marks, and the other interpretative devices now used for the book collection? If time and expense prohibit such cataloging of nonbook materials, how best can the public be informed of them? What methods can be devised for keeping like materials (in terms of subject matter) together when they are unlike in format? The problem has not yet been satisfactorily solved; the best solution to date is one of patron education to inform library users of the kinds of materials which will supplement and enrich the information they obtain from books. But much more education is needed; many patrons do not think of the library in terms of nonbook materials; it would not occur to them to ask if a film exists on the paintings of Tintoretto or for mounted reproductions to be examined in connection with a critical work about an artist. Until these materials can be used together, each making its particular contribution to understanding and enlightenment, the library does not realize its full service potentialities.

The tendency of many librarians to keep separate card catalogs and indexes for materials which are handled separately is one of the major bars to the most fruitful use of the collection by patrons. This practice is often followed even when materials are housed in subject collections and although films on art may be in the same department as books on art, the indexes to which the patron has access may not bring the two forms together. There is no reason why cards should not be made for films, for example, which could be interfiled in the main card catalog so that the patron seeking material on Degas would find not only such books as Ambroise Vollard's *Degas, an Intimate Portrait* but also the film, *Ballet by*

Degas. Current practice, which keeps the records of special form materials apart from book records, requires that the patron know of such special materials if he is to have access to them; it does not lead him to such materials in his routine check of library holdings.

SOME ADDITIONAL ADMINISTRATIVE PROBLEMS

We have seen how art has been defined for library purposes to cover a wide range of subjects and appeals; how the peculiar character of the subject matter has led to a variety of materials in different forms which the library must handle; and how the different appeals and the different forms of the material have led to a great diversity of uses to which an art library can be put. Out of these characteristics of the field of art — the subject matter, the form of the materials, and the use made of them — arise the distinctive problems which face the administrator of the art collection.

One interesting problem originating from the library definition of the arts is that of the degrees of excellence which are represented in any type of art. To the aesthetician, art means the "best" art; to the librarian, it usually means every manifestation of the art form in which a patron is likely to have an interest. When "Drawing" is included among the arts, the library must recognize cartooning, poster design, greeting card art, and similar forms of drawing as well as the drawings of the masters. For each type of art, this same wide-ranging coverage is expected. Yet, at the same time, the librarian usually attempts to be selective and to have the better examples on each of the several levels. This requires an ability to shift standards to fit the particular art form with which he is dealing; the "best" comic strip art cannot be selected by the criteria established for the "best" religious art of the fourteenth century. And it places the librarian in a strange position when he attempts to raise the level of his collection since a different set of standards is applied to the different parts of it. In order to keep his collection of reproductions on a high level, the librarian may decide, for example, to keep no Norman Rockwell paintings, yet he may feel obliged to maintain a small collection on how to draw cartoons. To the devotee of Rockwell, such a decision must always seem to be the rankest kind of discrimination.

The subject matter of the books in the field of the arts is usually the works of art themselves; but the subject matter with which the works of art are concerned may also be a source of difficulty for the librarian. The art department, like any other department of a library, is a potential target for censorship, and the pattern of censorship of the visual arts follows very closely the pattern in the literary field, that is, the censor is not concerned with the merits of the object as a creative work, but almost solely with the subject with which it deals. A "Comstock" period in art censorship generally takes the form of a kind of class legislation designed to protect the "lower orders." But public libraries are never completely immune from attack, and when the "immoral literature" runs low, works of visual art or illustrated books for art students may well provide the censors with material.

An added complication in the censorship problem connected with the arts is the current trend toward political and ideological censorship. While this censorship is infrequent, and does not necessarily mean that the library will be forced to withdraw pictures of controversial works from its collection, the pattern of censorship is so familiar that the librarian has no reason to believe that the full course, including the attempt to control library policy, will not be run. He must always be prepared for such attacks, and he can combat them best when his policy of selection is based on sound principles of artistic worth, when his collection meets the needs of the community in the field of art, and when his public is educated in an understanding of the library's aims and ideals.

The education of the public should not be the task of the art librarian alone, of course. Respect for public property, pride in the library's collection, recognition of library policy and obligations should be inculcated by all members of the staff in all departments. While censorship is not so acute a problem in the field of art as it is in the field of fiction, the art department should be vitally concerned whenever outside pressures force the withdrawal of a *God's Little Acre* from the circulation department, a *Nation* magazine from the reference shelves, or a *Boundary Lines* from the film collection. In such instances the library as a whole suffers and the library as a whole should unite to combat these attacks upon any of its parts. Through a well-defined and firmly administered overall policy the library can much more effectively meet these problems than through an inconsistent and individually administered system of day-to-day, department-by-department decisions.

The ways in which library materials will be used should shape the kind of policy which will be established for the control and dissemination of those materials. In a specialized art library, a certain uniformity in library usage may be expected: its patrons are more serious, more advanced in their knowledge of the subject, and more likely to use the materials to serve predictable instrumental and aesthetic purposes. In a public library the users and their purposes are more heterogeneous; their approach to art may range from the reverent to the completely indifferent; their reasons for using the materials may be based on professional or practical need, aesthetic interest, intellectual curiosity, academic coercion, social pressure, or even interest arising out of hostility. To organize and control the materials so that the maximum benefits may be derived in each instance is a complex administrative responsibility. In the special library the regulations which are established can be adapted to the use to which the materials will be put by the majority of the patrons, but the public library serves so many groups that no outstanding majority can readily be identified, and the rights or demands of one minority may often conflict with the rights and demands of others which are equally valid.

The nature of art materials and of the aesthetic experience creates certain patterns of use which raise problems for the library. Art objects, as has been pointed out before, are the primary materials in the field of art, and art objects are meant to be studied and examined in an entirely different way from books. This raises a question for many libraries: to what extent should the art objects themselves, or reproductions of them, be handled by the library? In other words, how much of the museum function should the library assume? Many of the newer libraries are equipped with a small gallery or an assembly hall which can be utilized as a gallery for the exhibition of works of art. In smaller communities the library often takes the lead in encouraging the production of art in the community itself, and if the works of the masters are not available, at least the production of art in the local community is fostered. Others, where no galleries are available, take their function to be the provision of books to be used in connection with exhibits held elsewhere and define the library's field in terms of the materials of print exclusively. Most libraries accept the obligation of providing prints and reproductions which can be circulated, but do not attempt to collect statuary, ceramics, and other art objects which can be used only as materials of an exhibit.

Even when this limitation is accepted, the library's role still needs defining. Clippings, or pictures mounted on cardboard, do not really provide a satisfactory experience of the work of art. Recognizing this, many libraries have introduced a new service, the provision of matted or even framed pictures which can be borrowed for a longer period than the usual loan term so that they may be hung in the borrower's home and be seen and enjoyed as a picture should be. Such a service is an extension of the usual library function which fulfills more adequately the purpose of the art library. It gives the patron a chance to experience art more naturally; it makes art works available to homes where the expense of buying good reproductions prohibits purchase; it makes possible a constant change of pictures so that experience of art works is broadened; and it has led, in many instances, to the purchase of good reproductions when the patrons have learned to like certain works and to acquire them. This service is certainly desirable, but it creates new problems of handling and storage which many libraries are not yet equipped to assume.

Even when the library elects to limit its art collection to books, the question of the kinds of books must be settled. If funds are limited the problem of selection is always present, and in the field of art it often resolves itself into a question of where to place the library's emphasis: on books which contain reproductions of the art works themselves, or on books about art? A case may be made for both sides. The value of expensive collections of reproductions is often unequal to their cost because the average layman is insufficiently familiar with the field of art to appreciate the picture alone. This is especially true of new and unfamiliar art, and many laymen need the guidance of a good art critic or historian to explain the problems of the artist and to clarify the criteria upon which judgments are based. Many librarians feel that the best service that can be rendered their public is the introduction to art through this kind of understanding so that they can appreciate and enjoy the works of art which are supplied by other agencies. The other side of the argument holds that the way to appreciate art is to have contact with the works of art, not with books about them. Although it is true that many laymen do not know all of the facts and factors which the critic knows, still they can learn from the contemplation of art works themselves, and to learn from art by experiencing it is better than to accept the judgments of others isolated from the works about which they are speaking. The compromise which most libraries make attempts to provide the best of both sides: the critical works and reproductions of the art works taken together can give the layman both the experience of art and the criteria with which to evaluate this experience, but in many instances, limited funds force an either-or decision which rests upon the librarian's definition of his institution's *major* function.

Another problem for the librarian in his selection of art books is that of expense. Books which contain well-reproduced color plates are generally much more expensive than general trade books; an average of $15 per volume is not unusual among ordinary art books. This means that fewer copies and fewer titles can be purchased and that replacement of titles is difficult. It means, too, that many of the more important works are almost prohibitively costly; and that to protect the investment of such amounts may impose restrictions upon use which limit the value of the book for library purposes. In the end, these problems come full circle, and the selection of illuminated volumes, fine editions, and rare items becomes part of the original problem of the library's function. A book may be a museum piece just as much as a statue or painting, and the library must decide here too just what its obligations should be in the provision of the materials of art.

Cost, and the difficulty of replacement, create a serious problem in the art library because use of art materials often takes the form of misuse. No library, in any subject field, is completely free of patrons who mutilate library materials, but the art department is particularly vulnerable. The reasons for mutilating art materials are many. Students are a constant source of difficulty; the removal of pictures from books and periodicals to illustrate papers, for example, is a recurrent source of trouble for libraries. Yet if students are denied access to illustrated materials, the library's usefulness to one of its largest groups of users is curtailed; while if the destruction of library materials continues, the library's value to all of its users is jeopardized. The dilemma is a difficult one because the culprit is not easily identified and cannot be held solely responsible even when identification is possible. The teacher who makes such assignments, gives extra credit for illustrated work, and fails to inculcate the necessary respect for public property is equally guilty. The librarian is faced with the necessity of soliciting cooperation from the schools as well as from the individual students who use the library if he is to combat such vandalism, and efforts to gain such cooperation from the schools have not to date proved particularly successful. Until some mutual understanding can be reached between the two educational agencies, the problem is likely to continue to plague librarians and their future patrons.

Illustrations and pictures are many times ruined inadvertently by students in their attempts to trace or copy pictures, again often for school assignment. The patron is often unaware that he is misusing library property; not until the tracing is completed does he realize that the pencil cuts through tracing paper to mutilate the picture below. The librarian can frequently solve this problem without interfering with the student's use of the materials. Most art libraries provide hard-surfaced, transparent material (isinglass, for example) which can be placed between the picture and the tracing paper to absorb the pressure of the pencil and save the picture from destruction. Once the student has learned of this device he is usually quite willing to comply with the librarian's request to save the picture for future users, whereas a blanket refusal to permit tracing often leads the student to obtain his own ends either by tracing in spite of orders, or by removing the picture entirely.

Deliberate mutilation of art books occurs frequently enough to present a serious problem even though those who engage in the practice form a very small part of the library's public. The problem is serious because the work of a single person can destroy the value of a book for all subsequent users, and where expense or unavailability makes replacement impossible, the damage is a permanent one. All too often the damage has been inflicted for no constructive purpose, and the vandal is less frequently an art lover than he is a self-appointed censor or a victim of neurosis.

In general, public libraries have reacted to the mutilation of library materials in one of four ways, none of which is completely satisfactory. One reaction is to ignore the problem, to recognize that it is the work of a small part of the total library clientele, and to refuse to expend the inordinate time and effort required to ferret out and punish the guilty persons. Such an attitude is unsatisfactory because it penalizes the average user who finds unusable the materials he needs and because it promotes vandalism by seeming to condone it, and by permitting bad examples to stand as guides to the conduct of others. Another reaction, at the opposite extreme, is to refuse to purchase books which contain materials that are likely to lead to such problems. This too is unsatisfactory because it allows the purchasing policy of the library to be dictated by that small element in the clientele which is least qualified to do so, because it accomplishes the very censorship that the picture-cutters desire, and because it penalizes the average user who is deprived of materials that the library rightfully should own. A third reaction is to set up a system for collating illustrated books or portfolios before and after each circulation so that destruction of materials may be immediately discovered. This is extremely time-consuming; it requires either additional staffing or the consumption of professional time in mere collating; and it is comparatively haphazard since there is no control over vandalism within the library nor over carefully manipulated removal of plates which cannot easily be seen on a quick check. The most common solution is to place all books for which such problems are anticipated on special shelves for use only by those whose purposes are deemed serious by the librarian. This system, coupled with collation of each volume upon its return, controls the vandalism to a certain extent and preserves more of the materials for the average user, but it adds a heavy work burden on the librarian who must provide for special handling, storage, and control of the problem books. Furthermore, it multiplies the red tape through which the patron must go for services to which he has a right, and it places a heavy responsibility on the librarian to screen the users of such materials. This is a responsibility which most librarians are reluctant to assume, as it forces them to restrict library services on a highly subjective basis. Since the kind of aberrant behavior being checked is not limited to any age, sex, income, educational or occupational group, the librarian's judgment cannot be anything but a personal reaction, and most librarians hesitate to withhold service on such a basis.

As in every problem area, the solution seems to lie in the eventual education of the public. The destruction of pictures in the art department is not a problem for the art department alone; it is a symptom of a widely held attitude which can be combatted only by the cooperative efforts of every department and every educational agency. Such a program of education cannot be accomplished overnight, nor can any single individual or department hope to reach more than a few members of the library's public. But the start is always made with a few, and the librarian should not allow himself to be discouraged by the immensity of the task nor the failure of others to carry their full share of the responsibility. Nor should he permit such a stopgap device as the restricted shelf to substitute for a dynamic educational program. It is only in terms of the latter that the individual tasks of librarianship take on their fullest meaning.

REPRESENTATIVE REFERENCE TOOLS IN THE FIELD OF THE FINE ARTS (700's)

Encyclopedias and Dictionaries

Adeline, Jules. *Adeline's Art Dictionary*. Enlarged ed. 1927. (Reprinted 1953)
Davenport, Millia. *The Book of Costume*. 2 vols. 1948. (Reprinted, 2 vols. in 1, 1954)
Maerz, A. J., and Paul, M. R. *A Dictionary of Color*. 2d ed. 1950.
Myers, Bernard S., ed. *Encyclopedia of Painting*: Painters and Painting of the World from Prehistoric Times to the Present Day. 1955.
New Standard Encyclopedia of Art; Architecture, Sculpture, Painting, Decorative Arts [*Harper's Encyclopedia of Art*], based on the work of Louis Hourticq. 2 vols. in 1. 1939.
Runes, D. D., and Schrickel, H. G. *Encyclopedia of the Arts*. 1945.
Sturgis, Russell, and others. *A Dictionary of Architecture and Building, Biographical, Historical, and Descriptive ....* 3 vols. 1901-02.

Bibliographies and Indexes

Outstanding art magazines for possible purchase may be selected from the lists of indexed periodicals in *Répertoire d'art et d'archéologie* (for scholarly libraries) and in *The Art Index* (for college and public libraries).

The Art Index; A Cumulative Author and Subject Index to a Selected
   List of Fine Arts Periodicals and Museum Bulletins. 1929-
Brooke, Milton, and Dubester, Henry J. *Guide to Color Prints*. 1953.
Ellis, Jessie Croft, comp. *General Index to Illustrations*; 22,000
   Selected References in All Fields Exclusive of Nature. 1931.
Gilbert, D. B., and Franc, H. M. *Guide to Art Films*. 2d ed. 1950.
Hiler, Hilaire, and Hiler, Meyer, comps. *Bibliography of Costume*;
   A Dictionary Catalog of About Eight Thousand Books and Peri-
   odicals; ed. by Helen Grant Cushing, assisted by Adah V.
   Morris. 1939.
Institut international de coopération intellectuelle. *Collections de
   reproductions photographiques d'oeuvres d'art*. 1927.
Lancour, A. H. *American Art Auction Catalogues, 1785-1942*;
   A Union List. 1944.
London. University. Courtauld Institute of Art. *Bibliography of
   the History of British Art*. vols. 1-5, 1934-45.
Monro, Isabel Stevenson, and Cook, Dorothy Elizabeth. *Costume
   Index*; A Subject Index to Plates and to Illustrated Text. 1937.
Monro, Isabel Stevenson, and Monro, Kate M. *Index to Reproductions
   of American Paintings*. 1948.
Répertoire d'art et d'archéologie. vol. 1- 1910-
Technical Studies in the Field of the Fine Arts. vols. 1-10,
   1932-42. (Published by the Fogg Art Museum, Harvard
   University; quarterly)
UNESCO. *Catalogue de reproductions en couleurs de peintures —
   1860 à 1955*. 3d ed. 1955.
——— *Catalogue de reproductions en couleurs de peintures
   antérieures à 1860*. New rev. ed. 1953.
See also September 15 issue of *Library Journal*, which each year
   since 1949 lists the new art books and "Fine Arts Reproductions."

   Biographical Aids

Bryan, Michael. *Bryan's Dictionary of Painters and Engravers*.
   New ed. rev. and enl. 5 vols. 1925-27.
Champlin, John Denison, ed. *Cyclopedia of Painters and Paintings*.
   Critical editor, Charles C. Perkins. New ed. 4 vols. 1927.
College Art Association of America. *Index of Twentieth Century
   Artists* .... vols. 1-4, 1933-37.
Fielding, Mantle. *Dictionary of American Painters, Sculptors, and
   Engravers*. 1945.
Mahony, Bertha E., and Whitney, Elinor. *Contemporary Illustra-
   tors of Children's Books* .... 1930.
Mahony, Bertha E., and others. *Illustrators of Children's Books,
   1744-1945*. 1947.

Mallett, Daniel Trowbridge. *Index of Artists, International-Biographical*; Including Painters, Sculptors, Illustrators, Engravers, and Etchers of the Past and Present. 1935. (Reprinted 1948)

———— ———— Supplement .... 1940. (Reprinted 1948)

Nagler, G. K. *Neues allgemeines Künstler-Lexikon.* 3d ed. 25 vols. 1924.

Thieme, Ulrich, and Becker, Felix. *Allgemeines Lexikon der bildenden Künstler* .... 37 vols. 1907-50.

Vollmer, Hans. *Allgemeines Lexikon der bildenden Künstler des XX. Jahrhunderts.* 2 vols. 1953-55.

Who's Who in Art. 1927-

Who's Who in American Art; A Biographical Directory of Selected Artists in the United States Working in the Media of Painting, Sculpture, Graphic Arts, Illustration, Design, and the Handicrafts.... 1935-

Directories

American Architect's Directory. 1955.

American Art Directory. 1952- (Continues the *American Art Annual*, q.v. under "Yearbooks")

American Association of Museums. *Handbook of American Museums*; With an Appended List of Museums in Canada and Newfoundland. 1932.

Mastai, Boleslaw. *Classified Directory of American Art & Antique Dealers.* 5th ed. 1953.

Print Prices Current; Being a Complete Alphabetical Record of All Engravings & Etchings Sold by Auction in London. vols. 1-21. 1918-39.

"Publishers and Distributors of Prints," *Library Journal*, LXXIV (September 15, 1949), 1347.

"Sources for Reproductions of Works of Art," *ALA Bulletin* (April, 1936), 287-299.

Where to Buy 2" x 2" Slides; A Subject Directory. Enoch Pratt Free Library, 1953.

The Writers' and Artists' Yearbook .... a Directory for Writers, Artists, Playwrights, Writers for Film, Radio and Television, Photographers and Composers. 1906 to date.

Yearbooks

American Art Annual. 1898-1948. (Continues as *American Art Directory*)

Libraries, Museums and Art Galleries Year Book. 1897-

Year's Art, 1880-1945/7;   A Concise Epitome of All Matters Relating to the Arts of Painting, Sculpture, Engraving, and Architecture, and to Schools of Design, Which Have Occurred during
the Year. 1880-1947.

Historical Treatments

Fletcher, Sir Banister. *A History of Architecture on the Compar-
ative Method*. 16th ed. rev. 1954.
Gardner, Helen. *Art through the Ages*; An Introduction to Its
History and Significance....3d ed. 1948.
Lester, Katherine Morris. *Historic Costume*; A Resume of the
Characteristic Types of Costume from the Most Remote
Times to the Present Day....Rev. and enl. ed. 1942.
Michel, André. *Histoire de l'Art*. 8 vols. in 17 plus Index. 1905-29.
The Pelican History of Art. (48 volumes, projected, each on a dif-
ferent subject and classified separately.) vol. 1, 1953-
Planché, James Robinson. *A Cyclopedia of Costume*; Or Dictionary
of Dress, Including Notices of Contemporaneous Fashions on
the Continent; and a General Chronological History of the
Costumes of the Principal Countries of Europe, from the
Commencement of the Christian Era to the Accession of
George the Third. 2 vols. 1876-79.
Reinach, Salomon. *Apollo*; An Illustrated Manual of the History of
Art Throughout the Ages; from the French, by Florence Sim-
monds....Completely Rev. and New Chapter by the Author.
1935.

Note: Books on gardening, photography, ballet, motion pictures,
sports and games, and other miscellaneous subjects are included in those art departments which follow the 700 section
of the Dewey classification precisely. For each of these areas
there are similar bibliographies, dictionaries, encyclopedias,
yearbooks, etc., for which see Winchell's *Guide to Reference
Books* and supplements.

music

INTRODUCTION

In most systems of aesthetics, and in popular thinking in general, music is recognized as one of the fine arts, along with painting, sculpture, and architecture. Certainly many works of aesthetic theory deal with concepts which are meant to be as applicable to the musical arts as they are to the visual; a statue, a symphony, and a painting are all considered to be works of art which reflect similar characteristics of beauty and lead to similar kinds of aesthetic pleasure. We have seen in the preceding chapter, however, that the term fine arts has come, in most practical situations, to refer to the visual arts only, and music is dealt with separately as though it were another category equal in importance to the field of the fine (i.e., visual) arts, but not part of it. Universities and colleges have a school (or department) of art and a separate one of music; the larger libraries usually separate the two departments; museums generally concentrate on the visual arts, leaving music to special academies and agencies; art publishers and music publishers are separate entities. While the broadest aesthetic generalizations are applicable to both art and music, our practice would seem to run counter to our aesthetic theories.

151

There are practical reasons for this separation in situations
where the materials of the two art forms must be handled. First,
there is the sheer bulk of the material. The literature of music
(and this need include only musical composition and not the books
about music) is almost as large as the field of literature itself; the
primary works of visual art are equally numerous. Merely to handle such a body of materials requires some expedient division into
homogeneous units. Secondly, the form of the materials for the
two arts differs sufficiently to make their handling complicated.
Sheet music, scores, phonograph records — by their format alone —
must be processed and stored in a different manner from paintings
and statues; the efficient organization of personnel to deal with
such materials dictates a separation of skills and techniques.
Thirdly, the visual arts are addressed to the sense of sight, the
musical arts to the sense of hearing, which means that to a certain
extent the audiences for the two arts will not be the same. Although
it may be true that those interested in the visual arts are more
likely to enjoy music than those who are not, the specialists are
likely to be limited to one field or the other, and many laymen
seem capable of appreciating one of the art forms, but not both.
The separation between the two art forms is then, to a certain
extent, dictated by actual use.

The separation of fine arts from music in this text is, therefore, a reflection of general library practice rather than of aesthetic principle. In most library systems which are large enough
to warrant departmentation, art and music are divided. Although
music is frequently relegated to a subordinate position within the
art department (often merely a reflection of the Dewey Decimal
system which makes music a tenth part of the total 700 section), a
separate librarian in charge of music is usually necessary. The
specialized background required of a good art librarian or a good
music librarian is such that there is hardly time for the librarian
to prepare for either field, let alone both. The work he will do in
one department differs in many ways from that in the other: there
is an entirely different set of reference tools in the field of music;
an entirely different group of master works and standard titles; a
different sort of administrative problem; and an almost completely
different clientele to be served. For most practical purposes, the
separate discussion of music is justified.

It is rewarding, nevertheless, to keep in mind the parallels
and the similarities between the field of music and that of the visual
arts. Many of the problems which face the librarian are similar;
many of the approaches in the literature follow the same pattern;
and many of the aesthetic concepts can be transferred — with the
necessary changes imposed by the altered form of the material —

from one field to the other. If the student utilizes his knowledge of
the field that he knows best to illuminate the field that he knows
less well, he can enrich his understanding and appreciation of both.

STYLISTIC PERIODS IN MUSIC HISTORY

In the chapter on the visual arts, a rough breakdown of the
general periods in the historical development of the arts was given.
The history of musical development is treated in essentially the
same manner, and the periods which are most universally agreed
upon parallel closely the periods used for the visual arts. These
periods, with their approximate dates, are as follows:

Primitive	to 1100 B.C.
Greek and Hellenistic	1100 B.C.-500 A.D.
Early Christian Church	300-600
Middle Ages	600-1400
Renaissance	ca. 1400-1600
Baroque	1600-1750
Classical (Viennese)	1750-1800
19th century (Romantic)	1800-1900
20th century	1900-

As in the visual arts, it must be recognized that such designations
are arbitrary and oversimplified; that the more specific and detailed the breakdown becomes the more disagreement among the
writers on musical history; and that such designations are utilized
here only because popular usage has made them part of the common language of the patrons and not because they can serve as infallible categories for pigeonholing the works of musical art. If
the student recognizes the limitations of such divisions, he can
benefit from the qualified utility of their generalizations.

Primitive

Our knowledge of early music, even for the period of the
Greeks, is much more restricted than our knowledge of early
painting and sculpture. Cave paintings, fragments of statues,
pieces of pottery, and other examples of the creative work of the
earliest artists and artisans are available to us, but the music is
not. The earliest songs were sung and passed on orally; when
some kind of notation finally came into being it was usually merely
a cryptic aid to memory which reveals little to the modern student.
Later notation named the notes, but such important aspects of
musical reproduction as pitch and interval are not clearly indicated

until late in musical history. While we know that music played an important part in the lives of the very earliest peoples, we are not able with any assurance to reproduce the music as it was played and sung at the time.

The fragmentary character of our knowledge of early music colors much of the scholarship in the field. Studies of primitive music are based mainly on observation of children or of contemporary primitives; the methodology is essentially anthropological, relying on field work with primitive groups in Africa, South America, and America and utilizing recordings of native and folk music as the basis for conjectures concerning the music of an earlier day.

Greek and Hellenistic

The study of Greek music is of a slightly different character, since archaeological research has given us only about a dozen pieces of music in Greek notation, most of them fragmentary and all of them of a comparatively late date. The study of Greek music then is based on the literary, plastic, and graphic monuments which show the high place music held in the education and general culture of the Greeks. These studies utilize the methods of historical research, depending on documents, literary allusions, graphic records, and indirect evidence to supply data concerning the place of music in Greek life.

Roman music, like Roman art generally, is based upon the Greek, and adds little except elaboration. Its importance to scholars of today lies mainly in the light it throws, however indirectly, upon the music of the Greeks, and as with Greek music the scholars are limited to the study of the theoretical, literary, and graphic documents rather than of the music itself.

Early Christian Church

Just as the early church adopted many contemporary beliefs and ceremonies so did it also adopt contemporary forms of art and music. The source of Christian liturgical song is in the eastern provinces of the Empire; Greek influences are still apparent in the Roman Mass; and the singing of hymns was taken over from the Jews. An understanding of early Christian music is, then, dependent upon the comparative study of the early music of non-Christian cultures as well as on the study of the Christian liturgy. In the latter field, tradition attributes to Gregory the Great (d.604) the collection and standardizing of historical musical formulas, the establishment of authentic antiphonal singing, and the first organized attempt to preserve and cultivate liturgical song. Under his influence Gregorian plainsong (nonmetrical chant melody) was used universally and exclusively in church services until the twelfth and thirteenth centuries; hymns were banished from the church (although retained in homes and convents); and a new method of musical notation was established which eliminated indications of rhythm but did show the rise and fall of the melody.

Middle Ages

When, in the eleventh century, Guido d'Arezzo added the lines of the scale, the names of the notes, and symbols to indicate rests, holds, and length of note to the Gregorian method, modern notation was created. With the introduction of notation and the system of solmization (so called for the names of the notes), the study of the music as it actually was played and sung becomes possible. While students of medieval music must still have access to treatises on music theory, literary studies of music, records of controversies over secular music and similar documents, the study of music as music becomes more important in this period and thereafter. Music literature from the Middle Ages to the present is a term which includes both the books about music and the transcriptions of music notation.

The great contribution of the Middle Ages to the development of music is the introduction of polyphony, that is, contrapuntal rather than monodic melody. The origins and rise of polyphony are still the subject of scholarly research; all actual evidence at present stems from the British Isles, but modern scholars believe that other countries also had contrapuntal composition, and the relation between polyphonic musical forms and the instrumental accompaniments of the troubadours and trouvères is the subject of scholarly study. Since we have very few of the melodies of the topical songs, laments, dances, rondeaux, and ballads which characterize the secular songs of the period, the student of music is limited to essentially the same materials as the student of literature.

In literature, there are two strains running through the period: the literature of the court and the upper classes of civilized society, and the literature of the people. In music there are essentially three strains: the music of the church, the secular music of the upper classes, and the popular music of the people. As secular music became more and more important to wider audiences, its influence began to be felt even in the realm of sacred music, until in the fourteenth century it was considered necessary to issue a papal bull prescribing stringent regulations against the increasing misuse of polyphony in the church. This conflict between

ecclesiastical and secular music continued throughout the later
Middle Ages and the Renaissance, and the literature of the controversy is important to any research collection in the field of music
history.

Renaissance

The innovations which were introduced in secular music continued to influence church music despite the church's resistance.
In the fourteenth century the so-called *Ars Nova* which added duple
time to the traditional triple time of church music had become
familiar; the Mass and motets for church use showed evidence of
the influence of many new forms; and hymns had returned to many
church services. Once more the church found it necessary to control the use of secular elements in church music, and the Council
of Trent (1545-63) attempted to establish a model for composition
which would embody the characteristics of beauty and dignity that
it considered suitable to the Mass. It found these characteristics
in three masses by Palestrina, whose influence upon subsequent
composition won for him the title of "Savior of Church Music."
Music literature in both its senses greatly increased during the
Renaissance for many of the same reasons that caused the development of other arts and sciences during the period. The invention
of printing, for example, made possible the wider dissemination of
music as well as of books and increased the international exchange
of styles and forms. The Protestant Reformation led to the demand
for resetting the church service and resulted in prolific composition of new church music, especially in England and Germany. The
use of color which distinguishes the painting of Venice was paralleled in its music, and the introduction of "chromatic" elements
led to the development of the modern scale. The use of the vernacular increased in musical composition just as it did in literature, and the emphasis upon individual creative craftsmanship
which characterizes the period is felt also in the many new forms
and the general "humanizing" of Renaissance music.

Baroque

The term "Baroque" as applied to the period of art production
from roughly 1600-1750 has often been used as a term of reproach,
designating a style characterized by excessive ornamentation, contorted forms, and a general deterioration of the Renaissance spirit.
In music, however, this is not as true as it is of the visual arts.
Certain excesses are apparent in some compositions of the period,
reflecting, in French clavier music for example, the same frivolous

elaboration which marks the rococo style in the visual arts; but the vastness of proportion and the splendor of color and ornamentation which are the hallmarks of the Baroque reach heights in composers like Bach and Händel which can hardly be described as contorted or excessive. In fact, the Baroque ushers in the period of great composition in the modern manner and marks a turning point in music history. Most nineteenth-century scholars and historians were so impressed with the greatness of the Baroque achievement that they tended to dismiss all earlier music as if it were a single stylistic whole and, despite the great variety of styles and the great developments in composition, to characterize it inclusively as pre-Bach.

Although modern scholarship has done much to clarify and differentiate the several facets of this "old music," the general public still tends to think in terms of pre-Bach music as a single entity and to practice either one kind of snobbishness or another: to look upon all music before the Baroque as primitive, or to look upon all music after the Baroque as too "popular" in its appeal. While contemporary scholarship rejects the oversimplification of the pre-Bach concept, the librarian should be prepared to find its influence in many of the requests he receives from the patrons of the music library.

Classical

A common error is the idea that classical music is any music not widely popular. Actually the period of classic composition in music in its more precise sense corresponds to the neoclassic period in the visual arts and covers the late eighteenth and nineteenth centuries. In the visual arts the classical period is that of Greek art and architecture, and the return in the eighteenth century to a formalism like that of the Greeks was, with reason, termed neoclassical. But little Greek music remains to us; we know of it mainly through psychological studies, like those of Aristoxenus and the Pythagoreans, for example, or through theoretical works from the Romans, Boethius and Cassiodorus. There is, then, no extant classical music from this period upon which a later age could build. The period called classical in music is that characterized by stress upon the formal elements (just as is classicism in painting), which reached its height in such composers as Haydn and Mozart. To call Rimsky-Korsakov's highly romantic *Scheherazade* classical is to be extremely inexact in the use of adjectives, but it is a common fault and one which the librarian soon recognizes. In responding to the requests of his patrons the librarian must analyze not only the wording of the request, but also the patron who

makes it, in order to know with some precision what really is
wanted.

Romantic

A reaction against the sedulous acceptance of tradition in
music took the form of a romantic revolt against the rules in favor
of untrammeled self-expression and the dictates of individual genius. As in painting, sculpture, and literature, this romantic revolt
existed side by side with the retention of classical symmetry, frequently in the same individual. Beethoven is often considered the
bridge between the classical and romantic styles because he employs the architectural form of the instrumental music established
by Haydn and Mozart, but introduces emotional sweep and personal
expression new to the music of his day. Similarly, composers like
Schubert, Mendelssohn, Brahms, and Franck retain the accepted
form of the sonata, but add lyrical and sentimental strains. Romanticism is pushed further by composers like Schumann and Liszt
who abandon the sonata form or adapt it to their personal needs.
The fervent nationalism which characterizes the Romantics in
painting and literature is also apparent in music in the polonaises
and marches of Chopin; the work of the Russian Five (Glinka,
Borodin, Cui, Moussorgsky, and Rimsky-Korsakov); the Scandina-
vian color of Grieg's music; and the utilization of folk themes,
songs, and dances by Brahms, Liszt, Tschaikowsky, Smetana,
Dvorak, and others.

Contemporary

The eclecticism which has already been noted in the visual
arts of the late nineteenth and twentieth century is apparent also in
the many stylistic schools and fads in music of the same period.
Realism in music, for example, introduces sounds which are imitative of the event or scene illustrated. Berlioz, Liszt, Richard
Strauss, and many of the moderns turned to new instruments, odd
devices for the use of instruments, and even nonmusical imple-
ments to create new tonal effects and sounds for this purpose.
Impressionism, in the tone poems of Debussy, Ravel, and others,
reflects the same intent to record fleeting impressions which
characterizes impressionistic poetry and painting. Many of the
moderns like Bartok and Stravinsky discard traditional tonality (as
traditional verse forms and literary styles are discarded by
modern poets and novelists) and deliberately seek the discords
which result from putting two tonalities together. Composers like
Schoenberg attempt to reject any reference to tonality and to

achieve atonality in much the same way that nonobjective painters attempt to reject objective representation.

Summary

It is not the intent of this rough outline to convey the idea that the development of music was a simple process, neatly divided into discrete periods which parallel precisely similar stylistic periods in other art forms. A fuller account of the many deviations, contradictions, and complexities that mark the historical development of music, however, must be sought in the several excellent histories of music which can devote the necessary space to its unfolding. The similarities have been deliberately stressed here to make more graphic the way descriptive terms are interchanged between the several arts, and the traditional period designations have been used in order to acquaint the student with the kinds of concepts commonly found in the literature about music and in the language of the patron of the general music library.

It should be recognized that the experts in music and musicology devote much of their time to the clarification and refutation of these very concepts and that research in the history and development of music is devoted to a reconstruction in specific detail of the periods which have here been glibly characterized in a phrase or two. A great deal of emphasis at present is on the so-called pre-Bach era of music, and the publication of much of this early music, the discovery of new manuscripts, and the re-evaluation of the composition and theory of this earlier time may well result in more accurate and enlightened attitudes toward its music. Primitive and Greek music are also the subjects of scholarly investigation that may soon provide new data on which to reconstruct the musical production of these periods. In those libraries which try to serve the needs of musicologists, scholars, and serious students of music, the historical studies and archaeological discoveries will fill out, extend, and greatly modify the simplified outline given here, and the student who intends to work in such a library must steep himself in the literature of music and its many auxiliary fields instead of relying on any superficial simplification.

MUSICAL LITERATURE

The literature of music is an extremely difficult field with which to deal because it is composed not only of the books about music, but of music itself and of recorded performances of that music. Each of these three represents a body of materials almost as large as the single field of books about the other disciplines. The music librarian is therefore faced with a three-fold task of becoming familiar with not only the major types of books, but of the music and of recorded performances; not only the major writers, but the major composers and performers; not only the leading book publishers, but the leading music publishers (they are seldom the same) and the major recording companies; and with the criteria for evaluating not only the worth of the textual discussions, but also the excellence of scores and sheet music, and the quality of recordings. And even if he relies on the familiar library substitutes for expert knowledge — the guides, bibliographies, indexes, and other sources of information — he must still become familiar with three different groups of such aids.

Books about Music

The literature about music may be categorized in much the same way that the literature of the visual arts has been in the preceding chapter.

The history of music displays a variety of types as great as that outlined for the visual arts. There are histories of music in general, national histories, histories of particular periods, histories of particular forms, histories of particular instruments and the music written for them, and biographical studies of groups of musicians and individuals. The historical viewpoint is a comparatively late development in the writing about music, however; until the seventeenth century most of the writers about music were concerned with establishing theoretical systems of musical knowledge, and these organizations of music theory reflect the philosophy of each particular period.

Music theory includes in its scope, beyond the accurate definition of technical terms used in theoretical instruction, the comprehensive systematization of musical knowledge. As early as the sixth century B.C., Pythagoras had worked out a mathematical-acoustical basis for the measurement of comparison of intervals, and later theorists combined theoretical speculations with problems of practical musical instruction. Theory deals with the rudiments of musical composition — the scales, intervals, etc. — and the other more complex elements like melody, rhythm, harmony, counterpoint, form, and instrumentation and orchestration. Such studies may be designed (a) to instruct the reader in how to compose or to perform, (b) to provide a basis for technical analysis of music for study or for appreciation, or (c) to assist in the analysis of aesthetic elements.

Musical aesthetics utilizes many of the concepts of general aesthetics, and the approaches to it can be as varied for music as

for the other forms of art. Often music is included in books which
deal with the other major art forms as well, but many books exist
which deal with the aesthetics of music alone, and the approaches
may be philosophical, critical, scientific, historical, artistic,
psychological, or any combination of these, dealt with either subjectively or objectively. And in each area — history, theory, or
aesthetics — every type of treatment may be encountered from the
very simple to the very complex, from the highly scholarly to the
extremely popular, from the most detailed to the barest outline.

In addition, the music librarian must be aware of the auxiliary
areas of knowledge which often must be represented in a collection
that attempts to serve the musician or student of music. The science of acoustics, for example, which is concerned with the nature
of sound, the physical basis of pitch relationships, and the application of this knowledge to the production and reproduction of tone by
various instruments and the voice, is extremely important to the
student. Physiology and psychology also have a bearing on musicology: the physiological processes involved in hearing and performing; the psychological foundations of the perceptions of interval, scale, rhythm, etc.; psychological testing of musical capacities
and limitations; educational psychology and its application to the
teaching of music; studies of emotional and physiological effects of
listening and performing — all of these are areas in which patrons
of the music collection have an interest. Finally, historical method
and the auxiliary sciences of anthropology and ethnology are basic
to the study and understanding of musical history, to comparative
musicology and to research in the field. The autonomous library
will attempt to represent all these allied subjects on its shelves in
addition to the materials which deal directly with music.

To keep abreast of current publication in the books about music
is not difficult. Most of the leading trade publishers of general
books issue books about music, and their catalogs and the standard
trade bibliographies keep the librarian informed of new titles and
editions. As in any field of book acquisition, the librarian learns
through experience which publishers specialize in particular kinds
of works, which ones are generally most reliable, which ones feature scholarly treatises and which, the popular books. For the
larger libraries and for purposes of research, scholarly works in
musicology are important, and the university and college presses
should be watched for their publications in this field. Several
series of publications exist in musicology — like the "Columbia
University Studies in Musicology" or the "Eastman School of Music
series" — in which important studies are made available. The publications of such university presses as those of Harvard and Oxford
and of such trade publishers as Macmillan, Knopf, and Norton

testify to the ready availability of worthwhile additions to the collection of music literature. Until recent years, the scholarship of
music centered in Europe and the works of the German scholars,
particularly, are basic to any research collection. So too are the
works of historical interest — the early treatises and documents
which can be found only rarely in the American market. For
scholarly materials in music, the librarian must be familiar with
the sources of foreign publication, the agencies through which
rarities can be obtained, and the trade bibliography of foreign
countries as well as of America.

Reviews of the books about music are also generally available.
Most of the publications of the trade publishers are reviewed in the
general reviewing media, and the smaller libraries particularly
are likely to find the majority of the titles in which they are interested reviewed in such sources as the *Saturday Review*, the *New
York Times Book Review*, the *Herald Tribune Books*, and the library literature. More scholarly works, as in every field, are
less widely evaluated, and reviews of them can often be found only
in the special and scholarly journals of music. It is even more
difficult to keep informed regarding foreign publications unless the
librarian has access to the periodicals and trade bibliographies of
foreign countries. A library with any pretensions to a research
collection would, of course, subscribe to scholarly journals from
abroad, especially in the field of music where so much of the research is done by European scholars. Even the more general
music libraries will find British periodicals like the *Music Review*
and *Music & Letters* of value, since they do not require knowledge
of a foreign language but do provide a more complete coverage of
non-American musical news and publication.

Music Proper

In the trade, a distinction is generally made between music
publishers and publishers of books about music. While a commercial publisher will occasionally attempt publication in both fields,
the usual practice is for the book publisher to confine himself to
the traditional book form, leaving to special publishers the publication of scores and sheet music and a few technical manuals on
such subjects as singing and counterpoint. The major drawback to
this arrangement from the standpoint of the librarian is that music
publication lies outside the traditional channels, depriving libraries
of ready access to its listings and to many of the services extended
by the book publisher. Music publishers, for example, are less
quick to provide catalogs of their publications or to make available
prepurchase examination copies. Another difficulty is the lack of

good trade lists of music in America except for the Library of Congress' *Catalog of Copyright Entries.* Even the European listings are inadequate; only Hofmeister's *Musikalish-literarischer Monatsbericht* is sufficiently detailed to give a chronological coverage of the field. The use of the copyright entries and the Hofmeister to aid in the selection of music is practical only in the largest libraries. The problem of careful selection and adequate coverage by the smaller libraries is difficult as there are few selective lists, and reviews of current music are not widely carried.

Since the *Publishers' Trade List Annual,* the *Cumulative Book Index,* and the *Publishers'* Weekly cannot be used as guides to current music publication, the librarians of smaller music collections must rely on the listings which they can solicit from individual publishers. This means that the librarian must know something about the integrity and reliability of the publisher from whose list he selects, but he deals much of the time with old and established firms of reputation and standing. Many of the larger publishing houses have a long history of music publication — Oliver Ditson was established in 1835, G. Schirmer in 1861, Carl Fischer in 1872, Theodore Presser in 1888 — and experience soon teaches the librarian the special services and subject emphases of the individual publishers. The Associated Music Publishers, for example, are sales agents for foreign publications; H. W. Gray is the American agent for the fine English house, Novello and Company; Theodore Presser is especially noted for its educational publications; E. C. Schirmer for its choral and a cappella music; Broude Brothers for its orchestra score series, etc.

Although the publishers may be reliable, the librarian still needs an evaluation of specific pieces of published music to determine their suitability for his particular collection. Unfortunately, the criticism of music usually takes the form of newspaper or magazine reviews of specific performances rather than of the music itself, and very few reviews evaluate published compositions in the way that books are reviewed. The composer Robert Schumann is an important figure in the realm of criticism as well as of composition because he introduced, in the magazine *Neue Zeitschrift für Musik* which he founded in 1834, the critical analysis of the compositions themselves as well as their performed interpretations. While reviews of music are still comparatively rare, the Music Library Association's *Notes* and the British publication *Music & Letters* provide good evaluative criticisms of published music, and the more popular magazines, *Musical America* and *Musical Courier,* feature shorter annotations. For music useful for school performance — band numbers, operettas, etc. — the *Educational Music Magazine* is the most complete and detailed, listing new publications with some annotations, and grading them as "easy," "medium easy," "medium difficult," or "difficult."

In the scholarly libraries, interest in antiquities is greater than in current publication, and the problem is not one of finding an evaluation of a new work or a new edition but of obtaining copies of works of which the value is well known. Early music and holographs appear only rarely in the American market, and the European libraries have often guarded their holdings with an understandable but regrettable jealousy. Recent years have seen an advance in international cooperation, however, which is beginning to open up the resources of the great collections to other libraries. The larger research centers in the United States are also working toward the reproduction, transcription, and editing of their rarities for wider use of scholars everywhere. The famous *Denkmäler deutscher Tonkunst, Denkmäler der Tonkunst in Bayern* and *Denkmäler der Tonkunst in Oesterreich* are now available on microfilm; the Library of Congress music microfilm archives make reproductions of holographs available to subscribers; the Smith College music archives series provides transcriptions of old music; and since World War II, the famous Breitkopf and Härtel editions of the complete works of Bach, Beethoven, Brahms, and Mozart have been reproduced in photolithograph by J. W. Edwards. In 1942 the complete contents of Petrucci's *Odhecaton* — the first successful printing of polyphonic music from movable type (1501) — were made available in modern score for an extremely low price in an edition by Helen Hewitt. A grant from the Carnegie Corporation and the American Council of Learned Societies made this contribution to world scholarship possible and the Medieval Academy of America published it. As an example of the work which can be done by musicologists for the benefit of scholars everywhere, it stands as a model for further research and altruistic endeavor which it is hoped may be copied by libraries both here and abroad.

Phonograph Records

In recent years, particularly since the introduction of electrical recording and the perfection of long-playing discs, excellent recordings of all the standard classics and many infrequently heard compositions have become easily obtainable on records. While the average layman probably finds most of his wants readily filled by the releases of the major companies — Victor, Columbia, and Decca — the more selective or more scholarly record collections use many additional firms both here and abroad who specialize in old music, little-heard music, and less popular materials. Another important source is the Library of Congress phonoduplication service, made possible by a grant from the Carnegie Corporation in 1940. The Carnegie money was used to install a complete sound laboratory for the making and duplication of phonograph records; and folk music recorded in the field, transcriptions of radio broadcasts, original recordings of performances of music available in the Library of Congress, readings of poetry, and other unique pressings are now obtainable by libraries. It should be remembered, too, that recordings exist for other aspects of musical interest in addition to the performance of master works. The Seashore Measures of Musical Talents are an example of one type which music collections might wish to add; other types include recordings which illustrate the characteristics of the different instruments for the instruction of the beginner, records of sound effects, readings of poetry and the drama set to musical accompaniment, and compositions for ensemble from which one instrument has been omitted to allow the student to perform with the recording.

Especially notable for library collections are the "anthology" albums which illustrate musical history or specific kinds of music. The six-volume *Columbia History of Music* edited by Percy Scholes, for example, and the English (Parlophone) album, *2000 Years of Music*, are extremely valuable. The monumental *Anthologie Sonore*, edited by Curt Sachs (issued irregularly and not in chronological order) is devoted to music not recorded elsewhere and seldom performed and with its accompanying program notes is of inestimable value to the record collection which is devoted to providing new and broadening experience to the listener. A new historical series, called "Archive Production," and sponsored by the History of Music Division of the Deutsche Grammophon Gesellschaft, is planned for some seventy discs to cover twelve "research periods" from Gregorian chant and the Middle Ages to the Mannheim and Viennese schools of the eighteenth century. Special collections include such albums as *Liturgical Music of the Catholic Church*, featuring the choirs of the Sistine Chapel and the Dijon cathedral, the French albums, *Seven Centuries of Sacred Music* and *Three Centuries of Organ Music*, and many others which deal with as many different aspects of musical history as do the books about music. There are albums devoted to the music of a particular geographical area (Oriental music), to music of a specific instrument (harpsichord music) or of a specific period (music of the Renaissance), etc. These collections of records are often designed specifically for educational or musicological purposes and are not always known to the average record buyer or local music shop.

Fortunately the increased popularity of recordings has brought a number of excellent guides to records (discographies) and has

led to the inclusion of reviews of current records in many popular
magazines. In such volumes as Hall and Levin's *The Disc Book*,
The New Guide to Recorded Music, or Bernard Haggin's *Music on
Records*, to name only a few, one finds evaluations and comparisons
or recordings (often highly personal in their critera) which are
useful in helping to select from the vast stock of available recordings. Reviews of current releases are also carried in the *Saturday
Review*, the *Library Journal*, and other sources easily obtained even
by the smallest library. The Music Library Association *Notes*
contains an "Index of Record Reviews," which like the *Book Review
Digest*, gives full bibliographic information concerning latest releases and the sources of reviews and indicates the general tone of
approval or disapproval of each review. About twenty different
reviewing media are indexed, ranging from popular and widely held
sources such as the *Consumers' Union* and the *Nation*, to more
special publications like the *American Record Guide* or the *Review
of Permanent Music*. The "Index" serves then not only as a guide
to current music and its critical acceptance, but also as a guide
to reviewing media which might well be added to the library
collection.

Periodicals

According to Luening[1] there are about ninety special music
magazines in the United States and four purely scholarly ones
which contain historical evaluations, theoretical studies, and reviews, studies, and comments on contemporary musical activities.
Although this list is in itself a formidable one, the research collection must consider also the major scholarly music magazines
from foreign countries and magazines which are no longer published
but which were of importance in the field of music in their day.

The extremely important periodical literature of music presents a serious problem to the librarian because so little of it is
indexed. Among the general indexes — *Readers' Guide*, *Education
Index*, and *International Index* — only nine separate magazines were
analyzed in 1956. In 1949 the long-awaited *Music Index* began publication, and while it analyzes some eighty American, English, and
foreign periodicals and plans to increase its coverage if sufficient
support is found for the project, it does not cover earlier publications. For these, only the *Bibliographie des Musikschrifttums*
includes any information, and it goes back only to 1936. For

---

[1] Otto Luening, *Music Materials and the Public Library; a Report to the Direc-
tor of the Public Library Inquiry*. (N. Y., Social Science Research Council,
1949), p. 29.

indexing prior to 1936 no tool exists. What this means to the research scholar can be deduced from the list published in the Music
Library Association *Notes* for November, 1938, in which the important periodical titles in print at any time prior to 1936 are noted.
The list contains the names of 175 magazines, 51 of which are in
English, and all of which are considered by the Association to contain matter of interest to the musicologist. The Music Library
Association has long been calling for the compilation of an index
to supplement the *Bibliographie,* but has had no success in bringing such a project to completion. The Newberry Library, with
WPA assistance, began an index on cards of some 111 periodicals,
but had to abandon it in 1942. H. W. Wilson considered a similar
project, but rejected it as unprofitable. Until such an index can be
compiled, the reference value of music periodicals is much curtailed, and a great deal of important information is on the shelves
but essentially unavailable.

Films

The addition of sound to films has made the motion picture
another tool of value to the music library, although to date film
has been used more as a teaching aid than as an implement of research. The documentary-factual film can be used in the teaching
of musical history, as an introduction to specific instruments, for
instruction in notation, and to increase appreciation of specific
compositions. The ability of the camera to concentrate on details
in close shots and from many angles makes the film a useful means
by which the scholar and the student can study intensively the
technique of great artists. As contemporary films become of
historical interest they may become invaluable in recreating the
experience of great performances and in preserving the techniques
of contemporary artists for future generations.
The general guides to films can be used for reviews of musical
films as well. Special reviews are contained in the *Educational
Music Magazine* for the specific subject field of music, but the library which wishes to have a really strong collection will probably
go outside the field of music proper in adding to its film holdings.
Films on the dance, for example, are certainly pertinent in a music
library, as are the many films which recreate a historical period,
films on the physics of sound, and others whose subjects do not
classify as music but do contribute to the better understanding of it.

Reference Materials

The reference tools of music fall into the usual categories of reference tools in any subject area: bibliographies, dictionaries, encyclopedias, yearbooks, biographical dictionaries, etc. As in any other subject area, these tools are adapted to the peculiar charac- ter of the subject: there are dictionaries of musical themes, for example, collections of program notes, and directories of collec- tions of musical instruments as well as the standard type of gen- eral encyclopedias and dictionaries of terms, names, and summa- ries. The short list which appears at the end of this chapter, limited as it is, gives some indication of the variety of purposes served and the range of subjects covered by the reference materi- als of music.

The student will readily recognize the eclectic character of the list, which is intended to convey a sense of the great scope of interests covered by the tools in the field. Musicologists will need to supplement the few scholarly tools with many of the more spe- cialized ones which deal exclusively with ancient and early church music, with Oriental as well as Occidental music, and with a much wider range of bibliographical references. The nonspecialist lay- man will find many of the titles here too esoteric; he will want more biographical treatments, stories of the operas, and contem- porary and popular indexes. Many will find too few of the valuable foreign language tools here, while others will consider the inclusion of even these few German titles inappropriate. Each library situa- tion will require a revision of the list — the omission of some titles, the addition of others. The use of Winchell's *Guide to Reference Books* and other general bibliographies, and of the separate bibli- ographies on the list and those included within other listed titles, will be necessary when the specific needs of the particular library are known.

TYPES OF MUSIC LIBRARIES

The nature of the library collection is dictated by its users and the purposes for which it was established. In many music li- braries of Europe, the collection consists of music manuscripts rather than of books, and the holographs and rarities are not in- tended for general circulation. In many American libraries, on the other hand, the music collection consists solely of books for the use of the layman borrower.

In general, the major types of music libraries are: (1) the scholarly research collections which strive to gather together the original musical manuscripts and treatises on music necessary to the scholarly analysis of primary materials; (2) the libraries of music schools, universities, and colleges which collect both re- search and general materials for students of music and musicology;

(3) music departments in public libraries which may make some provision for research, but in general place greater emphasis on popular and nonspecialist materials; (4) commercial lending libraries which make available scores and parts for the use of performers; and (5) libraries of motion picture studios and of radio and television stations which provide the music and recordings needed in the production of films and broadcasts. The dissimilar publics served by these libraries, and the varied needs which they represent, make different demands upon the librarian and the collection and require an organization and interpretation of the materials suited to their specific needs.

Research Collections

The music libraries, or departments, which attempt to provide the necessary scholarly materials for research in musicology collect many more kinds of material than does the average music library. Although the collection of contemporary publications is essential, incunabula are of great importance as are books printed before 1800, and research libraries must make special effort to find and preserve these rarer items. The older musical scores and manuscripts, and those of the great masters of music, are of especial research interest, and as in the field of literature, the holographs and original manuscripts which indicate the composer's original intent are an essential corrective for the later revisions and editions. Not only music and the books about it but also librettos are objects of study for musicologists. Collections of old instruments, especially those that can be played, are a valuable research tool. Pictures of old instruments, of musicians, and of music being performed often provide information which textual descriptions do not; for example, much of our knowledge of the state of ancient music is based upon bas-reliefs and other pictorial representations. Any personal or public documents which relate to music and musicians have their place in the historical reconstruction of music's development as they do in any historical research. Today, motion pictures and sound films of musicians' performances and of the dance are additional research aids.

European libraries have had an advantage over most of the American libraries in the amassing of early manuscripts, holographs, instruments, and pictures. Many European collections date from the days of the early Christian church when liturgical music was brought together in cathedrals, chapels, and monasteries. Others were begun by private collectors among the nobility and royalty who fostered the production of music and had access to autographs and original manuscripts. The holdings of musical

holographs, manuscripts of the music of the troubadours and trouvères, music of the Middle Ages and the Renaissance, court operas
and librettos and the like in the great music libraries of Germany,
France, Britain and Italy — the Prussian State Library in Berlin,
the Gesellschaft der Musikfreunde in Vienna, the Bibliothèque
Nationale, the Bibliothèque de l'Arsenal, the library of the Paris
Opera, the British Museum, etc. — represent centuries of careful
accumulation. A few American libraries, however, have assembled
groups of materials which place them among the leading research
collections of the world. The Library of Congress is now outstanding for printed material, and the New York Public Library music
department is the most widely used of any world collection. Important collections are held also by the Yale School of Music, the
Boston Public Library, the Eastman School of Music, the Henry
Huntington Library, the Newberry Library, the Harvard University
Library, the John Carter Brown Library in Providence, and others.

Through the use of microphotography, photostating, and other
means of reproduction, the rare and unique items of music can be
made available to scholars anywhere. The collection of such reproduced materials is an important aspect of any research library's
activities, and the promotion of cooperation between research collections is a primary task of the scholarly libraries. The research
library should provide facilities for reproduction by microfilm or
other devices, reading machines for their use, and guides to collections of such materials.

An important reference tool for the research library are the
catalogs of the great collections which serve both as a bibliography
of musical literature and a guide to source materials. The compilation and publication of such bibliographies and catalogs is a
considerable contribution to scholarship and an important task of
the scholarly libraries. The larger libraries particularly, in com-
piling indexes to the materials in their collections, can make information available to musicians, students, and other libraries
which could be found in no other way. Other obligations beyond the
traditional preservation and dissemination of materials are also
often assumed by the research library. In some cases the libraries
have made older and rare works available for performance, not
merely by reproducing the pages mechanically, but by transcribing
old works into modern notation, bringing valuable works up to
standard instrumentation, and copying parts into scores and transcribing scores into parts. The Library of Congress' collection of
Stradivarius instruments is an outstanding example of the museum
function assumed by many scholarly libraries. Lectures and concerts, often featuring music and instruments seldom heard elsewhere, are also often sponsored by libraries which can provide the

music and the instruments for them. The research librarian in the field of music fosters such programs in his own library whenever possible and — almost equally important — keeps abreast of similar activities and services in other libraries in order to guide scholars to the best centers of resources and information in the field of their special interest.

The librarian of a scholarly music library needs a strong background in musicology as well as training in library techniques to perform these services. He must be able to speak with musicologists and musicians in their own technical language; he must be able to recognize important research materials relating to music in all of its aspects; he must be able to evaluate conflicting demands upon his budget in terms of research value and musical importance; and he must be able to interpret his collection in the terms which will have the most meaning for scholars in the field. While it is probably not necessary that he play a musical instrument, the music librarian in the scholarly library should be able to read musical notation and know something about the technique of musical performance. His knowledge of musical history and theory should be wide; he cannot confine his experience to the "One hundred favorite pieces" which are the staple of "pop" concerts and radio broadcasts. Foreign languages are also an essential part of his equipment since the greater part of musical history, musical scholarship, and important composition has been, until recent years, the product of Europe. German, Italian, and French are a minimum requirement despite the universality of music itself. It is small wonder then that the librarians of the research collections have so often been notable scholars in the music field; names like those of O. G. Sonneck, Otto Kinkeldey, Carleton Sprague Smith, and W. Oliver Strunk, for example, are important in musicology as well as in music librarianship.

School and College Libraries

School libraries[2] which specialize in music may be attached to independent music schools and conservatories, schools of music joined to a university, or music departments within a general library of a college or university. Depending, then, upon the curriculum of the individual educational institution, libraries of this type may range from those which provide scholarly materials for advanced research to those which provide only the most general

---

[2] The term "school libraries" in this section is used as a general term to stand for libraries attached to any kind of educational institution, whether a college, a university, or a special school of music.

musical materials for the cultural background of the nonspecialist. The duties of libraries serving the scholars are essentially those mentioned in the preceding section, but all libraries attached to educational agencies have certain other characteristics in common.

The characteristic which all school libraries share, whatever their subject matter, is a dependence upon the curriculum of the parent institution. Certain libraries will have acquired, through gift or purchase, collections which may be only remotely connected with the subject fields stressed by the school to which they are attached, but in general the subject emphasis of the collection will reflect the subject emphasis of the course materials, and certain areas may definitely be omitted because the school does not offer instruction in them. This relationship between library holdings and course offerings is a useful guide to selection and acquisition for the librarian. He can concentrate on building up inclusive collections of certain types of materials without feeling the necessity to represent other types essential to a well-rounded collection of generalia, and he thus tends to become a specialist in the bibliography of the needed fields.

Most colleges, and many universities, prepare their students of music to be teachers rather than performers. The emphasis, therefore, is on the more familiar and simpler pieces of music proper and on musical pedagogy in the literature of music. Educational psychology, teaching techniques, curriculum studies, teacher training, and similar aspects of the field of education as they apply to the teaching of music receive greater stress here than they do in the scholarly libraries, or in the general public libraries. Music for performance is generally selected for use by student and school organizations like the bands, choral groups, glee clubs, and musical-dramatic societies which so many schools promote. In most cases, these groups purchase their own music and house it separately from the music department of the library, but the library should still feel responsible for making publishers' catalogs and bibliographical tools available to assist in the selection and purchase of such materials.

In the universities, conservatories, and special schools of music, the heavier emphasis is upon research in musicology and in the training for musical performance. A much wider selection of instrumental, orchestral, and vocal music will be required, and a greater emphasis will be placed upon the needs of research and less upon pedagogy. Little-heard music and music designed for less familiar instruments and ensembles will be collected. The stress will be more upon the study of music in a documentary sense; less on the "appreciation" of the best-known pieces traditionally performed.

In libraries attached to educational institutions there will be
an attempt to extend the appreciation of good music to those who
are not majors in it. General and popular works on the history,
biography, and introductory theory of music will be present in the
collection, depending on the curriculum of the school and its general objectives. In many colleges, music appreciation courses are
offered to introduce students outside the school of music to some
of the standard music which, in the opinion of the faculty, should
be familiar to anyone calling himself educated. These courses
usually utilize recorded performances of music and attempt to
interest the general student in listening to unfamiliar as well as
familiar works. Record collections, in such instances, become an
important part of the music library, and college and university
libraries have included listening rooms and circulating record
collections to a greater extent than have public libraries.

One of the major influences in popularizing the record collection in the school library was the gift from the Carnegie Corporation of a basic library of records, phonographs, scores, and books
about music. Between 1933 and 1940, 183 college music sets were
distributed, consisting of an electric phonograph, 953 records, carefully chosen to represent an anthology of ancient and modern music,
both Oriental and Occidental, scores, books, and a printed descriptive catalog. These Carnegie sets formed the nucleus of the music
library in many instances; in a few cases they remain essentially
the only music collection the school possesses. But in many other
cases the Corporation's aim was realized; with the set as a start,
the music library has grown and expanded, demonstrating the cultural and educational value of such materials to the institution as
a whole.

The degree of emphasis upon musicology and research in the
individual school will help to determine the kind of background
needed by the librarian. A broad general knowledge of musical
history and musical theory is essential, in any case, and some
familiarity with foreign languages. Work with students will necessarily be on a more elementary level; they will require assistance
for term papers and short reports, advice on readings, reference
aid in the general tools. The librarian will probably spend more
time in publicizing general materials and services and building up
a working relationship with faculty and students than in gleaning
the rare book and manuscript market or analyzing and transcribing
the materials of scholarship. The basic library techniques in reference work, book selection, technical processes, and reader assistance will be utilized much more frequently than knowledge of
esoteric aspects of the subject field. The librarian of a research
library should be a musicologist with some training in library

techniques whereas the librarian of a school or college library is first of all a librarian with a strong musical background.

Departments in Public Libraries

Three major types of public library music departments may be differentiated. The first is the large research collection to which most of the generalizations made in the section on research collections are applicable. Music libraries like those of the New York Public Library, the Boston Public Library, the Free Library of Philadelphia, the Grosvenor Library in Buffalo, and a few others represent a kind of service in music which most public libraries cannot possibly hope to achieve, but they are an important segment of the total public library picture and should not be forgotten when the public library's contribution to music is assessed.

More typical, unfortunately, is the small public library with inadequate funds, where the music collection is only one of a variety of subject fields and services for which the general librarian is responsible. Some fine music programs have been developed even under these adverse circumstances when sufficient interest and energy have been substituted for adequate support and staffing. But the development of a respectable collection of books about music, music proper, and recordings — and a program of services related to music — usually requires the full-time attention of a subject expert. The incidental attention of a librarian charged with a variety of other responsibilities is not enough for a field as complex as music which appeals to an audience so heterogeneous.

A third class of music library is that represented by a special department of music (or a special section for music in the fine arts department) in the medium- and large-sized public libraries. In these libraries the major emphasis is upon a well-rounded collection of music materials for the use of the general public, local musicians, and students of music. Its research resources are limited, although an attempt is usually made to provide a small collection of basic research tools. Its music department is under the supervision of a music librarian, and special attention is given to the promotion of public interest in the materials of music and the use of the library's facilities. It is to this type of library that this section refers when dealing with the public library.

Most public libraries cannot possibly collect manuscript music, incunabula, holographs, and similar rarities. The best service that they can hope to render the scholars in their communities is to provide general bibliographies, indexes to the major source collections, and service through interlibrary loan and other cooperative schemes. This knowledge of research sources, however, is specialized knowledge of a useful order and should not be regarded as unimportant. The librarian is often the only person in the community who has such knowledge and access to the channels through which it can be obtained, and the ability to direct the scholar to the place where the information can be found is often almost as important as being able to supply the information directly.

Direct services are supplied to the musicians, students of music, persons connected with organizations which use music (radio stations, churches, schools, etc.), and laymen interested in listening to music and increasing their appreciation of it. Public libraries supply the music used by local symphony orchestras and other groups of performers in many instances; they provide the material for program notes on concert programs, radio commentaries, club papers, and elsewhere; they make available scores for study, for practice, or for use in following performances in concert or on the air; they provide the background reading with which many listeners and performers alike increase their appreciation and understanding of music; they provide recordings of great music for the enjoyment of many who would have no other opportunity of hearing it; they foster lectures and concerts just as many research libraries do. In addition, many public libraries can contribute to the growing body of bibliographical materials in the field by keeping homemade indexes with a local or regional emphasis. The concert activities of the community and their programs; the activities of local composers, performers, teachers, or groups and organizations in the field of music; the publications of local publishers and compositions of local writers; and the folk music of the locality are often collected nowhere else, yet may be of great research value. A vast collection of rare items is not the only source of research materials.

The major problem for the public library, as it is for almost every library, is the inadequacy of funds available for building up services in the field of music. As has been pointed out earlier, music is still too frequently treated as a less important part of the total fine arts section, and it must make a fraction of that total budget do for all the services it would like to provide. This is becoming less frequently true as a wider audience for music is making its needs known, but there are still many communities where the traditional notion that "music isn't books" militates against the establishment of a fully independent and adequately supported music department.

The satisfactory provision of music services in a public library is an expensive process. There are, as noted above, three collections of materials (books, music, and recordings) instead of just one which must be provided, and the cost of the materials of music

is high. Their expense is increased by the fact that they require
special handling and must be more frequently replaced. Sheet music and scores, for example, if bound in such a way that they can
be placed on a music stand or a piano rack are predestined to early
physical disintegration. Records, until the introduction of vinylite,
were subject to breakage and scratches which fast made them useless. The storage of musical scores, recordings, and sheet music
requires special shelving and cases. Record players are expensive, and listening rooms and soundproofing are even more so, to
say nothing of the administrative problems they present in planning
space, manning recording machines, and controlling discs. If records are allowed to circulate, the listening rooms may be eliminated but additional problems are posed: the wear and tear on
records is much increased, special carrying cases or protective
coverings must be supplied, additional personnel must be made
available to collate the records when they are charged out and returned.

In view of these several difficulties in the way of establishing
music collections, it is not surprising that many libraries have
gladly accepted gifts and bequests as a source of supply. Until
recently it was not unusual for music and record collections to
consist solely of donations, and as is too often the case, the quality
of the gift materials was frequently below the standard which the
librarians would have imposed had they made the selection. Many
collections still reflect the personal bias or haphazard selection of
well-meaning donors. But blanket condemnation of gift collections
is completely unwarranted; some of the best collections, both for
research purposes and for general use, are based upon donations
and bequests. The Drexel Collection in the New York Public Library, the Allen A. Brown Collection in the Boston Public Library,
and the Edwin A. Fleisher Collection in the Free Library of Philadelphia are especially notable, and in the last two instances, the
continued interest of the donor and the trustees has been of great
importance in maintaining the eminence of the music collections in
the two libraries. Almost every large library in the country can
point to instances of private generosity which helped to develop a
collection or form the nucleus for later additions. It is not the gift
as a gift, but the undiscriminating acceptance of any kind of gift
which has led in many cases to an ill-assorted and low-standard
collection.

Where the library controls selection, the standards in the fields
of art and music, especially in those parts of the collection which
represent reproductions of the works of artists, have generally
been higher than those maintained in the same library in the field
of fiction. Many libraries which purchase a fairly representative

collection of popular potboilers for their fiction shelves would not think of providing a similar level of production in their musical recordings. The expense, the comparatively limited clientele, and the popular tradition concerning appreciation of the arts have tended to preserve a more discriminating attitude in music selection. For the general library this is probably a good thing, but it should be recognized that popular materials are also valuable in later research, and that the complete disappearance of popular songs, sheet music, and other aspects of the cultural history of a period would be a great loss. Many collections of research value are formed of items which would have been rejected by libraries at the time of their publication as being beneath the standard of quality desired. While it may not be the province of the medium-sized public library to collect substandard materials for future researchers, some musical Farmington Plan should be agreed to which would guarantee the preservation of at least one copy of every music publication in some library in the country.

The training required for the librarian of the public library's music department is essentially the same as that of the school librarian. Much of the public library's work is with students of schools, conservatories, and colleges who require assistance in the preparation of papers, the use of standard materials, the selection of readings. Other users of the public library include local musicians, composers and publishers, laymen whose interest in music is cultural rather than professional, and groups and organizations whose interest in music may be primary or only incidental. While the range of interests served is wider than that served by the usual school library, the kinds of needs are almost identical: materials of history and theory, technical how-to-do manuals, music for performance and listening, general reference aids in music and its allied fields, and popular literature to aid in the understanding and appreciation of music. The librarian in the college or university, of course, may rely upon the assistance of the music faculty in the selection and evaluation of materials, but it is not unusual for public libraries to utilize the special knowledge of musicians, teachers, and scholars in the local community for advice and suggestions in much the same way. Particular emphasis is placed in most public libraries upon cooperation with groups and activities in the community; the libraries usually attempt to provide materials to accompany concerts and recitals and space for publicity concerning musical activities. Some libraries have even acted as a clearing house for the exchange of musical services and the announcement of positions open or wanted. In addition to the basic library techniques and a knowledge of music, the public library's music librarian should also have a strong interest in community activities and public relations and a willingness to work with individuals and groups in many ways.

Special Libraries

The commercial lending libraries and the libraries of motion picture studios and radio stations are highly specialized in their holdings, but often do not employ a professional librarian. The lending libraries may contain either sheet music, music in score, or phonograph records, and many times they represent the widest selection of these materials in the community. About fifty of the larger music publishers also maintain rental libraries of contemporary orchestral pieces and older compositions in manuscript. The libraries of small radio stations may consist of phonograph recordings and transcriptions only; or, in the large stations, of scores and parts, books about music, and recordings and transcriptions. Extensive collections of all kinds of musical materials including transcriptions of broadcasts, collections of scripts, and other materials related to broadcasting compose libraries of the large networks. Motion picture studios maintain music libraries of the sound tracks of their film productions and large collections of sheet music, scores and other materials to be used in the production of films. Occasionally such libraries are called upon to do difficult historical research, involving music and instruments typical of a particular period and place; and such requests, relying as they do upon collections of book materials, are usually relayed to the large research or public libraries. In all of these special libraries, there is likely to be as heavy an emphasis upon popular and dance music past and present as there is on the classics and the works of the masters. Although the professional librarian may not administer these special collections, his awareness of their existence and familiarity with their holdings may often be of great value to his patrons and to the definition of his own library's function. Certainly, whenever it is possible to promote cooperative relationships with such libraries, mutual benefits should result.

THE ORGANIZATION OF MUSIC MATERIALS

To arrange, index, and interpret the great variety of materials on each of the three levels of music literature is not easy, especially as several different organizations of the material are possible and plausible. Different needs of different patrons dictate different approaches to the subject matter, and since each of these several approaches contributes in its special way to the understanding of the subject, room should be made for them in any organization of the literature. The historical approach by stylistic periods (as reflected in the Bücken and Norton series in the bibliography) is only one of the possible ways of presenting a historical study. National and biographical organization of the material is also useful, and in music as in the other humanities the individual creator receives a great deal of attention. The organization of music in terms of the tools and materials employed (as in the visual arts — water color, oil painting, wood carving, etc.) is useful since the instrument is of primary importance. Room must be made for the literature which deals with the particular instrument: music for the piano, for the violin, for the organ, for the voice, etc. The breakdown by form, as in literature (novel, drama, poem, essay), is paralleled in the field of music, where a great part of the writing is also devoted to specific forms (symphony, oratorio, opera, cantata, fugue, etc.). The categorization by purpose, as used in the field of architecture (public buildings, ecclesiastic and religious buildings, residences, etc.), is also used in music classification in the division between theater music, sacred music, dance music. Yet while each of these divisions has a value which classification attempts to make manifest, the several categories are not discrete: vocal music may also be sacred music, theater music for the ballet is also dance music, and any one of the subdivisions may be subject to historical treatment — by period, by country or by biographical studies. Such complexity is typical of every subject area, but the three-way split in music literature multiplies the problems faced by the classifier and cataloger and complicates the task of devising a usable scheme of classification and cataloging processes.

Classification

Neither of the two most widely used classification schemes — the Dewey Decimal system and the Library of Congress Classification — is completely satisfactory. McColvin puts it strongly: "Dewey's music section, with its haphazard over-classification and the confusion of music and musical literature, could scarcely be worse. As for the Library of Congress scheme . . . for general purposes drastic alterations would be required."[3]

There are several weaknesses in the Dewey system. Music has been limited to the few numbers comprehended between 780-789, in order that it may be included in the schedule as part of the fine arts. As so often happens in the Dewey classification, such an

---

[3]Lionel R. McColvin and Harold Reeves, *Music Libraries: Their Organisation and Contents* ... Vol. I (London, Grafton, 1937), p. 25.

organization is schematically defensible, but practically inadequate. The fine arts are divided into sections representing each of the arts: the 720's for architecture, the 730's for sculpture, the 750's for painting, and the 780's for music. This is a neat schematism, but under such an arrangement, music is no more prominent in the total scheme than landscape gardening, and no more room is left for the books devoted to the history of music than is left for those dealing with bowling and skittles. Clearly this is not an accurate reflection of the comparative volume of publication in the several subject areas, nor does it provide sufficient space for expansion to allow for a more detailed breakdown by types in those areas where publication is prolific.

Another major weakness is the "confusion of music and music literature" mentioned by McColvin. While certain sections of the 780's seem to have been designed primarily to describe books about music, others are arranged to reflect musical compositions themselves. Yet there is no distinction made — the number 786.41 may be used to designate a book about piano sonatas or a sonata score. In libraries which use the Dewey classification, music itself is often marked with an "M," so that 786.41 would indicate a textual discussion of the sonata and M786.41, a composition in sonata form. The use of the M symbol for music proper is fairly successful, but a difficulty still remains in the descriptive categories of Dewey. The book about music is not always accurately described in terms that are adequate for a musical composition: books about sacred vocal music for solo contralto are rare, although there are many such musical compositions.

Since the use of Dewey does not eliminate the necessity for combining letters and figures in the call number in any case, the Library of Congress solution to the problem is much more adequate. Here a large section under the letter M provides for a breakdown by the categories most descriptive of musical compositions, while a separate section under ML makes available an equally expandable classification scheme for music literature in which the categories can be designed to fit the nature of textual materials in the field. The ML section can devote as much space as is needed for aesthetics, history, acoustics, and other subjects in the books about music. By the same token, the M section can utilize all the space that is needed to allow for the many forms and types of musical compositions.

Even so, the full description of a musical work through a classification number requires a much more complex combination of symbols than that provided by the Library of Congress. Several attempts to devise such a classification have been made by librarians at one time or another; a good example is that created by

Dickinson, whose scheme uses letters, figures, and arbitrary symbols to make up a highly informative notation.[4] Using this scheme,
it is possible to classify a piece of music, not only as a Beethoven
piano sonata, but to indicate as well that the particular piece of
music is the Fourth sonata, that it is edited by Jensen, is arranged
as a chamber piece for a trio consisting of piano and strings from
its original form as piano solo, and that the part described is for
the violin. Such a notation looks like this:

> p5121-3=11
> B39
> So(4) J
> p21

and is probably too complicated for the average music collection.
Yet most of this information is of importance to music students and
performers. The difficulty is that different aspects of the information are important under different circumstances. Where the music is to be played, the fact that it is the violin part of a trio arrangement is highly important, and for the player to have all such
pieces of music together would be a great convenience. If the music is to be studied rather than performed, however, the original
form of the composition is more important, and this work probably
should be placed with the other piano sonatas rather than with violin
music. The editor and arranger are also of importance to the student of comparative arrangements. While the Dickinson scheme
can be adapted to emphasize any of these aspects, it cannot be
made to change emphases to meet changing demands.

The classification of phonograph records can be as complex
as that of music books, but most libraries attempt to keep the
classification scheme simple. Where the collection of phonograph
records is small, classification is often omitted altogether, and
recordings are filed in alphabetical order by name of composer or
in some other simple arrangement. As the collection grows larger
and the variety of approaches to the music makes it difficult to turn
readily to the recording which will meet the request, classification
is added — often in the form of a simplification of the particular
classification (Dewey or Library of Congress) used for books in
the same library. The judgment of the librarian, based on his
knowledge of the kinds of uses to which his record collection is
put, will dictate different schemes in different libraries. There is
no one system which is universally "best"; the librarian deals with

---

[4] George Sherman Dickinson, *Classification of Musical Compositions; A
Decimal-Symbol System* (Poughkeepsie, Vassar College, 1938).

phonograph records, as he does with other nonbook materials in his collection, in the simplest manner consistent with efficient use of the materials by the particular audience.

Cataloging

The problem of cataloging has been most satisfactorily attacked by descriptive cataloging which through subject headings, collation, and notes can give equal emphasis to each aspect of the work that requires it. Although fuller classification has the advantage of minimizing the amount of time which the patron must spend at the card catalog, most music libraries find that the advantages of simpler numbers and more complete catalog descriptions outweigh those claimed for the elaborate classification. With the growth of record collections within music libraries, the descriptive catalog has gained further favor since many librarians consider it advisable to have patrons approach the record collection through the catalog rather than through direct access to the files of records themselves.

The principles upon which the cataloging of music are based are essentially those used in the cataloging of books, and the special rules for music cataloging which have been devised by the Music Library Association attempt, insofar as possible, to retain the rules and the forms employed in traditional catalog practice. Certain special considerations and problems related to music publication, however, require a modification and an elaboration of the usual cataloging rules.

It will not be the purpose of this chapter to list all the regulations pertaining to the cataloging of music. These are given in detail, with examples, in the Music Library Association's *Code for Cataloging Music*.[5] But cataloging problems throw light on the nature of the materials, the conditions of publishing in the field, and the kind of work the music librarian does, and certain examples are cited here because of the insight they help to provide into the complexities of music librarianship.

The entries in a card catalog for musical pieces are composed, essentially, of the same elements as a book entry. There are the author (composer), title, place of publication, publisher, and date. In addition, there are many variations, just as there are for books: anonymous works, works which are edited, translated, or rearranged by a later composer or editor, works which are issued in several parts, etc. In music, however, the variations and exceptions appear more frequently than they do for books. The title of

    [5]Music Library Association. *Code for Cataloging Music;* compiled by a committee of the Music Library Association. Preliminary version ... 1941-42.

the work, which generally causes little confusion in the average book, is not nearly so simple as one would anticipate. For works of music, for example, there are certain works (songs, operas, oratorios, etc.) which have a distinctive title like that of a book: "Erlkönig," *Il Trovatore*, *The Creation*. But there are many more works which have a generic title: symphony, quartet, violin concerto. In addition, many of the generic titles have characteristic elements which are necessary for their identification like opus numbers, serial numbers, and key indication, and many compositions have catch titles which have become attached to them: "Jupiter" symphony, the "Moonlight" sonata, etc. This confusion is further compounded by the fact that opus and serial numbers are not consistently assigned either by the composer or his editors; that the same works are marked by different series of numbers; that publishers arbitrarily assign numbers based on their own publications rather than on the total composition of the composers; and that no consistent form is followed by composers or publishers in titling or referring to musical works: a single work may be called, on different title pages, *Symphony no. 8 in B Minor*, the *B Minor Symphony*, *Schubert's 8th Symphony*, the *Unfinished Symphony*, etc. Key is a distinguishing characteristic only for works composed since around 1700, as music before that time was based on other systems of tonality. The language of the title is also confusing; it is common for a title page to be printed in full in German, Italian, French, and English, or in some other combination of languages, and even when only a single language is used, the librarian must decide whether to use the language of the title page or the language of his public. (In the case of literature, retention of the foreign language title of a work usually indicates that the work is in that language, and the translation of the title into English indicates a translation of the book. In music no translation of the music itself is needed; the title is translated only for the convenience of those who do not understand the language.) In music cataloging then it has become necessary to utilize the device of the conventional title — a form of the title for each piece which will be consistently supplied as title entry no matter what the form on the title page. Only in this way can all the editions and copies of a single work be kept together.

While publisher and place are usually given on music title pages, the date of publication, especially for nineteenth-century and German works, is often difficult to find. For scholarly libraries and those which contain special collections, first editions, and other rarities, the dating of these works becomes highly important and calls for a special kind of research. In most music libraries, the music is in reprint and date is not so important; certainly it

seldom repays the amount of time and effort required for its verification. Students should be aware, however, of some of the sources
of information for dates: publications like the annual volumes of
Hofmeister's *Handbuch der Musikalischen Literatur*, thematic indexes like the *Köchel-Einstein Mozart Verzeichnis* (the source of
the K. [Köchel] numbers which are now a standard identification
for the works of Mozart), the *Brahms Thematisches Verzeichnis*
by Ehrmann, and publishers' advertisements in nineteenth-century
journals.

The collation of music is complicated by the special problem
of parts which are not successive as they are in literary publications, but simultaneous. Publication of parts varies; sometimes the
complete score and the separate parts are issued at one time;
sometimes individual parts are issued separately after publication
of the score; sometimes, although rarely, individual parts may be
issued without the complete score. This is confusing to the cataloger because in the bibliographic sense, a volume is a single
physical object, whereas in music the publication is complete only
if all the parts are present, but is useful only if the parts remain
separate physical entities. A volume of music may, therefore,
consist of several physical objects. How to enter such materials
in a catalog, how to bind and preserve them, and how to count them
in an inventory of accessions or holdings are all difficult administrative problems in the technical processing of music.

Added notes on the catalog card for music serve the same general purpose served by added notes on any catalog card: they supply essential or useful information not given in the title, imprint,
or collation. The nature of musical compositions makes certain
kinds of notes essential, and when not included on the title page,
such data as the following should be added: (1) the species of the
composition, as, for example, ballet, opera, tone poem, etc.; (2)
the kind of publication, that is, score, score in parts, or parts; (3)
the medium of the performance, that is, the instrument(s) for which
the particular copy is intended and the original medium (if ascer-
tainable) if the copy in hand is an arrangement; (4) the key and/or
opus or series number, since these may constitute the one absolutely distinctive way of identifying the work; where such information is not given on the title page, considerable research is often
required to find it; (5) the voice range represented in vocal music;
(6) the language or languages of the text; (7) the author of the text;
(8) the translator of the text; and (9) the kind of notation, if it differs from modern staff notation. It can be seen from this list of
items that the cataloging of musical compositions requires a good
knowledge of music, both early and contemporary, and a sense of
the needs of performers and students.

The establishment of subject headings, too, as in any subject field, is a difficult and challenging task, and a double one in music cataloging since headings must be devised to describe music as well as books about it. In small collections, the standard guides to subject headings like Sears or Library of Congress lists are probably satisfactory, but in special libraries it has been found necessary to devise new and more detailed lists. Several attempts have been made, through the Music Library Association and by specialists working independently,[6] but there is still disagreement among the experts, and no single schedule of headings has yet been accepted by practicing librarians as sufficiently satisfactory to be taken as a standard.

Phonograph records

The cataloging of phonograph records poses many of the same problems with additional complications arising out of the nature of recordings. As in cataloging music, the conventional title is generally used in order to bring the several issues of a single composition together. Modern packaging of record albums and long-playing records have introduced additional variations in titles, the prolific use of catch and popular titles, and special album titles to complicate the problem. While such notes as those relating to score and parts and voice range are not required, additional information is valuable. The performer is of particular importance in the description of recordings, and by performer is meant not only the soloist, but also the conductor, the orchestra or ensemble, the individual players in ensemble groups, the individual performers in operatic performance, and so forth. The type of record — 33 1/3, 45, or 78 r.p.m., and automatic or manual — is especially important where records are allowed to circulate, since borrowers can only use the records which can be played on their home machines. Additional complications arise when more than one number is cut on a single side of a record, as is often the case for songs; when an album is given an inclusive title, with each record containing a different number and sometimes different performers (as in the album *Stars of the Metropolitan*); when an album of a larger work utilizes a single side for an additional smaller piece; when only an excerpt from a larger work is recorded with a separate title for

---

[6]See, for example, Ruth Wallace, *Care and Treatment of Music in a Library* (American Library Association. Committee on Cataloging. Contribution no. 1, Chicago, The Association, 1927); Music Library Association, *Subject Headings for the Literature of Music* [mimeographed] (Rochester, The Association, 1935); Hazel E. Ohman, *A Music Subject Heading System* (Long Island, N. Y., The Author, 1932.)

the part (like the "Andante Cantabile" from Tschaikovsky's *String Quartet, no. 1, D Minor, Opus 11*).

Albums, and even single recordings, in other words are very much like literary anthologies for which a great number of analytics must be made and a great number of cross references must be supplied. But the number of approaches to recordings is greater than those to printed anthologies; in addition to each author and title, there is the possible need for references to performers, instrumentation, variations in title, etc. For such an album as *An Anthology of English Church Music from the 15th Century to the Present Day*, for example, added entries can be justified for the British Council under whose auspices the work was recorded; for the Rev. E. H. Fellowes, who compiled and edited the collection; for twenty-one titles, three larger pieces from which three of the numbers are excerpted, fifteen composers, seven choirs and their seven conductors. Subject headings will also be needed for sacred music, masses, and whatever other descriptive headings seem useful to the individual library.

The logical escape from such an overwhelming task is the utilization of printed sources which already perform these services. In many libraries it is the practice to eliminate analytics that would duplicate the information already available elsewhere; books which are analyzed in the *Essay and General Literature Index, Index to Plays in Collections, Play Index, 1949-1952,* or the *Index to One-Act Plays,* for example, are not analyzed in the card catalog. In the field of music it would be possible to rely on the catalogs of record companies, the *Gramaphone Shop Encyclopedia,* its supplements, and similar sources to provide many analytical services. The main difficulty here is that the printed sources appear late, and while delays are typical of published sources in all fields, they are particularly serious in the field of music. In some cases, the library would be without analytics for many of its recordings for as long as two or three years, and in the case of the *Gramophone Shop Encyclopedia,* nothing would be later than 1954, when the supplements discontinued publication. On the other hand, where such elaborate indexing is available as that provided by the Victor and Columbia record catalogs, it seems a wasteful duplication of effort in a busy and understaffed library to duplicate all the cross references and analytics of the commercial catalogs, even though these analytics are not completely satisfactory. One caution must be given: if the library does restrict the number of its own analytics in favor of analytics in printed sources, it should make sure that the public knows that this practice is followed, so that the user of the card catalog will not miss those items which the library owns but which are analyzed elsewhere.

Binding

Problems like those mentioned above which arise in the handling of special materials are the most immediate ones facing the librarian of a music library. Sheet music, scores, miniature scores, and recordings complicate seriously the usual routine technical processes, not only because their form is different from that of the usual library book or magazine, but also because the way that they are used requires special preparation. One of the more pressing of these problems concerns the binding of printed music, as the great number of references in the literature amply testifies. While the question of whether to bind in cardboard or in cloth may seem like a trivial matter to engage the attention of a professional administrator, the smooth operation of the library, the satisfaction of the library's patrons, and the preservation of the library's materials may all rest upon its answer.

There are several reasons why the binding of music is a greater problem to librarians than is the binding of ordinary books. The first relates to the way printed music is used. A score or a piece of sheet music is not held in the hand like a book; it must lie flat on the music stand or piano rack. The publishers' original bindings are consequently deliberately flimsy to make them loose and flexible, whereas library rebinding, in order to preserve the materials, is stiffer, tighter, and more durable. There is, then, a conflict between the one purpose (preservation) and the other (use), and the resolution of this conflict is often difficult to attain satisfactorily.

Music made up of more than one part raises another problem of use. To be of any value to the performers, the three parts of a trio for piano, violin, and cello, for example, must be kept together, and in ordinary library practice, the way to keep things together is to bind them in a single cover. But while the parts must be kept together, they must also be detachable for distribution to the individual players; therefore to bind them into one volume interferes with their use. Several different ways of handling this problem have been tried, the most usual being that of binding as an ordinary volume one of the parts (the piano part, for instance) and placing the unbound parts in a pocket inside the cover of the volume. This works fairly well with pieces for smaller groups, but for large orchestral works this is not satisfactory because of the great number of parts. Many libraries do not attempt to bind the larger works, putting them all in a package instead (for example, a square of muslin which is wrapped around the complete set of parts and tied with tape), thus protecting the music, keeping the parts together, and still making it possible to separate them. In any of these methods, the problem of collation arises: before and after each circulation it is necessary to check the work to determine that each of the parts is present. This type of check is time-consuming, since it is not enough merely to count the parts, but is also necessary to check each one to see that parts are not interchanged from other scores or that in some way or the other the total work has not been disturbed.

The form of printed music presents another binding problem. Most sheet music and many smaller works often have too few pages to permit a binding which will provide a spine sufficiently large for marking and lettering. Yet if the music is to stand on the shelf like a book it needs to be titled and numbered on the back. One method for meeting this problem is to bind in a sufficient number of blank pages to fill out the needed width of a binder's cover; another is to provide an extension back which is pinched in but may be pulled out accordionwise to allow for lettering. Sheet music is often placed in cardboard covers such as are used on pamphlets or in boxes, cases, folders, and portfolios, most of which have to be specially constructed to fit the various sizes of the music.

Complete works of a composer and definitive editions often are published as a single volume, and, in addition, libraries frequently collect individual pieces by a single composer, for a single instrument, or in a particular form to make up a collection. These "made-up" collections have the drawbacks and advantages of any anthology; they keep like things together, but they limit multiple use of the several items. In music they also cause a confusion in the counting of holdings, since libraries have not yet agreed upon a consistent method of inventory of such individual pieces. Certain libraries make a very impressive report of holdings by counting each title in such a collection as an individual work, whereas others count only each physical volume irrespective of the number of pieces contained within it. Comparative figures on music collections are therefore meaningless unless the particular method of inventory is known, and to date no arbitrary decision has been made which will impose consistency on practice.

Finally, there is the item of cost, and while this is always a consideration in the rebinding of library materials, the binding of music again presents additional difficulties. While the several parts of a single piece of ensemble music are usually counted as a single volume by the library, each of the separate parts plus the portfolio that contains them is considered a volume by the binder. The binding of a quartette, for example, brings a charge for five volumes. Under such circumstances it is not surprising to learn that in 1937 binding absorbed two-thirds of the annual appropriation of the music department of the New York Public Library's circulation branch.[7] If anything, such a figure would now be an underestimate in view of the rising costs of materials and labor since 1937.

In the light of these several difficulties, the question might be raised: why bind music at all? The answer to the question is, of course, that binding is necessary as a protection for the music both while it stands on the shelves and while it is in use. The flimsy paper covers and the loose binding which characterize sheet music and scores make them particularly susceptible to physical deterioration, and the most routine handling of them soon loosens the pages, crumples and tears the covers, and results in losses of parts and destruction of sections which render them useless to the patron. That this can be a serious loss in the case of old and rare music hardly needs to be stated, but even pieces of contemporary publication cannot always readily be replaced. The preservation of music is important to the librarian, not because the physical object as such is peculiarly sacred, but because the librarian tries to make it available to as many of his patrons as may wish to use it. If a piece of music is missing, or damaged, or partially destroyed, future users are deprived of it, and the librarian is not satisfied with the consolation that its destruction gives evidence of use. He wishes to maximize its use by preserving it for future patrons as well as making it available to a patron at the moment. It therefore becomes necessary to provide whatever safeguards are available which will not interfere with use at the present — and binding is one of the most practical of these.

PROBLEMS OF THE MUSIC LIBRARY

The Users of Music Materials

While the nature of music materials creates many problems for the librarian, the nature of the audience for these materials is equally a source of problems. The audience for music, like that for the visual arts, is almost universal. People who do not attend concerts or own record players are still exposed to music in one form or another — at church, at school, in the theater or the cinema, over the radio and on television, or in public places and vehicles as members of a captive audience. "For most Americans music has not only become accessible; it has become unavoidable."[8]

---

[7]Dorothy Lawton, "Binding Problems in Music: Methods and Costs," Music Library Association *Notes* No. 5 (November 1937), p. 26.

[8]Arthur Prichard Moor, "The Library Museum of Music and Dance ..." p. 2 in *Columbia University. Teachers College. Contributions to Education,* no. 750, 1938.

This presents a problem because such a wide variety of interests and backgrounds is represented and because tastes and preferences in music are strongly predetermined, even though the individual is not consciously aware of it. Users of the library's collection will include scholars, teachers, students, composers, performers, and critics, as well as members of the general public who have had no musical training at all. The needs of such a varied group are themselves extremely varied, and the collection which attempts to meet them all would have to be all-inclusive. The situation is not helped by the very definite preferences of patrons, ranging from the complete anti-romanticism of many students of modern or ancient music, to the complete aversion for anything not romantic which characterizes the taste of so many laymen.

The all-inclusive collection is not possible, of course. Only within certain narrow limits is it possible to gather a definitive collection, and we have seen that certain kinds of libraries have set such limits upon their collections and their clienteles. But the general public library, while it delimits its collection also, cannot be so narrowly selective, and the limitations it sets are usually those which will allegedly be felt by the few rather than the many.

To determine who those few shall be involves the translation of the library's objectives into practice, since the selection of some items at the cost of eliminating others can be justified only in terms of the aims to be served by this retention and rejection. For a long time, for example, many librarians defined the function of their institution to be the provision of books and periodicals, and holding strictly to that definition, resisted the inclusion of sheet music, scores, and phonograph records. With the current trend towards the redefinition of the library as a communication agency, the inclusion of scores and records becomes acceptable, although the economic factor must also be considered, and many libraries feel that although they would like to supply all forms of musical materials, they can afford to purchase some but not all. Under such circumstances, the librarian must answer the difficult question: what forms can be eliminated?

Most libraries are traditionally committed to the provision of books and periodicals as their primary stock in trade. Few public libraries would seriously consider eliminating their books about music in favor of music itself. Many might feel that either scores or records but not both can be provided. As an exercise in policy formation, the student might suppose that he is faced with this decision and, taking any library that he wishes to study, try to determine whether scores or records should be the one form of music to collect. If he wishes to reach the greatest number of people, he may decide in favor of recordings, since few of his patrons can read even the simplest musical score whereas both musicians and nonmusicians can listen to records. If he wishes to provide music for serious study rather than for entertainment, he may decide that the printed music reaches a more selective and purposeful group. If he feels that the library should try to provide new and wider experience to its patrons, he may decide that printed music merely caters to patrons already sufficiently motivated and that records have a better chance to introduce new listeners and new users to the benefits of music experience. But if he feels that the library should provide those materials which are not readily available elsewhere, he may decide that recordings are easily found through many other agencies, while printed music is much less accessible. Each of these reasons has a certain validity; in weighing their comparative merits the student may find not only that the nature of the collection is affected, but also that alterations must be made in the aims which he has enunciated for his library.

The Levels of Appeal in Music Materials

Once the decision has been made as to the form of materials appropriate to the particular library, the librarian is faced with the perennial question as to the nature of their content. The music field presents as wide a range of appeals as do the fields of literature and of art and imposes the same kinds of decisions upon the library selector. Should the library emphasize the familiar or the unfamiliar; the popular or the little-known; the simpler or the more difficult? McColvin discusses at some length the dilemma of the selector who attempts to provide "the most important works which are likely to be most used"[9] but finds that "most important" and "most used" are not necessarily the same thing. It is a difficult decision to make: how low should the floor be below which "popular" works will not be added to the collection? How high can the ceiling be, above which "important" works will be too little used to justify their purchase?

One of the complicating factors in the selection of music is that the "popular classics" embrace a large field of standard works which are meritorious. Certainly no library would be justified in omitting Beethoven's *Fifth Symphony* or Händel's *Messiah* from its collection on the grounds that they are popular. Yet the library may often feel that to provide more and more duplicate copies of recordings which are heard almost daily over the air is unnecessary when so much important music is seldom or never played.

---

[9]McColvin and Reeves, *op. cit.*, p. 8.

The problem becomes even more acute when that great area of
"semi-classical" music is considered: the operetta and show
tunes, the lighter occasional pieces, the recital songs, and others
which certainly qualify on the requisite of "use" if not on "importance." In the selection or rejection of these items there is a certain danger that personal preference or intellectual snobbery may
play a part in the ultimate decision and that some pieces will be
rejected because "too many people" like them, or because the
individual selector happens not to care for them. Again it becomes for the librarian a matter of seeing selection and use in
terms of the library's aims.

The Use of Music Materials

The peculiar character of music raises an interesting question concerning the library's philosophy about the use to which its
materials will be put. It is generally agreed that the library will
not use tax money to provide text books, professional literature,
or other materials which should properly be purchased by the individual benefiting personally from them. The everyday needs of
professional men, the tools of a trade, or the materials with which
individuals make their living are not provided at public expense.
Yet in the realm of printed music, public libraries do provide
pieces (and in some cases, even the instrument and the practice
room) which can be used for practice or for public performance by
students and professional musicians. Certainly it would appear on
the surface that here the library is providing a highly specialized
service at public expense to a small segment of the population.

The justification for this apparent contradiction probably lies
in the nature of printed music, which must be interpreted by an
expert if it is to be enjoyed by any but the select few. Anyone can
read a novel as it was written by its author or see a picture as it
came from the painter's brush. But only the highly skilled can
experience music by looking at the score as written; it is the distinctive characteristic of music that it reaches its audience through
the indirect medium of an interpreter. On the grounds that others
benefit by the services rendered the musician, the expenditure of
public money can be justified, just as the assistance given to a
teacher or a minister, the materials provided the researcher, the
acting copies of plays for public performance can be defended as
enriching the community indirectly through the borrower.

Many libraries, however, attempt to stress the documentary
use of printed music and channelize their selection in terms of the
study value of the music rather than of its practical value for re-

hearsal and performance. This distinction is not a mere academic quibble; an entirely different collection of music is built up if one collects materials suitable for local recital performances than if he collects those essential to a study of composition and musical history. That some of the latter happen to be played or sung by patrons instead of silently studied is not the library's concern, but it makes a difference if the collection, so to speak, must duplicate innumerable piano accompaniments to "Kiss Me Again" instead of purchasing William Byrd's *Psalmes, Sonets and Songs of Sadnes and Pietie*.

The provision of musical instruments pushes the special services in the field of music one step farther. Usually if phonograph records are made available a player is also provided, and in some cases, the library's records may only be played within the building and are not allowed to circulate. Many libraries, even though they allow their records to be borrowed, also conduct record concerts in the library for the benefit of those without record players, or in the interests of building a sequence of listening less random than that of the ordinary borrower. The phonograph may be justified on much the same grounds that the reading machine for microfilm is justified — the material cannot be used without it. But if the record player is a legitimate piece of library equipment, should the library assume responsibility for other musical instruments as well? Printed music demands an instrument also, just as a recording does — should the library begin to install practice rooms, and pianos and other instruments? Most public libraries draw the line here, just as they would if it were suggested that easels, paints, brushes, and a properly lighted studio be part of the equipment of the art department, but the library of a music school or department in a university frequently makes such facilities available for the use of its students. Radio and television, on the other hand, are being accepted by public libraries, and library-sponsored meetings built around particular broadcasts and programs are not considered outside the province of the public library.

Such developments suggest that attitudes towards the library's proper function will continue gradually to change and that many services may be introduced which would have shocked the librarians of 1876. In the field of music, particularly, where the audience is made up of many small groups whose interests cannot be served in the customary manner through the traditional book alone, services and materials may be introduced which will alter greatly the old-fashioned idea of the library.

REPRESENTATIVE REFERENCE TOOLS IN THE FIELD
OF MUSIC

Bibliographies of Books about Music

Bibliographie des Musikschrifttums. 1936-
Duckles, Vincent Harris, and Nicewonger, Harriet Schneider. *A
    Guide to Reference Materials on Music.* Rev. ed. 1952.
Forkel, Johann N. *Allgemeine Litteratur der Musik.* 1792.
"Guide to Books on Music," annual listing in a January issue of
    Saturday Review. 1943-
Lichtenthal, Peter. *Dizionario e bibliografia della musica.* 4 vols.
    1826. Vols. 3-4 are a translation of Forkel's *Allgemeine Lit-
    teratur der Musik.*
National Association of Schools of Music. *A Musical Literature
    List for Music School Libraries.* 1935.
———— ———— Supplements, 1936- in its *Bulletin.*
"Quarterly Book-List" in *The Musical Quarterly.* April, 1929-
Scholes, Percy A. *A List of Books about Music in the English
    Language, Prepared as an Appendix to the Oxford Companion to
    Music.* 1940.
U. S. Library of Congress. *Catalogue of Early Books on Music
    (Before 1800).* 1913.
———— ———— Supplement (Books Acquired by the Library 1913-
    1942). 1944.

Bibliographies of Music

Deutsche Musikbibliographie. 1829-
Gleason, Harold. *Music Literature Outlines.*
    Ser. 1. *Music in the Middle Ages and Renaissance.* 2d ed.
        1951. (3d Printing 1954)
    Ser. 2. *Music in the Baroque.* 2d ed. 1951. (Reprinted 1954)
    Ser. 3. *American Music from 1620-1920.* 1954.
    Ser. 4. *Chamber Music from Haydn to Ravel.* 1949.
Haywood, Charles. *A Bibliography of North American Folklore
    and Folksong.* 1951.
Jahresverzeichnis der deutschen Musikalien und Musikschriften.
    1852- (Title varies)
Sonneck, Oscar. *A Bibliography of Early Secular American Music.*
    Rev. and enl. by W. T. Upton. 1945.
U. S. Copyright Office. *Catalog of Copyright Entries. Part 3:
    Musical Compositions.* 1891-

Bibliographies of Periodical Literature

A Bibliography of Periodical Literature in Musicology and Allied Fields and a Record of Graduate Theses Accepted.
    Vol. 1. October 1, 1938 - September 30, 1939. 1940.
    Vol. 2. October 1, 1939 - September 30, 1940. 1943.
The Music Index. 1949-

Dictionaries and Encyclopedias

Apel, Willi. *Harvard Dictionary of Music.* 1947.
Baker, Theodore. *A Dictionary of Musical Terms.* 21st ed. 1923. (Reissued as 23d ed., n. d.)
Barlow, Harold, and Morgenstern, Sam. *A Dictionary of Musical Themes.* 1948.
—— *A Dictionary of Vocal Themes.* 1950.
Ewen, David. *Encyclopedia of the Opera.* 1955.
Grove, Sir George, ed. *Dictionary of Music and Musicians.* 5th ed., ed. by Eric Blom. 9 vols. 1954.
Moser, Hans J. *Musik Lexikon.* 1935.
Pratt, Waldo Selden. *The New Encyclopedia of Music and Musicians.* New and rev. ed. 1929. (Reissued 1951)
Scholes, Percy Alfred. *The Concise Oxford Dictionary of Music.* 1952.
—— *The Oxford Companion to Music.* 9th ed. rev. 1955.
Slonimsky, Nicolas. *Thesaurus of Scales and Melodic Patterns.* 1947.
Thompson, Oscar, ed. *The International Cyclopedia of Music and Musicians.* 6th ed. rev. and enl., ed. by Nicolas Slonimsky. 1952.

Biographical Aids

American Society of Composers, Authors and Publishers. *The ASCAP Biographical Dictionary of Composers, Authors, and Publishers.* 2d ed. 1952.
Baker, Theodore. *Biographical Dictionary of Musicians.* 4th ed., rev. and enl. 1940. Supplement, 1949, by Nicolas Slonimsky.
Detheridge, Joseph. *Chronology of Music Composers.* 2 vols. 1936-37.
Eitner, Robert. *Biographisch-bibliographisches Quellen-Lexikon der Musiker und Musikgelehrten der christlichen Zeitrechnung bis zur Mitte des neunzehnten Jahrhunderts.* 10 vols. 1900-04.
Ewen, David, ed. *The Book of Modern Composers.* 2d ed., rev. and enl. 1950.

—— *Composers of Yesterday*. 1937.
—— *Dictators of the Baton*. 2d ed. 1948.
—— *Living Musicians*. 1940.
Historical Records Survey. District of Columbia. *Bio-biblio-graphical Index of Musicians in the United States of America from Colonial Times...* 1941.
Reis, Claire. *Composers in America*. Rev. and enl. ed. 1947.
Thompson, Oscar, comp. *Tabulated Biographical History of Music*. 1936.
Who's Who in Music. 1937; 1950. (Ed. for U. S. and Canada has title: *Musicians' International Directory and Biographical Record, 1949-50*.)
Young, Percy Marshall. *Biographical Dictionary of Composers*. 1954.

Yearbooks

The Billboard Encyclopedia of Music. 1939-   (Annual supplement to *The Billboard*. Title varies.)
Music and Recordings. 1955-
The Year in American Music. 1946/47-

Analytical Indexes

Cushing, Helen Grant, comp. *Children's Song Index*. 1936.
Sears, Minnie Earl, and Crawford, Phyllis, eds. *Song Index*. 1926.
—— —— Supplement. 1934.

Historical Treatments

Bücken, Ernst, ed. *Handbuch der Musikwissenschaft*. 13 vols. in 9. 1949-50. Includes such titles as:
    Die Musik der Antike, by Curt Sachs. 1930.
    Die Musik des Barocks, by Robert Maria Haas. 1929.
    Die Musik des Rokokos und der Klassik, by Ernst Bücken. 1931.
Davison, Archibald Thompson, and Apel, Willi, eds. *Historical Anthology of Music*. Rev. ed.
        Vol. 1. *Oriental, Medieval and Renaissance Music*. 1949.
        Vol. 2. *Baroque, Rococo and Pre-Classical Music*. 1950.
Láng, Paul Henry. *Music in Western Civilization*. 1941.
Nef, Karl. *An Outline of the History of Music*. Tr. by Carl F. Pfatteicher. 1935.
New Oxford History of Music. 1954-
    Vol. 2. *Early Medieval Music up to 1300*. 1954.

The Norton History of Music Series, including such titles as:
    Music in the Renaissance, by Gustave Reese. 1954.
    Music in the Baroque Era, by Manfred Bukofzer. 1947.
    Music in the Romantic Era, by Alfred Einstein. 1947.
The Oxford History of Music. 2d ed. 8 vols. 1929-38.
Slonimsky, Nicolas. *Music since 1900.* 3d ed., rev. and enl. 1949.
Spaeth, Sigmund. *A History of Popular Music in America.* 1948.

    Program Notes

Bagar, Robert, and Biancolli, Louis. *The Complete Guide to Or-chestral Music.* 2 vols. 1954.
Boston Symphony. Program Notes (or similar releases by other symphony orchestras). See also the one-volume Philip Hale's *Boston Symphony Programme Notes.* 1935.
Kobbé, Gustav. *The Complete Opera Book.* 1950.
———— ———— Ed. and rev. by the Earl of Harewood. Rev. ed. 1954.
Newman, Ernest. *Stories of the Great Operas and Their Com-posers.* 3 vols. 1928-30. (Reprinted frequently in one-vol-ume ed.)
———— *More Stories of Famous Operas.* 1943. (Reissued 1955)
O'Connell, Charles. *The Victor Book of Symphonies.* New rev. ed. 1948.
———— *The Victor Book of Overtures, Tone Poems, and Other Orchestral Works.* 1950.
Seaman, Julian, ed. *Great Orchestral Music, a Treasury of Pro-gram Notes.* 1950.
Veinus, Abraham. *Victor Book of Concertos.* 1948.
The Victor Book of Operas. Newly rev. ed. by Louis Biancolli and Robert Bagar. 1953.

    Guides to Phonograph Records

American Record Guide. 1935-
Barbour, Harriot B., and Freeman, Warren S. *The Children's Record Book.* 1947.
Clough, Francis F., and Cuming, G. J. *The World's Encyclo-paedia of Recorded Music.* 1952. (Includes First Supplement)
———— ———— Second Supplement (1951-1952). 1953.
Cumulated Index of Record Reviews. 1948/50-
DeLaunay, Charles. *New Hot Discography; the Standard Dictionary of Recorded Jazz*, ed. by Walter E. Schaap & George Avakian. 1948.
Eisenberg, Philip, and Krasno, Hecky. *A Guide to Children's Records.* 1948.

Gramophone Shop, Inc., New York. *The Gramophone Shop Encyclo-pedia of Recorded Music*. 3d ed., rev. and enl. 1948. Con-tinued by the monthly *Record Supplement*, 1948-54.
The Guide to Long-playing Records. 1st ed. 3 vols. 1955.
   Vol. 1. *Orchestral Music*, by Irving Kolodin; vol. 2. *Vocal Music*, by Philip L. Miller; vol. 3. *Chamber and Solo Instru-ment Music*, by Harold C. Schonberg.
Haggin, Bernard H. *Music on Records*. 4th ed., rev. 1946.
Hall, David, and Levin, Abner. *The Disc Book*. 1955.
Kolodin, Irving. *The New Guide to Recorded Music*. 1950 ed.
Lebow, Bernard, ed. *The American Record Index*. 1950-
Myers, Kurtz, and Hill, Richard S., eds. *Record Ratings*: the Mu-sic Library Association's Index of Record Reviews. 1956.
U. S. Library of Congress. Music Division. *Folk Music of the United States and Latin America*; Combined Catalog of Phono-graph Records. 1948
(See also *Music and Recordings* under Yearbooks; the catalogs of the commerical recording companies, especially the Victor and Columbia catalogs; reviews in the *New York Times* and the *Saturday Review*, and in the starred magazines listed below.)

Directories of Record Manufacturers

Myers, Kurtz. "Phonograph Record Trade List for Library Use," Music Library Association *Notes* (Second Series), III, No. 4 (September, 1946), p. 417-21.
Record Retailing Yearbook & Directory. 1948-

Leading Periodicals

Acta Musicologica. 1928-
American Musicological Society. *Bulletin*. 1936-48. (Succeeded by the *Journal of the American Musicological Society*. 1948-)
The Diapason. 1909-
The Etude Music Magazine. 1883-1957
Modern Music. 1924-46.
Music & Letters. 1920-
*Music Library Association. *Notes*. Second Series, 1934-
The Music Review. 1940-
Musical America. 1898-
Musical Courier. 1880-
The Musical Quarterly. 1915-
Opera News. 1936- (Issued weekly during the opera season and fortnightly Spring and Fall by the Metropolitan Opera Guild.)
La Revue musicale. 1920-
Rivista musicale italiana. 1894-

chapter five

literature

THE DEFINITION OF THE FIELD

Literature has been defined as "the reduction of thought to writing," but clearly such a definition is essentially valueless for the librarian. Since words function not only as the materials with which the literary artist works, but also as a means of communicating ideas for any kind of knowledge, the entire range of library materials (exclusive of pictures and recordings) becomes the stuff of literature, regardless of its subject matter or its form. By the terms of the definition, there is nothing in print which is not literature.

Yet so extreme a view is not unknown among literary scholars. Edwin Greenlaw, for example, makes the claim, "Nothing related to the history of civilization is beyond our province,"[1] and the trends in literary scholarship which require the study of politics, economics, social conditions, psychiatry, and biography before admitting the possibility of an appreciation of literature are committed to a

---

[1] Edwin Greenlaw, *The Province of Literary History* (Baltimore, Johns Hopkins Pr., 1931), p. 29.

similar philosophy. If the librarian were to follow it to its logical conclusion, his literature department would have to represent on its shelves the subject matter of all other disciplines, and traditional classification systems would become meaningless.

For practical purposes this definition is not only too much, but also too little. While a pragmatic concept of literature must place more stringent limitations upon subject and treatment, a true study of literature cannot confine itself to *written* documents alone; there is a highly important oral literature in the history of literary forms and genres. The oratory of the Greeks is an essential part of their literary contribution, and even their plays and poems meant to be read were meant to be read *aloud*. The folk tales and ballads handed down by the bards, the minstrels, and the troubadours were literature long before they were permanently transcribed. It may be objected that even in these cases such literature does not become the charge of the librarian until it is written down, but the modern librarian considers it more logical to retain as literature the recordings of a T. S. Eliot reading his own poems than the written records of mathematical formulas or chemical experiments.

Since written or oral is not a conclusive criterion for a work of literature, a definition in terms of literary forms is probably more useful. These terms limit the definition of literature to that of a work of art, but a work of art with features of its own determined by its medium, in which the characteristics of art objects in general are incorporated in a manner peculiar to the literary task. The kinds of literary forms which can thus be distinguished are known as *genres*.

The Literary Genres

The major genres were defined, essentially in the forms we now employ, by the Greeks. Aristotle's *Poetics* lists epic poetry (forerunner of our modern fiction); lyric poetry (our modern nonprose); dramatic poetry (our modern drama, whether in prose or verse); history; oratory; philosophy; and criticism. Today we would generally eliminate history and philosophy as literary property, although the line is a fine one, and few literary histories of eighteenth-century England, for example, could ignore the work of Berkeley and Hume, Bishop Butler and Gibbon, Edmund Burke and Adam Smith. But with these genres (fiction, poetry, drama, oratory, and criticism) as a guide, and limiting the term "literature" to imaginative writing in them, we come as close as possible to a workable definition which does not do too great violence to the infinite variety which marks the realm of literature.

Even when the field of literature is defined in terms of specific genres, it presents, as do the other humanistic disciplines, a many-faceted problem for the library collection. In the sciences and the social sciences, the library needs only the books about the subject field; it does not have science and social science as such on its shelves. In the field of literature, however, we have not only the books about the field, but also the very field itself. The subject matter of literature, as well as the books about it, forms the literature collection.

THE LITERATURE COLLECTION

The literature collection is composed, essentially, of four main groupings of materials. First, as mentioned above, there is the obvious field of the original literature itself. This comprises what may be designated, loosely, as the primary material of the field[2] — the plays, the novels, the poems — as individual creations of the literary artist.

The second field is that of the critical materials, those works which take the individual primary materials as their subject matter. Although it may appear simple to distinguish a book about a play from the play itself, another kind of confusion may arise. Many critical works are, in themselves, literature, and may be considered primary even though their subject matter is another primary work. Samuel Johnson on Shakespeare is a guide to both Johnson and Shakespeare; it is therefore primary material in its own right for the student of Johnson and critical material for the student of Shakespeare.

A third field may be designated as the "philosophical" — that which treats of literature in general terms rather than in terms of specific literary works or writers, concerning itself with general theories of literature which form the basis for individual criticism. But here again many of the great names in literature function as literary theorists as well as practitioners. The Preface to the *Lyrical Ballads* deals with the function of poetry, and even includes some specific criticism, while serving as a primary artistic work to any student of Wordsworth. Here the intention of the writer acts to clarify the distinction; the ballads themselves are primary literary works; the Preface is a philosophical-critical discussion of poetry and therefore not "primary," although probably of greater importance in the history of poetry than the ballads.[3]

---

[2] For many scholarly researches the truly primary material consists of the original holograph manuscripts and work sheets, but for ordinary usage, the printed text, even in reprint form, is sufficiently "primary" to the extent that it represents the complete and final form of the work as intended by the writer.

[3] But where, then, does one put Pope's *Essay on Criticism* — or even Hemingway's *Death in the Afternoon?*

The fourth field may be described as the historical-interpretative field, which in turn may be subdivided into three main parts. In the first fall the *histories* of literature in general, which attempt a sequential presentation of the substantive field of literature. In the second fall the *biographical* studies which deal with literary history in terms of the literary artists more than of their works. In the third fall the *interpretative* and *critical* studies which consciously apply criteria of judgment to color the study of literary development.

All histories of literature are related, as individual criticisms are, to general theories of literature. No study of literary history, however objective in intention, or outline in form, can completely ignore the application of normative judgments. The historian's selection of writers to list or works to include is an act of judgment which is based on some kind of criteria whether verbalized or not. The characteristic that distinguishes the interpretative group of works from the general and biographical histories is its conscious and admitted application of criteria in favor of which the writer advances arguments and explicit judgments.

The Classification of Literature[4]

The librarian's interest in defining a discipline and characterizing the materials which belong to it is prompted by pragmatic rather than academic interests. It is his task to devise a scheme of classification that will place like materials together in the subject categories which are most apt to be called for by patrons. For example, the Dewey Decimal classification for literature (800) recognizes the genre definition of literature and provides for the forms of literary invention: poetry, drama, fiction, essays, oratory, letters, satire and humor. But Dewey also recognizes a limitation upon practical usage: the language in which the literature is written. The 800's are therefore subdivided into national language groups, with the breakdown by genres within each language division. The 810's are devoted to American literature, the 820's to British literature, the 830's to German, etc. Within each group of ten, the same number is used to designate the genre: 811 is American poetry, 821 is British poetry, and so on, and the same sequence is followed throughout, with 812, 822, 832 for the drama of each country, 813, 823, 833 for the fiction, throughout the national and genre groupings.

---

[4]It is suggested that the student refer to a copy of the Dewey Decimal Classification and the P classification of the Library of Congress in connection with his reading of this section.

As is frequently the case in the Dewey classification, the
arrangement of the subject field into arbitrary groups of ten sometimes imposes a rather close restriction upon the treatment of individual writers, movements, and periods. Within each genre
grouping, for example, Dewey makes a chronological breakdown:
English poetry is divided into early English, pre-Elizabethan,
Elizabethan, post-Elizabethan, Queen Anne, later eighteenth century, early nineteenth century, Victorian period, and the early
twentieth century. This exhausts the available sections in the
decimal group; if Dewey is strictly followed, English poetry should
have come to a full stop at the end of 1949.

In general library practice, the fiction classification and the
special individual author classifications in any of the sections are
not followed. Most public libraries do not classify fiction at all,
but arrange it by author in a single undifferentiated section without
regard for chronology, nationality, critical status, or thematic
emphasis. This makes for some strange shelf-mates in the fiction
section, but it serves the practical purpose of allowing the seeker
of recreational reading a wide choice and making it a simple process for the student of a specific writer to find his works in straight
alphabetical sequence. The fiction classification number is used
only for the other types of literary materials: the critical and the
historical. In most libraries, a book classed in the 813's would be
a critical work about American fiction; if it were a work about a
single novel, it would be given a Cutter number for the author of
the primary work so that all critical works about the one novel
would be shelved together. For example, the Dewey and Cutter
numbers for *Moby Dick* would be 813 for fiction and M497 for Melville: 813 M497. In practice, *Moby Dick* itself would shelve with
all other fiction in alphabetical order under M for Melville without
call number, but Howard Vincent's *The Trying Out of Moby Dick*
would classify as 813 M497v, the final "v" for Vincent placing the
work in alphabetical order by author among the several books *about*
Melville's fiction.

In college and school libraries, fiction is more likely to be
identified with assigned rather than recreational reading and is
usually classified. Here the primary work and the works about it
are filed together. Since several works by an author, Melville, for
example, must be distinguished in some way, the Melville Cutter
number, M497, is followed by the initial letter of the title: 813
M497m for *Moby Dick*; 813 M497o for *Omoo*; 813 M497p for *Pierre*.
Critical works utilize an arbitrary letter, x, for example, following
the usual Cutter number for the novel itself to indicate that the
book is *about* Melville rather than by him, followed by the letter
for the critic's last name. Thus 813 M497m is used for *Moby Dick*

itself; 813 M497mxG for William Gleim's *The Meaning of Moby Dick*. In this way all copies of a novel are filed together, followed by all critical works about it in alphabetical order by author, followed by other works by the novelist in alphabetical order by title, each accompanied by its own critical commentaries.[5]

The Library of Congress classification arranges the literatures in groupings by language family: Romance literature, Teutonic literature, etc., with separate letter classes for English and American literature. Within each grouping, the breakdown is chronological, and within each century or period, the writers — of whatever form — are arranged alphabetically. This arrangement allows for much wider expansion to fit the state of publication than does the Dewey, but it solves even less adequately the problem of what is literature and what is not. Any writer in any subject field and in any prose form may be placed in the alphabetical arrangement for the century and language group in which he wrote.

In both Dewey and Library of Congress the introductory section of the literature classification is devoted to general works which do not properly belong in any of the language or national breakdowns. General works about literature and literary aesthetics; collections; reference tools like dictionaries, compends, manuals, and outlines are arranged at the beginning of the collection. The national (or language) classes then follow, divided as outlined above.

Historical materials, in Dewey, are handled in the literature section as they are in all sections of the classification. Borrowing the number *9* from his 900 classification for history, Dewey uses the form number *09* to designate a historical treatment of any subject. A history of general science is 509; a history of all the arts, 709; and a history of literature in general, 809. A history of American literature would classify as 810.9, of British poetry, 821.09, of French drama, 842.09. The Library of Congress classification, on the other hand, does not attempt a mnemonic system for dealing with the history of a national literature or a literary form, but merely utilizes its more expandable arrangement to make a place for history in each section. English literature (PR) devotes the numbers 81-479 to the history of English literature in general, with period breakdowns suitable to the development of that literature and with the numbers from 500-976 to the history of the different genres. American literature (PS) is organized in the same way, with space provided for general history and appropriate period breakdowns and for history of the several forms of literature

---

[5]In a similar fashion, the critical and historical works about individual poems or plays would classify in the regular poetry or drama section, the secondary materials filing after the primary materials with which they deal.

The Users of the Literature Collection

It has been stated above that a classification scheme should place materials in the categories which are most likely to be called for by those who use them. Consequently, as we have seen, some materials are classified in one way in one kind of library and in another way in a library serving a different public. But probably no other subject field exerts so wide an appeal as that of literature, which, however it is classified, will find its way into almost every kind of library.

It is obvious that the three major kinds of libraries — the public libraries, the school and college libraries, and the research libraries of large universities — will all devote a major part of their total collection to literature. In the public library the greatest use of the collection will be made by the general public seeking recreational reading and by students reading for class assignments. In the school and college libraries, more emphasis will be placed upon standard classics and less upon recreational reading; and users will be almost exclusively students. Some interpretative materials and learned journals will also be used in the college library by advanced students and by the faculty. In the university library, recreational reading will often be reduced to a minimum, although many of the materials used for recreational purposes in the other libraries will also have their place in the university library where their use will be scholarly rather than recreational. A far greater emphasis upon research materials and upon lesser-known writings of earlier periods will characterize the university's collection.

Literature also serves a recreational and scholarly purpose in special libraries devoted to nonliterary subjects. The creative literary artist interprets all phases of life and his views are often valuable to the student of the subject with which the artist deals. The social sciences turn constantly to works of literature for their reflection on social problems, and works as diverse as Bellamy's *Looking Backward*, Lewis' *Babbitt*, Marquand's *Point of No Return*, Farrell's *Studs Lonigan*, and Steinbeck's *The Grapes of Wrath* are considered social documents as well as literary works. The psychologist has found the prototypes of many of his concepts in the Greek drama and may well continue to seek out in the Hamlets, the Clyde Griffiths, and the Hans Castorps of literature the counterparts of scientifically gathered case histories. The historian considers many works of literature to be documents of great significance, and for some periods of history the literature is virtually the only insight we have into the life of the time. The anthropologist and the ethnologist have carefully examined folk literature in their studies of the total culture of different peoples. And when the scientist, the philosopher, the historian, and the sociologist turn from the serious pursuit of their professional interests, they then become general readers with interests in literature as diversion and entertainment. To the extent that all readers tend to prefer recreational reading that is allied to their personal interests, there may be a subject slant in the fiction, poetry, and drama which the scientist or the sociologist prefers that justifies the librarian's provision of recreational materials even in the highly specialized library. A good librarian will probably wish to supply Tolstoy's *War and Peace* and Cozzen's *Guard of Honor* in the library of an Army Command school; Lewis' *Arrowsmith* and Browne's *Religio Medici* in a medical school library; Rolland's *Jean-Christophe* and Davenport's *Of Lena Geyer* in the library of a school of music. All such works classify as literature in the general library, although the interest they arouse in the special reader may be completely nonliterary.

The librarian, despite his arbitrary assignment of a static call number to the books he selects, sees in each book a variety of levels and appeals. The number 812 tells us nothing about the excellence of a play, nor about the kinds of audiences to which it is most likely to have its fullest meaning. Yet these evaluations must also be made by the librarian when he selects books for his library and interprets them for the use of his public. Since, in selection, he relies frequently upon works of criticism and literary history to help him to this judgment and evaluation, let us turn first to these parts of the literary collection.

LITERARY CRITICISM

In the task of criticism there seem to be two points on which judgments may differ. First, two critics may not have been cognizant of the same elements in a given work of art. Although they use the same criteria, they may reach different conclusions as to the worth of a play, for example, because one critic may not have been sensitive to the role of a certain character in the development of the plot. On the other hand, the criteria used by critics may vary and affect their judgments. And since the different criteria may lead to a different selection of significant points or elements in the work of art, there are two possibilities here: an apparent agreement on the elements for discussion but a difference on their significance and a difference on both elements *and* their significance. Finally, although two critics may agree in general on the worth of a work, they may do so for different reasons. Here, again, they may use the same or different elements or criteria.

At the outset this looks like hopeless confusion and indeterminacy. But if we can in some way plot and understand exactly how these factors enter the critical task, we shall be in a better position to understand a given critical work, the several facets of a work of literary art itself, the many approaches to the literature which the librarian must serve, and the use of works of criticism in the librarian's task of selecting the primary literary materials for his collection.

The principles and criteria of literary criticism can best be distinguished perhaps in terms of the critic's conception of art. The discussions of art, broadly speaking, consider it either (1) as an activity which is universal in its application and must be considered in competition or cooperation with other activities, or (2) as an activity having peculiar principles and subject matter which must be discovered by an examination of the products of artistic activity.

In the first view, art is considered under the same principles as any other subject, be it morals, politics, or metaphysics. Critics of this persuasion may pass judgment on a play in terms of the moral quality of the characters or the principles of morality contained in the story. They may judge a novel in terms of its effect on the political community or by the political ideas expressed, or examine it as a manifestation of a certain political ideology. Finally, they may judge the work in terms of the scientific truths it contains, or of its propriety as a method for exploring the nature of things.

In the second view, the art object is taken as a proper subject matter, distinct from other subject matters and having principles and methods of investigation appropriate to it. The object is a whole or unity of some sort, and the task is one of stating the principles of that unity in terms of the relation of the parts to one another.

The Platonic and Aristotelian Schools

The contrast between these two methods of literary analysis is clearly illustrated in the critical writings of Plato and Aristotle, and writers on literary criticism frequently identify a contemporary critic as either Platonic or Aristotelian, depending upon the general tone of his major emphasis. The Platonic view sees art as no different from any other subject matter and employs the same method in investigating it as is employed for any other. In the *Republic*, poetry is evaluated just as other institutions are, in terms of its contribution to education, its value in the making of good citizens, and its fidelity to truth. Since poets deal only with imitations, claiming to present truth but achieving instead only shadows or distortions of truth, poets are exiled from the state. What holds for other arts and other institutions holds for poetry; there is no limited subject matter with peculiar principles and terms of analysis.

Contrast this with Aristotle's treatment of tragedy in the *Poetics*. Tragedy is isolated as a kind of whole or unity and is analyzed in terms of the relation of the parts to the whole in forming this unity. The elements are identified, and the principles for the proper ordering of these elements are stated. To take principles of criticism from the artist, the audience, or from other disciplines would be irrelevant, since the work of art has its own rules arising out of its own distinctive nature.

To the so-called Platonic school belong those critics whose interest, while ostensibly in literature, has been primarily ethical, moral, social, political, or religious. The Marxist critics, for example, have tended to reject writers and works, quite apart from their literary talent, if they do not adhere strictly to the critic's belief in the interdependence of literature and economic law. The "new humanists" have judged literature by the degree to which it reflects specific moral qualities. Many critics (and more especially, many reviewers) have judged a work by the degree of its doctrinal orthodoxy in the matter of specific religious belief.

To the Aristotelian school belong the aestheticians and the analysts of literary technique. Critics of this persuasion are typically amoral in their judgment of literature, indifferent to the political orientation of the writer, and unconcerned with the social value of the work. Their major concern is with the "laws of art" and the restrictions of form; with the relationship of the parts of literary work to the whole and to each other; with the artistic problems facing the artist and his means of solving them. At one extreme stand the critics of the "art for art's sake" school, some of whose exponents have rejected the necessity for literary art even to communicate to the reader so long as it is true to its own formal needs. Others have been more concerned with identifying the technical devices employed by the artist quite apart from any over-all system of aesthetic necessity. At the ultimate reach one might place the technical manuals which are concerned with the problems of how to write and which provide rules for the aspiring novelist or playwright. Even a collection of "tips" for writing short-stories-that-sell is in the tradition of Aristotle in that its concern is with the proper relation of the parts to each other and the whole for the achievement of certain effects. While its aesthetic theory may be adjudged to be on a comparatively low level, its criteria are more precisely defined than are those of many "more philosophical" analysts of literary art.

Critical Theories

A recognition of the general theories underlying specific criticism is essential for the librarian in order to make literary history intelligible; to make the significance and bearing of critical writing clear; and to provide the ground for useful firsthand description and judgment of individual works of art. These theories may be roughly distinguished in terms of the relationship which is, in each case, of basic concern. Since works of art are (1) produced by someone, (2) represent, or imitate, or set forth, or at least have a relation to some subject, and (3) are experienced by readers, four sorts of relations may be explored for any work of art. These are (1) its relation to its maker and through him to its period, (2) its relation to readers, (3) its relation to the reality it reflects, and (4) the relationships of its various parts in the unity which makes it a work of art. The particular concern of any general theory is an outgrowth of the conception of the nature of art in that theory, and that conception is in turn an expression of the basic concern the theory represents.

It thus becomes pertinent to analyze any critical evaluation of literature in terms of the location and nature of the basic concern of its underlying theory. Is it with the traits of authors, or the characteristics of an author's time reflected in him? Is it with the effects on readers: pleasure, or instruction, or moral guidance, or psychological renovation? Is it with the kinds of things literature imitates: individuals, classes, societies, internal and external action, the eternal verities, or some combination of these? To raise such questions has value, not only in clarifying the basic theory which gives direction to the critical judgments expressed, but also in suggesting the wide range of interests and values which may be found in the primary works of literature themselves. While a scheme for identifying the different critical tasks which critics set themselves cannot alone provide the librarian with the competence he needs to handle literary materials intelligently, it can promote a preliminary appreciation of the possibilities presented by different critics. Some schools of criticism may ultimately be rejected by the librarian, but the approach to critical works which is advocated here will allow the librarian to get as much as possible from the variety of critical work coming to his attention.

This is not to say that each critic is completely preoccupied with only one aspect of a work, but rather that one is usually basic in the sense that decisive considerations arise from it, and other aspects are analyzed in relation to it. The critical theory of Sidney, for example, is basically concerned with moral improvement as the essential effect which literary art should have upon its audience. He deals also with the traits of literary works and the interrelations of the parts of such works as these traits and relationships affect readers; with the subjects treated, and the kinds of persons and events reflected or imitated in literature, as an analysis of these things throws light on the effects on readers; and with the nature of the writer's creative activities as these relate to the effects he produces. Aristotle's *Poetics*, to take another example, is basically concerned with the parts or elements of a literary work and their relationships in a unified whole, and this basic concern determines the kind of attention given to the nature and kinds of imitation in literature, the kinds of pleasure literature may appropriately induce in readers or in a theater audience, and the interests and attitudes of writers which explain formal differences among literary works.

The history of literary criticism is marked by a slowly shifting emphasis through time from one of these factors to another. Broadly speaking we may characterize early criticism by its consideration of the effect of the work upon its audience, as in Plato, where literature is evaluated almost exclusively in terms of its moral and spiritual effect on the citizens of the republic. The concern with those literary traits which produce the desired effects led to more emphasis upon the characteristics of the work per se, which in Aristotle is reflected in a synthetic analysis of existing form, and which, in the classicist followers of Aristotle, became a dictatorial prescription of specific literary devices. With the rise of romanticism interest shifted to the individual artist and the events or periods in his life which influence the work he produces. From this concern it is but a small step to the interest in the social milieu out of which the artist comes, which characterizes the psychological, social, and political orientation of so much contemporary criticism. With the emphasis upon the social milieu the audience comes back into a central position; criticism seems to be completing the cycle to return again to consideration of the social, moral, and political effects of literature upon its audience. Although representatives of each of these points of view undoubtedly can be found in every age, the leaders of critical schools and the great bulk of critical work have followed the pattern outlined here.

The Use of Critical Writings

Since the librarian relies frequently upon critical evaluations by others to assist him in the selection of materials for his collection, and since the critical materials that are available to him vary enormously in scope, in depth of analysis, and in form, it is necessary that he himself be both a critic and a judge of criticism.

Critical works may cover the principles of literary aesthetics which are applicable to any period, place, or form; they may be concerned with a single form in a single period; they may be limited to the consideration of a single aspect of a single work. They may attempt a detailed analysis of the work under scrutiny; they may attempt to compare the work with others of a similar nature or by the same author; they may report personal impressions; they may merely present a summary outline of plot or theme. They may be embodied in whole volumes, in short essays, in single-paragraph "reviews" in magazines and newspapers. Many of them — and not only the shorter and more ephemeral examples — do not consist of carefully formulated argument from critical principles, but depend for their persuasiveness on assumptions concerning the critic's sensibility and experience, or on the status of the publication in which his judgments appear.

The student — the librarian-to-be — should remember that it is not the critic's function to tell him what to like or dislike. The critic's importance lies in his ability to point out aspects of the work which can assist in a fuller appraisal or reappraisal. Criticism deliberately objectifies the work under consideration, identifying what is new and what is old in the work, making comparisons with other works to show in what respects it surpasses or falls short of those works, clarifying the author's intent, and improving, in whatever ways are pertinent to the individual work, the process of assimilation. Mere enthusiasm in the critic, then, is not enough. His elucidation of values should be in terms of specifics and his criteria should be clearly identified and defined. The final evaluation is left to the individual reader whose insights are sharpened by comparing his own discriminations with those of the critic.

Many of the critical writings to which the librarian turns for judgments on contemporary works are short and sketchy, and only a knowledge of the critic's longer works, or of a variety of his works, can help to identify the basic principles. If one's acquaintance with critical writings is wide, he may often be able to uncover the unidentified principles by analogy with other writings by the same critic, by comparison with similar critical opinions in works which do a more complete analytical job, or by building up a more complete picture of a critic's viewpoint through a collection of his particular criticisms. There is no shortcut to the kind of literary experience which wide reading provides, and this chapter can do no more than draw attention to some of the purposes which such reading can serve.

In the class work which accompanies this chapter, therefore, the major emphasis should be placed upon works of criticism from which the student, as from a middle ground, can work back to the aesthetic theory upon which the critical evaluation is based, and forward to the literary work itself, which is the object of the evaluation. It is hoped that the student will bear constantly in mind the triple distinction between literature proper, criticism, and theory, so that the intensive study of one may operate as an extensive overview of all three. Ideally, if the significant differences among the several critical theories can be clearly worked out, then the variety of possibilities of firsthand understanding and evaluation of literary works, a useful grasp of the variety of critical approaches exhibited in the critical writings about these works, and an insight into the histories of literature are most likely to be developed. On the basis of some comprehension of general theory, the student should be able to engage profitably in the discussion of a sufficient variety of particular works of art to increase his competence to deal at first hand with literary works. Light should be thrown on problems of book selection by the guidance provided by these principles for description and evaluation of fiction, on both the "popular" and the "critically respectable" levels. Not only book selection would be improved, however; certain problems of classification and especially cataloging should be clarified, and reference and general advisory services in the field of literature should benefit.

The ideal is an ambitious one, and is not likely to be attained completely in this or any number of courses in a library school. But the use of criticism as a bridge which connects theory with the primary works and makes possible the easy movement from one to the other is a device which the librarian can continue to use to increase his competence after he leaves the library school. This chapter can only provide some of the tools with which the librarian will work; his proficiency with them will come from practice and experience.

Of the great critical writings of the past, the selection by Smith and Parks in their volume, *The Great Critics*,[6] is perhaps as good a representation as can be found within the covers of a single book. The student is urged to read widely in the volume and in the works listed in the bibliography for a summary of the different and shifting emphases which mark the influential critical writings of the past. For contemporary criticism, a similar compendium is Morton Dauwen Zabel's *Literary Opinion in America*[7] which also presents both a representative sampling of different points of view and an excellent bibliography of additional works of importance.

---

[6] James Harry Smith and Edd Winfield Parks, *The Great Critics*: *An Anthology of Literary Criticism*. 3d. ed., rev. and enl. (N. Y., Norton, 1951).

[7] Morton Dauwen Zabel, *Literary Opinion in America*, Rev. ed. (N. Y., Harper, 1951).

Reading in these two volumes, and in the primary works to which
these volumes refer, will provide the student with a sense of the
factors and considerations which lead to specific critical judgments
on specific literary works. It will help to identify the principles
underlying the major critical theories and will furnish some graphic
examples of the application of these principles to the critical evaluation of literary art.

LITERARY HISTORY

The literary historian, like the literary critic, organizes his
materials around some general theory of literature and its major
values. Like the critic, he may see the history of literature as a
separate phenomenon demanding special treatment suitable to its
distinctive subject matter, or he may consider it one with all history, political, social, or economic. If the former, he may trace
the history of the elements in literary works (type characters, for
example), or the growth of particular styles, or the evolution of the
genres. If the latter, he may see literary history in terms of its
environment and the political and social movements out of which the
literature is thought to arise. Or, following the prevailing mode
during the last few generations, he may see literature in terms of
the individual who produced it and will write chiefly literary biographies. Lastly, he may treat literary history in terms of its
effects on its audience and will be more interested in the readers
than in the writers.

Because of the complex variety of the field of literature, few
historians attempt a universal history of literature in all its forms.
Some organizing principle is usually required to reduce the chaotic
confusion of writers and titles to a comprehensible unity and to
deal with the materials intensively enough to be more than a mere
listing. What he selects for omission or inclusion, the categories
he elects to designate, the divisions of the subject which he chooses
to emphasize will grow out of his theories concerning the nature,
origins, and functions of literary art. Literary history is usually
a kind of literary criticism, even when no overt evaluative judgments are made. To understand and to appraise the histories of
literature with which he will deal, the librarian will rely as much
on his familiarity with critical theory as he does in the selection of
the acknowledged works of critical evaluation mentioned in the
preceding section.

The Development of Western Literature

The survey following is an eclectic summary of the development of the literature of the western world, which points up some of the characteristics that are stressed in the several histories of literature. It is an encyclopedic consensus based upon certain high lights usually emphasized in the histories and is not meant to represent an adequate survey of that history.

The literature of the Greeks provides an interesting microcosmic history of the development of literature in most countries. It begins with religious songs and war ballads and broadens, as the language becomes refined and the people more sophisticated, to embrace most of the forms of literary art which now exist. Out of the war ballads and legends grew the epic poems, the *Iliad* and the *Odyssey*; out of the religious festivals developed the great tragic and comic dramas which still stand — in Aeschylus, Sophocles, Euripides, and Aristophanes — as models of the genre. The poetry of the Greeks reflects the changing character of their civilization: during the period of the monarchy and the tyrants, the warlike past of the race and the lore and tradition of the past were the subjects for poetic treatment. With the rise of democracy in Greece, the individual became more important, and poetry began to reflect the inner thoughts, feelings, and reflections of the individual poet in such forms as the elegy, the iambic, and the lyric. But by the time of Philip of Macedon the literature of Greece had reached its greatest heights in all the several forms, and the "Hellenistic" period is marked by imitative and artificial work which added little that was new or truly creative.

Much of the extant literature of Rome is derived from Greek models. The Roman tendency to make literature ancillary to politics and to objects of practical utility is made obvious by the important place which speeches, letters, and history hold in Roman literature and in the conception of history as a continuous and progressive development of the state which marks not only the oratory and political writings, but such poetic works as Virgil's *Aeneid*.

During the so-called Dark Ages literature was subordinated to scholarship, and the famous work of the copyists of the period was essentially devoted to making Latin copies of Roman works which were in turn copies of the Greek. Literature did not die during the period: the introduction and diffusion of legends and folk literature were an important contribution. The transition, in the more formal literature, from the religious to the more secular marks the difference between the Dark and the Middle Ages. The characteristic form which highlights the change is the epic treatment of legendary heroes and history: the *Song of Roland* in France; the *Cid* in Spain; the *Nibelungenlied* in Germany; and *Beowulf* in England. Also typical of the period is the tradition of courtly love, which can be

traced through the troubadours of Southern France and the Minne-
sänger of Germany, the *Chansons de Geste* of the trouvères, the
allegorical romances like the *Roman de la Rose*, the mariolatry
tradition in Italy, *The Faerie Queene* of Spenser, down to its per-
sistence in the love story of the twentieth century.

As we approach the modern era, from the sixteenth century
onward, the literature of criticism and interpretation becomes
more complex. The closer we come to our own day, the more
varied and prolific are the strains which we can distinguish in the
literature and the approaches which the critics may take to them.
The sixteenth century is characterized on the one hand by the return to classic formalism in such neoclassicists as Du Bellay,
Ronsard, and Malherbe in France, Jonson in England, and Vida and
Scaliger in Italy, but on the other hand, it boasts the non-Aristotelian romanticism of Shakespeare and Lope de Vega, and the
sprawling synthesis, *Gargantua and Pantagruel*.

The seventeenth century is ushered in by the great picaresque
novel, *Don Quixote*. It reaches the high point of neoclassicism in
Boileau, in Corneille and Racine, in Dryden and in Pope, and of
worldly sophistication and polish in the Cavalier poets and Molière.
It is characterized both by the great puritan epics of Milton and the
bawdy excesses of the Restoration theater in Wycherly and Con-
greve which come as a reaction against the repressions of the
Commonwealth.

The eighteenth century is dominated by reason in the dictatorial
regulations of Samuel Johnson, in the scientific interests of the En-
cyclopedists and in the revolt against irrationality by Voltaire. But
it is equally an age of romanticism and sentimentality in the novels
of Richardson and Sterne, in Rousseau, and in the *Sturm und Drang*
writers, Herder, Goethe, and Schiller; and a period of revolution
against decorous complacency in Gay's *Beggar's Opera*, in Defoe's
Moll Flanders, and in the bitter denunciations of Swift.

By the nineteenth century we have an even greater multiplica-
tion of strains, from the extreme sentimentality of the early Romantics to the studied objectivity of the later naturalists; from
social criticism in Austen, Dickens, and Thackeray to placid acceptance in Macaulay and Tennyson; from concern with art for
art's sake in Pater, Wilde, and Baudelaire; from interest in the
ancients in Keats, in medievalism in Walpole, in the mystical and
strange in Coleridge, Poe, and Hoffman, to a concern with the problems of heredity and environment in Balzac, Hardy, and Gissing.

The twentieth century is still too close to us for a definitive
evaluation of dominant currents, but already there are historians
who have pointed to the rise of realism and naturalism in the first
decades of the century, the increasing social criticism which

followed the first World War, the "Lost Generation" and "Jazz Age" tendencies of the twenties, the proletarian emphasis in the thirties, and the loss of faith and idealism in the forties.

The Organization of Literary Histories

A variety of literary histories have grown up which, although they deal with essentially the same subject matter, are completely different in the scope of the material with which they deal, the aspects of it which they consider important, and the relationship between parts which they postulate. The influence of social forces, of the spirit of the age, of individual genius, of historical events, of national characteristics — each of these has been taken as primary by some historian who then views the development of literature in its terms.

Some literary histories, for example, are essentially little more than chronological arrangements of titles and authors, like Anne C. Botta's *Handbook of Universal Literature*. Others, while more detailed, still emphasize historical sequence, like Wendell Barrett's *Traditions of European Literature, from Homer to Dante*, which treats literature by historical epochs — Greek, Roman, Christian, medieval — in chronological succession.

A concern with the historical context of literature leads to the occupation with the history more than the literature, and a large school of literary thought exists which sees literature as an expression of the period out of which it arises. The twelve-volume *Periods of European Literature* edited by George E. B. Saintsbury devotes each volume to a different period, written by an expert on that period, and fits the literature to the period pattern. Taine's familiar formula, "race, milieu, moment," as applied in his *History of English Literature*, is the most famous expression of this concern with the influence of environment upon letters.

A special aspect of the period approach sees literature as the expression of the *Zeitgeist*, the "climate of opinion," the intellectual atmosphere, which acts as a kind of abstract force unifying the artistic production of any given age. Here the spirit of the time is abstracted from the characteristics of the other arts, as in Curt Sachs' *The Commonwealth of Art*, and literature is merely one art among many; or it is derived from other nonliterary and nonaesthetic movements, and literature is seen as a social phenomenon, as in Parrington's *Main Currents in American Thought*, or in Alfred Kazin's *On Native Grounds*. From Kazin, Parrington, and others it is but a short step to the more extreme Marxist view of literature which sees it as an expression of completely nonliterary forces, a historical phenomenon like political movements which arise out of historical events and which should be studied in these terms. Granville Hicks's. *The Great Tradition,* which interprets all American literature since the Civil War in terms of its identification with the class struggle, is this type of study. These extrinsic studies of literature soon lead to so-called literary studies which are not interested in literature as such at all, but which turn the entire process upside down to make literature a tool for examining society instead of the study of society a tool for understanding literature. In F. A. Walbank's *England Yesterday and Today, in the Works of the Novelists,* the social history of the past century in England is reconstructed through vignettes extracted from English novels, and the novel receives no consideration as an artistic and integrated unit.

The *Zeitgeist* approach leads to a study of literature as a history of movements, either literary or nonliterary. Romanticism, for example, which cuts across national lines and informs the literature of Germany, France, and England during the late eighteenth and early nineteenth centuries, becomes a glass through which an understanding of those literatures can be seen more clearly. Mario Praz's *The Romantic Agony* traces the influence of the "Gothic" movement on the literature of the nineteenth century and shows its characteristics in different writers and different literatures. These movements are often seen also as universal in their influence, but modified by national characteristics. English romanticism is a different thing from German romanticism, and can be properly understood only as the result of the national genius reshaping an international current. Georg Brandes' monumental *Main Currents in Nineteenth Century Literature* discusses the great writers of the period in terms of the national modifications of the "school": "The Romantic School in Germany"; "The Romantic School in France"; "Naturalism in England," etc. The extreme view confines itself to a single national literature, isolated from the literatures of all other nations and sufficient in itself. The well-known Cambridge histories of English and American literature, while not as strictly chauvinistic as that, do set up national boundaries to the literature with which they will deal.

On the other hand, literature may be viewed as the creation of individual genius, which demands the biographical and psychological analysis of the author as a basis for understanding his work. Sainte-Beuve, reacting against the "naturalistic" interpretation of Taine, gave the fullest pioneering expression to this school of literary thought; Van Wyck Brooks's series on American literature continues in the tradition, and Burton Rascoe's *Titans of Literature from Homer to the Present* deals solely in terms of a few great writers and their influence on literature: "Sophocles and Greek

Drama," "Cervantes and the Spirit of Mockery," etc. An extreme reflection of this school of thought is the psychoanalytic and psychiatric approach which sees literature in terms of the personal aberrations and maladjustments of the artist. Ludwig Lewissohn's *Expression in America* and Edmund Wilson's *The Wound and the Bow* are examples of this type of interpretation.

The "Great Books" approach to the study of literature minimizes the importance of nation, period, or individual genius. The works are seen not so much as results of influences or as influences upon others but as the best that is known and thought about problems of universal contemporaneity. The books become individual monuments rather than successive aspects of a continuous development.

Still another approach is that which studies literature as a history of genres. *The History of the Novel* by E. A. Baker confines itself to the single form and is concerned with the technical limitations set by the structure of the particular genre, while E. K. Chambers' *The Medieval Stage* adds a time limitation to its study of the forms of dramatic art.

Such delimitations and intensifications characterize many literary histories, adding richness of detail and masses of evidence to a narrow field and — usually — a narrower interpretation. A single current of the literary stream may be diverted for special attention as in Brown and McDermott's *Survey of Catholic Literature*. A national and theme boundary may be imposed, as in Norman Foerster's *Nature in American Literature* which traces the treatment of a specific subject matter in a single national literature. A national-time-genre limit may be placed on a work, as in Georg Witkowski's *German Drama of the Nineteenth Century*. And, of course, there are the many studies of single writers, like Amy Lowell's exhaustive study of Keats, which employ the technique of the historian to create a documented study similar to the detailed biographies of rulers and statesmen in the books on political history.

Such single-track studies of literary history have a certain usefulness, as much when they fail to fit a particular piece of literature into any given period as when they succeed. They constitute a key to the stereotypes which mold the thinking of many writers and readers in the field, and should therefore be known to the librarian in order that he may understand the concepts which his patrons bring to the library. They also mark off, in broad and general terms, the high points in the literary output of the different periods, thereby serving as points of reference by which the several deviations from the standardized pattern may be distinguished. Used in this way, these approaches can broaden appreciation of individual literary works by underlining certain characteristics directly and others indirectly. They are dangerous only if they impose stereotypes upon appreciation and lead to the rejection of any works which do not fit the predetermined pattern. Without denying their utility, the librarian should be careful not to accept too narrowly the limiting boundaries of any one of the organizational principles. As in the field of criticism, he should seek to discover the values in the several approaches and should attempt to provide as broad and varied a sampling of the historical literature as he can afford.

THE PRIMARY WORKS

Important as the literary histories and works of criticism are, they are not the materials with which the average user of the literature collection is familiar. To most general users of the library, literature connotes the novels, poems, and plays themselves rather than the books about them, and in most cases the patron forgets that these secondary materials even exist. The real core of the collection is the primary material, and the secondary sources have their major value in their ability to interpret this material or to lead readers to it.

Of the several forms of literature, the most commonly known and most frequently used are poetry, drama, and fiction. The Dewey Decimal system provides for sections on essays, oratory, letters, satire and humor, and miscellaneous forms of literature in each national grouping, but none of these genres is significant in bulk or popularity. For general purposes, literature means poetry, plays, and novels (and short stories) to the patron and to the librarian.

Poetry

The earliest extant literature of almost all countries is poetry. The folk literature with which we are familiar, not only from the past, but in contemporary primitive cultures, usually is embodied in songs, ballads, and other poetic forms. Children are attracted early to rhythm, meter, and rhyme, and find pleasure in jingles and verses long before they have a sense of literary form of any other kind. Because of this there is a tradition among the students of literature that poetry is the most moving form of literary art, the most closely related to basic needs, the form which speaks most powerfully to the minds and hearts of all men of whatever station and background. The Romantics' view of the poet as the "unacknowledged legislator of mankind," while recognized as a slightly exaggerated one, is still widely and favorably quoted by writers on the place of poetry in human life.

Despite these clichés about the ability of poetry to touch all men deeply, library experience would tend to show that the majority of average readers today are indifferent if not actually hostile to poetry, and that to many, poetry is considered to be an esoteric interest of literary aesthetes and not the common denominator of literary communication. Poetry in our day has become pretty much an academic subject, read by students and scholars, but of little interest to the average patron. What little poetry does have an audience of any size is usually not the "best" poetry by critical standards, and much of it is quite obviously doggerel by any standards. An occasional *John Brown's Body* or *The Cocktail Party* finds a comparatively wide audience both in the library and outside it, but on the whole, the public library will number few devoted readers of poetry among its clientele.

On the other hand, the importance of poetry in literary development makes it incumbent upon even the smallest public library to give a place to some of the acknowledged classics and masterpieces written in poetic form and to attempt to select from contemporary poets the materials likely to hold a permanent place for future students of literature. In the larger libraries, and particularly in college and university libraries, the poetry collection has much greater importance, and many special collections exist for the use of scholars interested in this special segment of the field of literature. The establishment of a Chair of Poetry in the Library of Congress in 1937 gave official government recognition to the importance of poetry, but such a post is an unusual one. Even in the research libraries there are few collections large enough and of sufficient importance to require special handling or the services of a special librarian of poetry alone. A notable collection such as the Lockwood Memorial Library of worksheets and letters in the University of Buffalo is not administered by a special librarian, and the Modern Poetry Room of the University of Chicago, while important, is not typical.

Drama

The drama — that form of literature distinguished by its dependence upon *performance* by living players for its fullest effect — is as venerable as poetry in its historical lineage and as effective as poetry in its power to involve its readers (spectators) emotionally. Many primitive dances and rituals are essentially dramas in that they portray, through bodily movement, gesture, facial expression and sound, a stylized imitation of some human activity.

Children's play also reveals the same basic delight in imitation and imaginative portrayal of persons and actions.

These attempts at dramatic presentation are, of course, only vague foreshadows of the drama as the formal artistic creation we know today. The formal art of play-making, however, is also connected from its beginnings with the basic needs and interests of the people. The Greek drama, upon which much of our contemporary concept of drama is based, originated in the religious ceremonies of Greece and throughout its history was as much a religious ceremony as it was a mass entertainment. Similarly the theatre of the Middle Ages, which revived the drama after its disappearance during the Dark Ages, had its origins in the religious ceremonies of the Church. Modern drama began as a purely religious presentation illustrating portions of the service enacted by the priests and other churchmen, and only gradually evolved through the mystery, miracle and morality plays to the completely secular plays written and acted by laymen in theatres unconnected with the church. The Renaissance revival of interest in Roman and Greek literature helped to reintroduce the complicated plot structure and stock characters of Roman comedy and to revive the concept of the play as entertainment. From the Renaissance to the present, the drama has been centered in the secular theatre and has moved farther and farther, both in space and in spirit, from the cathedral where it began.

The drama collection of today is in reality dedicated to two different aspects of the drama. One is the drama as literature, seen as an art form employing language for the communication of ideas. The other is drama as "show business," in which the emphasis is upon theatrical presentation and the techniques of production. The audiences for these two kinds of material may overlap to a limited extent, but the purposes served by each of the two approaches are sufficiently distinct to require special handling and special abilities on the part of the librarian. Those dramas with status as literature may also be studied from the standpoint of production, and many little theatre groups, school dramatic societies, and other organizations interested in presentation will feel the need for interpretative studies of the literary as well as the theatrical form of the plays. But many contemporary plays are of interest as theatre only and make no pretensions to literary immortality. In the allied literature on stagecraft and the technical aspects of production, the drama librarian finds himself in a field far removed from the literary and more closely related, in many of its phases, to the technological. A key to the variety of aspects of the subject which may receive attention in the library's theatre collection is provided in the volume *Theatre Collections in*

Libraries and Museums.[8] It is recommended that the student examine this book as a guide to the outstanding collections in the field of the drama and as a partial subject index to the materials which form a drama collection.

Another characteristic of drama materials which has implications for the librarian has been indicated in the definition of drama given at the head of this section. Plays, in most cases, are intended for live performance more than for individual reading. While the great plays of the past — Shakespeare, Goethe, Molière — are read by students, and an occasional playwright directs his attention to the reader (Shaw, for example, especially in his Prefaces), the average library user prefers to see a play rather than to read it, and the interest in materials written in play form is highly specialized. In general, the users of drama in book form will be students of literature or of playwrighting and production, and amateurs and professionals engaged in the production of plays. The drama typically fulfills its function as recreation and entertainment on the stage rather than within the covers of a book.

Fiction

Broadly speaking, all imaginative literature is fiction in that it is invented and fashioned by the mind of the creator. Popular usage, however, specifically applies the term to prose works in narrative form like the novel (and its variants, the novelette and the novella) and the short story, and public libraries have accepted the popular terminology. When the "fiction collection" is referred to in library publications, it is the collection of novels and short stories that is understood.

The form of the novel which we know today is a comparatively new one in the history of literature. Historians are not agreed on the specific work which may be called the first modern novel, although a consensus would probably place its flowering in the eighteenth century. Certainly the epic poems of Greece must be recognized as forerunners of the novel in the sustained narrative they carry, and T. E. Lawrence has made a prose translation of the Homeric poems to support his thesis that they represent the "first novel of Europe." The Platonic dialogues also, in their reconstruction of character and dialogue, may be taken as early counterparts of the modern imaginative fashioning which we now call the

---

[8] Rosamond Gilder and George Freedley, *Theatre Collections in Libraries and Museums, an international handbook.* Published under the auspices of the New York Public Library and the National Theatre Conference, with the cooperation of the A.L.A. (N. Y., Theatre Arts Inc., 1936).

novel, and in the East, Lady Murasaki's *The Tale of Genji* reveals characteristics of the novel form as early as the eleventh century. By the time of the Renaissance, such works as Thomas More's *Utopia*, such pastorals as Sir Philip Sidney's *Arcadia*, and the chivalric romances approach very closely the novel we know today (modern novels about an ideal future society still are designated "utopias," for example, in recognition of their prototype in the work of More). When Cervantes undertook to burlesque the chivalric romances in his *Don Quixote*, the picaresque novel was already established as a form.

The novel, as a widely used form in which to point a moral, illustrate a principle, or embody a concept, probably won its popularity in part from the female readers who became an important segment of the audience in the eighteenth century. In such sentimental works as those of Richardson and Sterne we find many of the strains which critics have taken to be of particular appeal to women, strains which continue in the rental library staples of today. The characteristics of the succeeding periods, already noted in the summary on p. 213-16 (romanticism, naturalism, realism, aestheticism, etc.), are even more easily seen in the novels of the nineteenth century. Paralleling the romantic poets we have the romantic novelists like Scott, Hugo, and Dumas; paralleling the poets of the weird and fanciful, we have the Gothic novelists like Mrs. Radcliffe; realism is reflected in such varied writers as Austen, Balzac, Thackeray, and Stendahl; art for art's sake in such writers as Wilde; naturalism, most clearly of all, in Zola and Norris.

The short story is also a popular form. Although there are those who date its origin from the work of Poe, it must be recognized that the fables, folk tales, bestiaries, and fabliaux of the Middle Ages are short stories in a very real sense, and that many classics, like the *Decameron*, *The Canterbury Tales*, and *The Arabian Nights*, although held together by a frame tale device, are essentially collections of short stories rather than sustained novels. Short stories are characteristic of the folk literature of all lands and periods, from Aesop and the *Märchen* collected by the Brothers Grimm to the tall tales of the American West. While less pretentious than the novel, the short story is an extremely important form of fiction to which some of the greatest writers of all ages have contributed.

The audience for the other literary forms, like poetry and the drama, is limited to particular groups of readers, but the audience for fiction is almost limitless. Ranging as it does from the short stories of an O. Henry to the many-volumed studies of a Proust or a Romains, from simple folk lore to complexly constructed experiments with form, and from deeply thought-out philosophy to frivolous entertainment, the field of fiction has something for every taste, for every level of education, and for every kind of purpose. The needs which libraries are dedicated to serve — recreation, information, education, and aesthetic appreciation — can all be met for some readers through fiction alone. Slightly better than half of the circulation of even the largest public libraries — with their emphasis upon reference and research — is fiction, and as the size of the library decreases, the proportion of fiction circulation rises. In other words, fiction circulation in almost all libraries is larger than that of all the classes of nonfiction combined.

Fiction, of course, is no more a single homogeneous class than is nonfiction. There are also varieties and types within the field of the novel with different characteristics which appeal to different audiences and are meant to serve different purposes. It is therefore as difficult to establish a simple set of standards for a description and evaluation which will apply to all types of fiction as it is to establish a set of criteria equally applicable to books about automobile repair, the nature of God, and the paintings of Holbein.

The definition of popular fiction

In library discussions of fiction, much is made of the distinction between serious fiction and popular fiction. Most librarians agree that serious fiction has an important place in the library collection, but there is extensive disagreement concerning the inclusion of popular fiction. Yet a definition of either serious or popular fiction has not yet been satisfactorily made, and except for certain obvious specific examples — The Brothers Karamazov is serious, Tarzan is popular — most definitions break down when an application of their principles is attempted. Since it is the middle ground between serious and popular which is most difficult to define, it is probably more realistic to recognize at least three levels[9] of fiction:

1. The accepted "classics" which through time and a consensus of critical opinion have won a permanent place on the shelves of "great books."

---

[9] A fourth level could be set aside for the deliberately salacious and pornographic novels which seldom even reach the librarian's desk for review. There is a fairly prolific literature in this area, with a wider distribution than we have been able to measure because it is never reflected in sales or circulation figures. From the standpoint of the sociology of reading, however, this unmentioned level is very important and makes most summaries of contemporary reading incomplete. Since this literature is sufficiently sub rosa to present few problems to libraries, however, it will not be discussed here.

    2. The novels of apparently serious purpose which have not yet allowed us the perspective of time to temper our evaluations.

    3. The "popular" novels: popular in the sense not merely of large sales (many novels in the first two classes have been best sellers), but of being written for a wide audience *at the moment* and with no pretense to lasting values.

    The first class of novels need not be extensively discussed here. It includes the standard titles which are the subject of study in literature courses, over the importance of which little serious disagreement is likely to arise. We may assume that students who have reached the graduate level in their schooling have become acquainted with the "classics" of the past and the present, and that merely to mention such titles as *Don Quixote, Tom Jones, The Red and the Black, Wuthering Heights, The Scarlet Letter, Madame Bovary, Moby Dick, War and Peace, Huckleberry Finn, Remembrance of Things Past, Ulysses,* and *The Magic Mountain* is sufficient to indicate the sense in which the term "classic" is used here.

    The second class represents a more difficult problem. Many contemporary writers whose works are well reviewed, whose publishers are reputable, and whose readers are intelligent, seem established because of their very nearness. Yet each year sees promising writers disappear and well-reviewed books fade from memory. Our immediate reactions are not reliable gauges of probable permanence, and we hesitate to predict that the novel which moved us today will have anything to say to readers next year. Even works which hold us for a decade or two may seem shallow and second-rate with the passage of time. Many writers with established reputations would classify in group two: John P. Marquand, Somerset Maugham, Irwin Shaw, Carson McCullers, and John O'Hara, to mention a few. Another generation may place some of them in the first class, and it is this possibility which entitles them to a place in the second now.

    The third class may best be defined by the types which make it up. The major characteristic of these "popular" novels is their strong dependence on plot, as reflected in its major types: the mystery story, the Western novel, and the narrative generally defined. Of these classes, the first two are self-explanatory; the third is admittedly an ad hoc creation and includes at least seven sub-classes. The popular novel, in the more or less pejorative sense, may in general be defined as an imitation of some form of the serious novel, directed at a mass audience. We find the following types in the popular novel: the novel of manners *(If I Have Four Apples)*, the sociological novel *(Gentlemen's Agreement)*, the novel of character *(A Tree Grows In Brooklyn)*, and the thematic novel *(Green Light)*, all of which are varieties of serious fiction.

The popular novel may also be categorized in these additional types: the historical (Samuel Shellabarger), the romantic (Faith Baldwin), the suspense (Helen MacInnes), and the humorous (Thorne Smith). While a serious novel may exhibit the characteristics of these last four types, they usually appear as a subordinate aspect of the first four forms of the serious novel. Mark Twain's *Huckleberry Finn* has elements of humor and suspense, but it may be comprehended within the category of the novel of character.

Mystery and Western novels are established as separate categories parallel to the category of general narrative, partly because of the bulk of the material published in each of these forms, and partly because libraries and users of libraries have followed the lead of the publishers in recognizing such categories. The mystery novel as here defined is one in which the dominant element is the crime puzzle which must be solved, regardless of other literary accoutrements.[10] The use of the puzzle as the central point of the story is not limited to popular mystery novels, of course; serious fiction also employs it as a plot device. There is a puzzle in the Oedipus plays, *The Brothers Karamazov* revolves around a murder mystery, and Faulkner's *Intruder in the Dust* is definitely concerned with the standard mystery formula: a search for the murderer in order to save an innocent suspect. But in the popular mystery novels, the major emphasis is upon plot, and the reader is not expected to have any great interest beyond the solution of the puzzle. While there are often interesting characterization and much incidental information (see the material on bell-ringing in *The Nine Tailors* by Dorothy Sayers), the mystery novel is quite literally a "whodunit." W. H. Auden considers Raymond Chandler to be a serious writer rather than a writer of detective stories because he is concerned with a serious study of a criminal milieu and not just the ingenious solution of a puzzle. This introduces an interesting criterion which librarians might well bear in mind, especially in those libraries where the emphasis upon fiction is served by the simple expedient of rejecting all mystery and detective stories.

The Western novel is chiefly a product of the twentieth century although it obviously has its roots in such works as Washington Irving's *A Tour on the Prairie* and the novels of James Fenimore Cooper, especially *The Prairie*. The mass-produced Western with which we are familiar, however, is best represented by the books of Zane Grey, Ernest Haycox, Peter Field, Henry Herbert Knibbs, and Luke Short. It should be noted that the Western novel as the term is used here is not merely a novel with a western setting. It is one in which certain ingredients — a solid core of gun-play, cattle rustling

---

[10] The detective story is a special kind of mystery novel, but not the only kind.

villainous double-dealing, etc. — are considered indispensable and
of primary importance. Characters are usually fairly stereotyped
and so are situations, although modern writers of Westerns have
begun to introduce new material: romance, sex, and even some
highly literate descriptive matter. But by and large, the Western
novel is faithful to formula, and novels which depart from that
formula — Alfred Henry Lewis' *Wolfville* series or the novels of
Will James — are considered regional novels rather than Westerns,
while a novel like *The Ox Bow Incident* is clearly a thematic novel
in a western setting.

The types included under the heading "narrative" are probably
sufficiently defined by the sample titles or authors noted above.
An historical novel in the popular sense is usually an action ad-
venture tale in a setting that happens to be period. Although historical details may be accurate enough they are seldom integral,
as they are in such serious historical novels as *Kristin Lavrans-
datter* or *War and Peace*. The suspense novel is distinguished
from the mystery novel in that it concentrates on a single element,
that of terrified expectation which may be combined with puzzle,
but need not be. In a novel like *Wisteria Cottage*, for example, the
murderer is known and interest centers on the suspense created
by the reader's anticipation of the act itself. The romance usually
contains elements of other types — mystery, character, suspense —
but its major interest is in the love story and its goal is the happy
union of boy and girl. The humorous novel is generally concerned
only with funny action, although elements of satire, characterization, and even social criticism may appear in a minor way within
the framework of ludicrous plotting. In all cases of novels which
are called popular in this chapter, plot and action are of primary
importance and are essentially an end in themselves. A single
reading suffices, since once the reader knows "what happened"
there is nothing else to be had from the book. Contrast this kind
of audience reaction with that called forth by a work like *Hamlet*,
which reveals new depths and insights with each rereading (or re-
seeing) and which, although ingeniously plotted, is not at all adequately summarized by a mere outline of the story.

Popular literature as we have here defined it has always
existed side by side with the literature of the educated and the
elite. The literature of the court, of the aristocracy, of the upper
classes, while frequently the literature with which later generations
are the most familiar, is not the only — or even the most important
— aspect of the literature of any period. A play of Shakespeare is
a rare example of the meeting of both the serious and the popular
in a single work; in many ages our concentration upon the literature
of the court has led us to false generalizations about the place of

literature and its relevance to the total culture out of which it springs. That being so, the librarian is faced with a difficult responsibility in selecting, from all of the books in print, those which are most worthy of dissemination and preservation.

SELECTION OF MATERIALS IN THE FIELD OF LITERATURE

In the discussion of the three major forms of literature, an attempt has been made to define in broad terms the particular audiences to which each form appeals. This is important to the librarian in charge of selection because usually he is concerned with evaluating works, not solely in terms of abstract excellence, but also in terms of the audience which is likely to use the book. In the field of literature this is not an easy task. As we have seen, "imaginative" literature and the books about it cover a range of excellence from the most profound creative efforts of an Aeschylus to the most stereotyped potboiler of current mass production, and a range of matter from purely original expression of subjective feeling to objective reporting on the substantive content of someone else's creative work. Consequently it attracts readers with every conceivable subject interest, and from every educational, social, and economic background. The librarian should be able to recognize and understand the needs, the particular approach, the peculiar interpretations of each user and to adjust to them sympathetically and speedily. He must be able to recognize that Shelley's "To a Skylark" is an example of British poetry to one patron, an expression of nineteenth-century romanticism to another, a poem about a bird to a third, and a model of the lyric to a fourth. He must be able to place it in its historical context, its genre context, its subject context, and its form context, and to relate it to the pertinent supplementary materials suitable to each of these several approaches. In other words, any single title in the literature collection may be many things to as many men, and the librarian ought not to take a narrow view of the nature and functions of fiction, drama, and poetry.

The literary scholars have many different ways of studying literature. For the scholar this presents no problem since each may decide on the one which suits him best and follow his preference to the exclusion or denigration of all other schools of thought. The librarian, on the other hand, attempts to be receptive to them all and to interpret his collection for each individual patron in the terms with which the particular patron is in sympathy. The scholar may decide, for example, that literary history is a succession of individual writers and that the study of movements, or schools, or

trends is ridiculous and beside the point. Following this predilec-
tion, he may refuse to use any of the familiar terms with which
literary movements are designated and may brand as absurd any
interpretations which run counter to his own. The librarian, even
though he might personally agree with the point of view of such a
scholar, cannot reject the request of a patron who asks for a book
on the "Metaphysical poets," nor can he justify a failure — real or
feigned — to understand what is generally comprehended in the
term, "Metaphysical poets." He is expected to be familiar with
the many kinds of literature and the many approaches to them and
to be sympathetic to them all.

To maintain this kind of open mind the librarian must acquire
at least a preliminary appreciation of the possibilities presented
by different critical theories. He should know what different critics
look for in a work of art, how different literary artists interpret
the objectives of their art, what reasons the several interpreters
of literature have to justify the variety of periods, schools, and
styles which they have differentiated. A recognition of the many
factors which enter critical discussions will help him to understand,
not only the variety of judgments made by critics, but also the variety of judgments made by laymen whose criteria, often unstated or
unknown, are reflected in the more formal criteria of the critics.
In addition, a knowledge of critical theory will help him to understand the primary materials which critics discuss, enriching his
experience of the works themselves as well as of the evaluations
and interpretations of them. Hence the emphasis, in this chapter,
upon the study of literary criticism (see p. 206-13).

Reviewing Media

Most sources for evaluation of current works carry reviews
rather than full-scale literary criticism. This is not to say that
critical criteria are not applied in reviews, nor that book reviewers
are not serious in their evaluations.[11] It means merely that such
reviews are usually shorter, less formal in their statement of criteria, and presumably more hurried, so that the reviewer must
rely on his own background of knowledge instead of checking additional data and making detailed comparisons. For this reason it is
important that the librarian, who frequently relies upon the short
current review to assist him in the selection of books, should bring

---

[11] For a preliminary investigation of the comparative critical standards applied
in "popular" and "scholarly" reviews, see Walter B. Hendrickson, "A Review of
Reviews of Douglas S. Freeman's *Young Washington,*" *Library Quarterly* XXI
(July, 1951), p. 173-182.

to these reviews a general knowledge of principles and criteria
and a familiarity with the critical theory of the specific reviewer.
Evaluative judgments have little meaning as guides to selection if
the basis of the evaluation is not known.

The librarian turns most frequently to three kinds of periodicals for reviews of current literature. One is the periodical that
is devoted almost exclusively to the review of current books for a
general audience, of which the *New York Times Book Review*, the
New York Herald Tribune "Books," and the *Saturday Review* are
probably the most widely known. The second is the general magazine that carries a book review department, like the *Atlantic
Monthly*, *Harper's*, the *New Yorker*, the *Nation*, the *New Republic*,
and similar publications. The third is the library periodical, designed especially for the use of librarians and carrying short
evaluations of current materials. Among these, the *Library
Journal*, *The Booklist*, the *Wilson Library Bulletin's* "Readers
Choice of Best Books," and the *Virginia Kirkus Bookshop Service*
(primarily intended for the use of booksellers but widely consulted
by librarians) are the most frequently used. The so-called "learned
journals" and scholarly magazines, although they are of great value
to librarians for additional and more complete evaluations, usually
carry criticisms of current books too late to be of much help as a
guide to purchase.

For a general comparison of the scope and tone of these publications, the student is referred to Miss Haines's chapter on "Current Book Reviewing and Literary Commentary" in her *Living With
Books*.[12] Miss Haines characterizes these publications in a general
way, but only a careful reading of the individual review can make
clear the presence or absence of defined principles, the logic — or
lack of it — of the reviewer's conclusions, and the completeness and
specificity of any of these media when consulted for a judgment on
a specific work. The media vary in quality from review to review
in a single issue, and no blanket statement can be made concerning
the adequacy of any of them except in a general way. Constant use
of them teaches the librarian through experience which reviewers
seem most consistently to provide the kind of information needed,
and the individual librarian has his own preferences among reviewers and reviewing media for different kinds of literary materials.

As a test of a reviewer or a reviewing medium, the student
may find it instructive to check all of the major media for the reviews of some book with which he is familiar. It will be possible
for him to compare his own interpretation and knowledge of the
book against the information and evaluation supplied by the several

---

[12]Helen E. Haines, *Living With Books; The Art of Book Selection* (2nd. ed.;
N. Y., Columbia Univ. Pr., 1950), Chapter 6.

reviewers, and he will see, more clearly than any summary here can show him, the discrepancies between reviewers, the omissions and misinterpretations that different criteria bring about, and the special strengths of particular points of view and particular standards of judgment. No more graphic evidence need be adduced to underline the danger of relying on a single source or a single authority as a guide to the variety of appeals which a book may represent to the public served by a library. By extension, the need for a wide sampling of critical scholarship in the library's collection of literary criticism will also be apparent.

The student might, for example, study the several critical interpretations which exist for such a work as Henry James's *The Turn of the Screw*. Within a few selected critical pieces,[13] the student will find a variety of interpretations of the action: (1) that the book means literally what it says and that the ghosts exist; (2) that the ghosts exist only in the imagination of the governess for whom they represent fantasies of her repressed desires; (3) that the governess is a figure in an allegory representing the force of good warring against the forces of evil for possession of the innately innocent soul of man; (4) that the governess is really the source of corruption which infects the children; (5) that the governess is the innocent medium through which the evil spirits of Quint and Jessel corrupt the children; (6) that the governess is in love with the master, and is willing to sacrifice the children to clear her way to him; (7) that the governess is really in love with little Miles . . . , and so on.

This exercise can serve a useful function in forcing a close and analytical reading of the novel by the student himself in order that he may evaluate the several theories properly. He will begin to see the various levels on which a good novel can appeal; he will see how important the style of a work and the choice of language can be to the statement of a theme; he will see in operation the effect of critical theories upon interpretation. Such an experience

[13]See, for example, Oliver Evans, "James's Air of Evil: 'The Turn of the Screw,'" *Partisan Review* XVI (February 1949), p. 175-187; Robert B. Heilman, "Freudian Reading of The Turn of the Screw," *Modern Language Notes* LXII (November 1947), p. 433-45; Robert B. Heilman, " 'The Turn of the Screw' as Poem" in *Forms of Modern Fiction; Essays Collected in Honor of Joseph Warren Beach*, ed. by William Van O'Connor (Minneapolis, Univ. of Minesota Pr., 1948), p. 211-28; Katherine Anne Porter, Allen Tate, Mark Van Doren, "Henry James, The Turn of the Screw" in *The New Invitation to Learning*, ed. by Mark Van Doren (N. Y., Random House, 1942), p. 221-35; Philip Rahv, *The Great Short Novels of Henry James* (N. Y., Dial Pr., 1944), p. 623-25; Edmund Wilson, "The Ambiguity of Henry James" in his *The Triple Thinkers* (N. Y., Oxford Univ. Pr., 1948), p. 88-132; and Max Beerbohm, "The Mote in the Middle Distance," in his *A Christmas Garland* (N. Y., Oxford Univ. Pr., 1936), p. 3-10, for its demonstration of the use of parody as literary criticism.

will teach him the importance of careful reading, not only of the text of a primary work, but of its critical evaluations. And best of all, it will teach him to use critical reviews as aids to creative appreciation rather than as ready-made opinions to be echoed passively and unquestioningly.

It is suggested that the student also study the treatment of *The Turn of the Screw* in William Archibald's play version *The Innocents* or even in the libretto of Benjamin Britten's operatic version of the story.[14] Here one may raise the questions: what changes have been introduced? how do these affect the point of the story? what is gained and what is lost by such changes? how does this treatment alter your original idea of what James really meant? Consideration of these questions should provide an understanding of the demands of different literary genres and their effects upon matter and manner.

Nor is such an exercise limited in its value to the study of accepted classics. A similar study may be made of contemporary reviews of a popular novel. The reviews of a book such as Dashiell Hammett's *The Maltese Falcon*, for example, represent a fairly complete gamut of reviewing styles. There is the straight plot summary (*London Times Literary Supplement*, August 14, 1930, p. 654) which not only fails to evaluate the work, but — in this instance — even incorrectly summarizes the action. There is the short evaluative paragraph (*New York Times Book Review*, February 23, 1930, p. 28) which completely omits a summary of the plot and so inadequately defines its terms as to leave one unsure whether the book is considered good or bad. There is the more completely defined statement of values (*Outlook* 154:350, February 26, 1930) which, although short, gives one a sense of the reviewer's point of view. There is the longer critical analysis (*New Republic* 62:266, August 9, 1930) which relates the book to a clearly defined critical theory and tries to evaluate its place in the development of the genre. There is the full-scale analysis of the proper subject matter of the hard-boiled mystery story and Hammett's place in the tradition (Raymond Chandler, "The Simple Art of Murder" in Howard Haycraft, *The Art of the Mystery Story* [New York: Simon & Schuster, 1946, p. 222-37]). And finally there is a kind of "Poetics" of the detective story (W. H. Auden, "The Guilty Vicarage; Notes on the Detective Story, by an Addict," *Harper's Magazine* 196:406-12, May 1948), which places the particular genre in the hierarchy of literary art. This demonstration that popular culture

---

[14] Benjamin Britten, *The Turn of the Screw*. Op. 54. An opera in a prologue and two acts. Libretto after the story by Henry James, by Myfanwy Piper. Vocal Score by Imogene Holst. (London, Hawkes, 1955.)

is amenable to as serious study as is the culture of the elite may
help to counteract the tendency to literary snobbishness that is
sometimes inculcated by the special limitations of college literature courses. As in the critical analysis of more serious works,
the student will discover not only additional strengths in the novel,
but some surprising weaknesses in the reviews.

Reliance upon reviews can be justified only if the librarian is
very clear in his mind about two points: (1) the objectives of his
library which his book selection policy is designed to serve, and
(2) the standards upon which the reviewer bases his judgment. A
reviewer's condemnation of a book does not necessarily mean that
the book is unsuitable for the library; it may mean merely that the
reviewer has established certain standards for a literary work
which are not pertinent for the library. Conversely, the very points
which call forth praise from certain reviewers might be the points
which would make the librarian doubtful about the book's suitability
for the audience which his library serves. Merely to count the
number of pluses or minuses listed in the *Book Review Digest*,
therefore, is not book selection at all.

In general, library books are chosen to serve one or more of
the objectives which have been enunciated in the A.L.A. standards:[15]

> To facilitate informal self-education of all people in the com-
>   munity.
> To enrich and further develop the subjects on which individuals
>   are undertaking formal education.
> To meet the informational needs of all.
> To support the educational, civic, and cultural activities of
>   groups and organizations.
> To encourage wholesome recreation and constructive use of
>   leisure time.

Books in the field of literature may serve all of these functions and
often may serve more than one for a single reader, or a different
set for different readers. One man's recreation is another man's
information; for an audience as heterogeneous as that served by
the average public library a very flexible definition of such terms
as "educational," "informational," "cultural" must be established
if the library is to accomplish the potentialities of its service. For
an audience like that served by a specialized research library, on

---

[15]American Library Association. Public Library Division. Coordinating Com-
mittee on Revision of Public Library Standards of the A.L.A. *Public Library
Service: A Guide to Evaluation with Minimum Standards*. (Chicago, American
Library Association, 1956), p. 4.

the other hand, much stricter definitions will probably be set up, with certain categories — recreation, for example — relegated to a position of secondary importance.

In the end the individual reader makes the final decision concerning the purpose which any given book will serve. Many volumes, chosen by the librarian because they will widen the aesthetic appreciation of their readers, are read by some purely for recreation and are considered by others too difficult to read at all. The librarian's task is to anticipate the many reactions which any work may stimulate, the varied levels on which it may appeal, and the potential audiences which it may reach, so that the objectives of the library may be efficiently attained.

Informational Materials

Almost any good book will provide information of a sort to some readers. There are those who read *Moby Dick* to learn about whaling in the nineteenth century or *War and Peace* to learn about Napoleon's Russian campaigns. For the purposes of this discussion, however, informational books will be considered those whose major purpose is the presentation of factual information undiluted by additional appeals. While books of criticism may be said to provide information about the works under consideration, their major purpose is to increase the reader's aesthetic appreciation of the subject works, not to provide him with objective facts.

In every subject field there exist certain forms of informational tools which constitute the core collection of reference materials. The particular needs of different subject fields will dictate specialized reference aids, but certain types are basic to all fields. These are, generally speaking: (1) bibliographies, (2) dictionaries, (3) encyclopedias and handbooks, (4) biographical dictionaries, (5) indexes and abstracting services, and (6) reference histories. In selecting information materials for a subject department, the librarian should be sure that he has a representative sampling of these reference tools.

The specialized bibliography of any subject field is basic to the reference and research collection. It constitutes in itself a guide to other reference materials and may be used as an aid to purchase. In addition, it is a guide to students and scholars who can use it not only to lead to works unavailable in their own libraries, but also to supplement the library's catalog with more detailed analyses of works held by the library. In many cases, it provides evaluative and descriptive notes not available in the card catalog, and it brings works together in groupings designed to fit specific purposes.

The field of literature abounds in bibliographical tools, from those which attempt to be general and universal in scope, to those which concentrate on the several editions of a single literary work. In the present chapter, only the more general bibliographical listings in the field are given. The student should be familiar with the titles in the bibliography, however, because they are basic to any reference collection whatever its specialized orientation, and because within the pages of those books and periodicals he will find a wealth of references to the more specialized and particular bibliographies.

For miscellaneous information about many different aspects of literature — fictional names, allusions, plots, definitions, and similar matters — the dictionaries, encyclopedias, and handbooks of the field provide the most readily accessible source. These tools are of great value for quick reference questions where short answers are sufficient, and are used mainly to identify specific references. They are also often useful for dictionary-type data outside the field of literature, since many social, economic, and political matters provide essential background to the student of literature and are therefore included in reference books in the literature field. Some of the most widely used of these tools are listed in the appendix, p. 268.

Biographical dictionaries provide a short-answer information tool in the field. This information is much in demand by students, club groups, and others interested in the creators of literary works, and a wide variety of special tools exists for providing information about authors of the past and present. Of these, the examples on p. 269 provide a good cross section.

While biographical dictionaries supply the most concise and easily arranged sources for information about writers, the student should remember that other works in the field of literature, and many reference aids outside the field of literature proper, may be used as sources of biographical information. Biographical data about literary men are available from many of the general as well as the specialized biographical dictionaries: such publications as *Who's Who* and *Who's Who in America* number authors among the biographees. Similarly, the general encyclopedias and dictionaries, and of course the encyclopedias and dictionaries of literature, also include a great deal of general information about literary figures. Finally, literary histories provide information of this type, and one of the features for which the librarian looks in evaluating a new literary history is the ease with which such information can be found in it.

As in all fields, indexes are important informational tools in the field of literature. For magazine materials, the *Readers'*

Guide is useful for general periodicals and the *International Index* for the more scholarly and learned journals. But other materials are also indexed in the field of literature. For analytics of parts of books the *Essay and General Literature Index* is indispensable. The field of literature is marked by a great number of books which consist of anthologies, miscellaneous articles, symposia, and similar collections in which each of the individual items may be as important as the over-all title under which they are collected. It is possible for the catalog department to analyze each of these parts for the card catalog, but such works as the *Essay Index* obviate the necessity of this tedious task. Many libraries therefore do not make analytics for books which are indexed in the *Essay Index* (a list of additional volumes to be indexed is noted monthly in the *Wilson Library Bulletin*), and unless the printed indexes are used many wanted items are lost to the patron even though they are available on the library's shelves in a book of collected pieces.

Literary histories fall on the borderline between books which are strictly factual in their approach and those which attempt to interpret and analyze the facts. The more interpretive the history — the more it attempts to clarify the historical context out of which different literary works have come rather than to present a straight chronological sequence — the more it falls into the field of criticism and serves the objective of aesthetic appreciation rather than that of information. While this distinction may seem like a quibble arising out of the arbitrary organization of this chapter rather than out of the realities of library practice, it serves a useful practical purpose. In selecting a history for the literature collection, the librarian should decide which of the two purposes is likely to be served by it, and he may well find that a literary history which fails to make certain factual data available is useless as an informational work (strictly defined) but of great value as an interpretive record. He thus may revise his approach to it and evaluate it in terms of the audience which would derive the greatest benefit from it. To demand of all historical treatments that they be of primary usefulness as factual accounts would be to lose from the library many of the more important works in the field.

For reference purposes, of course, any history may prove useful at some time or another. A reference book is one to which one *refers* for specific information, and more specifically, one in which the facts are arranged in a manner to make them easily accessible. Only a few literary histories can be considered reference tools in the strict sense although any literary history contains facts which may be needed for answers to reference questions. Typical reference histories are thought of in terms of detailed indexing, well arranged and complete bibliographies, and a scope broad

enough to cover long chronological periods and many different
writers and works. Of these, perhaps the most widely used in
reference departments both large and small are those listed on
p. 270. Other notable historical studies like Georg Brandes'
Main Currents in Nineteenth Century Literature, Vernon Louis
Parrington's *Main Currents in American Thought*, Van Wyck
Brooks's five-volume series, *Makers and Finders: A History of
the Writers in America, 1800-1915*, may prove useful also for certain quick facts, but fall more logically into the field of critical
evaluation.

The informational tools considered here are those which cover
the entire range of literary genres. But for each of the major types
of literary form, a similar set of special reference tools exists.
While it is not the intention of this chapter to explore the field of
reference works for all the detailed particulars with which they may
possibly deal, the major fields of poetry, fiction, and drama are so
broad in themselves as to require special consideration. Most
general literature collections will contain the special as well as
the general reference works herein noted, but specialization within
the major genres occurs frequently enough in the larger and special libraries to justify the subdivision.

Reference books in the field of poetry

The nature of the poetic form is such that certain special kinds
of reference tools are needed to assist the students, scholars, and
general readers of it. Because it abounds in small and isolated
pieces which are very difficult to locate, even when the author or
title is known, indexes that will locate individual works are of great
importance. The way in which people use and remember poetry
also shapes a special feature of poetry indexes: many readers are
unable to identify a poem by author or title but frequently know it
by its opening lines. Most poetry indexes, therefore, are arranged
not only by author and title, as are indexes in other fields, but by
first line as well. And because poetry — and more frequently, poesy — is popular for use in speeches, recitations, and special programs, many patrons approach poetry in terms of the subject with
which it deals. All of the indexes listed on p. 271 provide subject
keys to the poems analyzed.

In addition, guides to quotations are an important aid for such
purposes. Quotation anthologies are not limited to quotations from
poetry, but it seems useful to list such volumes in connection with
the indexes to poetic readings and recitations to which they are so
closely allied.

Handbooks and manuals in the field of poetry are of the

how-to-do-it type and are not quick-reference tools in the sense in
which we have used the term. Any collection of books on poetry
should contain discussions of versification and of comparative verse
forms, and similar analyses of the genre which hover on the borderline between the informational, the critical, and the aesthetic.
Of the practical tools of reference in this field, the most obvious
is the dictionary of rhymes, to which the patron does refer in the
quick-reference sense. While most dictionaries — even the abridged
and collegiate dictionaries — contain a vocabulary of rhymes, the
reference collection should have at least one or two of the more
complete rhyming dictionaries which are devoted to a greater
variety of corresponding sounds.

Finally, because of the nature of poetry, a widely ranging anthology of shorter pieces constitutes in itself a reference aid of
some importance. One of the most frequent reference questions in
both general and specialized libraries is that which seeks the exact
wording of a famous phrase, a quotation, or a complete poem. For
this purpose, a good anthology is often a valuable and easily used
source of information, and although it does not fall into the category
of "factual information" which we have set up for reference tools
generally, it supplies the "facts" of precise wording in an easily
used form. Most reference desks find it useful to have at least one
or two outstanding collections of poetry constantly at hand, of which
the list on p. 271 provides a representative but far from exhaustive
selection.

Anthologies, which make available the content of several volumes for the price of a single one, are often used to build up the
poetry collections of the smaller libraries. A few well-chosen
collection volumes often cover a much wider range of materials
than the librarian could afford to represent on his shelves in any
other way. In addition, many librarians are glad to shift the burden
of selection to the anthologist and to assume that such collections
represent the works most worthy of preservation. But such collections, while they serve a useful function in many ways, have certain
weaknesses from the standpoint of the library which should be recognized. First, since so great a number of miscellaneous poetic
works are kept within the covers of a single book, the circulation
of the book to one borrower deprives a number of readers of access
to wanted poems. Secondly, in order to provide the wide coverage
and comparative inexpensiveness which is their special asset, anthologies are often printed in heavy volumes, on thin paper, in
double columns, and in fine print which makes them difficult to use
and more quickly subject to deterioration and wear. Thirdly, there
is a tendency for the several anthologies to repeat each other and
to reprint the same selections in volume after volume so that the

actual range of individual works covered by a collection of anthologies is less than would at first appear. And finally, a much more
complete selection of the poems of the major poets is desirable in
even the smaller libraries, so that the anthology does not completely satisfy the readers' needs, while multiplying the number of
copies of certain "favorite" selections. The anthology serves best
as a tool of ready reference which keeps a great variety of small
pieces together in a single place; it is least useful when it is used
as a substitute for a carefully chosen collection of individual works
for the readers of poetry.

Reference books in the field of fiction

In the field of fiction, short stories are comparable to poetry
in that they too are often lost in collection volumes. Similar indexes have to be supplied in order to locate the isolated smaller
pieces of fiction which the card catalog generally does not analyze.
The Short Story Index compiled by Dorothy E. Cook and Isabel S.
Monro, 1953, locates most of the better known stories in the most
widely held collections. For children's collections, and for the
student of folklore, the *Index to Fairy Tales, Myths and Legends*
by Mary Huse Eastman (2d ed., rev. and enl., 1926) and *Supplements*
(1937 and 1952) are also useful.

Indexes to novels, on the other hand, answer an entirely different purpose. The *location* of the novel is handled through bibliographies and finding lists, which are indexes of a special kind.
But the need for a guide to subject content is not sufficiently answered by the general bibliographies. In readers' advisory work,
for example, there is a great demand for a guide to novels about a
particular period, locale, event, or on a particular theme. The
librarian working with high school and college students will need
to supply historical novels to supplement the nonfiction reading in
history classes, novels about vocations to stimulate student interest, and fiction of many kinds to arouse student interest in subjects
quite unrelated to literature. To serve these needs, a group of
indexes to fiction have come into being, of which the most widely
used are listed on p. 273. For recent works, it should be remembered that the *Book Review Digest* provides a subject matter index
to the fiction reviewed in its pages.

Such indexes are, of course, essentially selective bibliographies of a special kind. The normal pattern of selective bibliography in the field of fiction is one which is selective in a "qualitative"
sense, attempting to list the "best" books in terms of evaluative
criteria outside the subject matter of the novel. These guides are
represented also in the list on p. 273.

Finally, a special handbook much in demand in connection with the study of fiction is one giving an outline of the plot of famous novels and stories. The most widely known of these aids are listed on p. 273.

Reference books in the field of drama

Dramatic works raise special problems in addition to the characteristic ones noted for fiction and poetry. Shorter plays are difficult to find just as short stories and poems are and special "analytical" indexes are needed to aid in their location. In addition, amateur play groups often wish to know specific production facts about plays: how many scene changes are required, how many characters of each sex, what is the playing time, etc. Therefore play indexes often supply such information in addition to the usual author, title, and subject data, and the librarian should be aware of which indexes supply which kinds of information. (See p. 274.)

A special periodical index — *Dramatic Index* — appears in the quarterly numbers of the *Bulletin of Bibliography*.[16] It analyzes materials about the drama and the theatre and is particularly useful as a guide to critical notices about current plays. For many libraries, however, the *Readers' Guide* is a sufficiently complete index for reviews of the popular theatre, while *International Index* covers the scholarly approach to the drama as literature. No special drama collection would be complete without all three.

Because the theatre is so essential a part of the field of the drama, many of the reference tools of drama depart from the usual literary pattern of the tools devoted to the other genres. Biographical dictionaries, for example, place as much emphasis (if not more) upon stage people as upon playwrights. Similarly, handbooks and yearbooks of the drama are generally more closely related to the theatre than to the bookshelf, although they are used by students of the literary play texts as well as by followers of stage productions. Such reference books as Burns Mantle's *Best Plays ... and Yearbook of the Drama in America* (1899 to date), George Jean Nathan's *Theatre Book of the Year* (1942/43 to 1951), and Bernard Sobel's *Theatre Handbook and Digest of Plays* (3d ed. 1948) are essential in drama and theatre collections, whether their emphasis be on dramatic literature or on show business.

Research Materials

Not all literary scholarship requires formal research. Perhaps

---

[16] Annual cumulations of *Dramatic Index* were also issued separately, and as part II of the *Annual Magazine Subject Index* from 1909-1949.

the most important aspect of literary scholarship — the creation of original works of literary art — seldom involves the scholarly collection of data, and when it does, its research need not be limited to the fields of literature or even to that of the humanities. The librarian of a literature collection cannot, except in the provision of other works of art or of technical how-to-do-it manuals, attempt to foresee the kinds of materials for which the creative literary artist will be seeking.

Formal research is pursued mainly in three major areas of literary study: in the writing of literary history, in the study of linguistics, and in the critical analysis, interpretation, and assembling of the original works of literature. And even in these areas there has been much important writing which has depended upon *a priori* reasoning, individual insights, and subjective reaction rather than upon objective and controlled investigation of verifiable data. In the nineteenth century, however, because of the success of certain research methods employed by the physical and biological scientists, the students of literature began to try to transfer the methods and concepts of natural science to their own discipline. The scientific school represents not only an acceptance of the methods of the laboratory, but by and large a rejection of the schools of aestheticism and historicism. To replace the intangible and amorphous subjectivity which could define poetry as "the thrill down our spine," the scientific school determined systematically to organize a body of knowledge, objectively established, using the methods of the sciences as models.

Science-inspired scholarship has produced some outstanding achievements: in the establishment of a "science" of linguistics; in the making of trustworthy texts, bibliographies, and variorum editions; in the fully documented historical studies which have increased our knowledge of the chronology and authenticity of many literary works; and even in the writing of imaginative literature itself, where the naturalistic writers attempted to employ the same kind of objectivity and impersonality which marks the scientific study. Nevertheless the so-called scientific method has been condemned by many literary scholars for its unimaginative grubbing among small details, its confusion of means with ends, and its narrow concern with the letter rather than the spirit of literary art. Although the emphasis in the following pages may be placed upon the scientifically-oriented research of the last century, it should be remembered that such research is not the only kind which literary scholars accept and that — indeed — it is completely rejected by many.

In the pages that follow, the kinds of research attempted in each of the areas — literary history, linguistics, and textual analysis

— will be outlined, and the kinds of library materials which each requires will be suggested. If this chapter, directed as it is toward practical preparation for librarianship, stresses the scientific researches, it is because the librarian can reasonably be expected to prepare for the needs of the scholar who wishes to compare two early editions of an Elizabethan play, but can hardly build the kind of collection which will surely aid the recorder of the "soul's adventures among masterpieces."

Literary history

The research methods employed by the literary historian are essentially the same as those used by any writer of history. He begins with the accumulation and collection of documents, and his concern — usually — is to establish a chronological scheme in which they can be placed. He collects, arranges, and sifts the facts, insofar as they can be determined, in order to arrive at a system of organized knowledge.

The earliest historical studies in the field of literature were of the type which has been condemned as "antiquarianism": a devotion to the past because it is the past, and the indiscriminate collection of unrelated facts which might someday be organized into some kind of unified scholarship. This method tends to ignore the present as unworthy of study and to become involved in the minutest details of parallel hunting, source digging, and the like. In the nineteenth century, this "historicism" led to a revolt which turned in the two directions we have already noted. One, the direction of aestheticism, put its entire stress on the individual experience of the work of art, rejected the "facts" and documentation, and led to no new body of knowledge. The other, scientism, attempted to transfer the methods of the natural sciences to literary study in order to act as a corrective of mere subjectivism. But by the beginning of the twentieth century, a partial swing back began in literary study. A respect for fact had now been firmly established in literary scholarship, but there was an increasing recognition that historical methodology may have as much validity as that of the natural sciences for reaching a system of organized knowledge and that routine application of techniques without insights contributes little to the understanding of literature. Today, literary scholarship employs a variety of methods, attempting to utilize whichever seems most suitable to the particular problem at hand. There are still those who insist that only deductive reasoning — or only inductive reasoning — or only the rejection of reason — can lead to an understanding of literary history, but no one school of thought can be said to have exclusive control in this field.

The historians of the nineteenth century borrowed from the
scientists not only their techniques but also their way of looking at
their subject matter. Adopting the analogy of the theory of evolution, for example, the literary historian attempted to see in the
history of literary forms a sequential process like that governing
organic complexes, which undergo "successive phases of germina-
tion, expansion, efflorescence and decay which are independent of
the volition of the men who effected them."[17] The development of
literary forms was seen as an example of the same doctrine of
mutations as is demonstrated in botany, and a formal classification
based on the Darwinian theory was applied to the phenomena of
literature. For these scholars, the materials of science are almost
as important as the materials of literature, and discussions of
methodology and theory are more important than biographical materials concerning literary writers. If literary phenomena are
essentially like natural phenomena, then the laws that govern them
are independent of the individual artists who happen to have brought
them into being.

If one believes that literary forms are developed in a sequential
process necessitated by conditions to which the creative artists
themselves are subordinated, then it becomes necessary for him
to study those conditions. Literary study under such circumstances
requires a knowledge of the "beliefs, institutions, conditions of life,
intellectual inheritance and all that is most truly the outgrowth of
the period to which the work belongs."[18] The novel, for example,
is seen as a reflection of the "spirit of the age," and an understanding of it must therefore be based upon a complete re-creation of
that age in all of its aspects, nonliterary as well as literary. Obviously the materials which will satisfy the needs of scholars of
the *Geistesgeschichte* school cannot be found in a literature collection alone; the complete coverage of political, economic, and social
history must be sought through many collections. But such a
scholar will expect to find some of the basic texts in each field; he
will certainly expect to find those works which attempt to relate
literature to its historical setting, or to illuminate political history
through reference to literary works which reflect or comment on
it, and he will want, especially, the printed guides and bibliographical assistance which will lead him to the needed materials in other
subject fields that are housed elsewhere.

Another type of historical study is the biographical, in which

---

[17] J. A. Symonds, "On the Application of Evolutionary Principles to Art and Literature," p. 39-40, in his *Essays Speculative and Suggestive*. New ed. (London,
Chapman and Hall, 1893).
[18] Greenlaw, *op. cit.*, p. 122-23.

literature is regarded as the product of the individual artist. Taine
was an important influence in promoting the use of literary works
as "documents" by means of which the scholar could reconstruct
the mental structure of the author, but Taine soon rejected the pri-
macy of individual genius and placed his emphasis on race, milieu,
and moment as the factors which shape the artist. It is Sainte-
Beuve who stands out most prominently in the development of the
biographical approach to literary history and criticism, calling for
a study of each author, each "talent," in order to make possible a
proper classification of him in the hierarchy of art. When literary
history is considered the story of the individual writers, the demand
will be for the kinds of documents that illuminate the writers' lives
and times. Marriage and birth registers are examined; diaries,
journals, letters, and notes are carefully studied; even laundry
slips, bills, and receipts are combed for clues about the artist. A
research collection which attempts to assist in these studies must
assume many of the characteristics of the museum, gathering up
not only worksheets and notebooks, but nonliterary memorabilia as
well. The efficient selection of such materials is a difficult problem since anything remotely connected with the writer may provide
a fruitful fact to the astute scholar, yet indiscriminate accumulation
of nonliterary artifacts can crowd out more pertinent materials
which properly belong in a library.

A special aspect of the biographical approach to literature is
that of the psychoanalytical school. Actually the psychoanalytical
study of literature dates from Aristotle, but it is not until this
century that organized data were available to the scholar. With the
publication of Freud's *The Interpretation of Dreams* in 1900, a
method was opened to the literary scholar for finding in the work
of the artist clues to his neuroses and psychoses. Freud himself
demonstrated the application of his discipline to the analysis of the
arts in his studies of Da Vinci and Dostoyevski, and a vast literature now exists in which both literary scholars and psychoanalysts
have used literature as the disguised fulfillment of repressed
wishes amenable to the same kind of analysis as that applied to
dreams. To serve the needs of these scholars, the writings of
many an M.D. are as important as those of a Lit.D., and a representative collection of the works of Freud, Jung, Adler, and other
psychologists, psychoanalysts, and psychiatrists is basic.

The literary historian may also direct his attention not to the
period and not to the man, but to the literary text itself. To many
students of literature, this would appear to be the only proper object of literary study. We shall deal more fully with this aspect of
literary scholarship below under the head, "Textual Analysis,"
but it should be noted here that the assembling and preparation of

a literary text calls upon all of the historian's skills as well as those of the critic. Questions of chronology and authenticity often rely upon a knowledge of printing procedures, proofreading practices, and methods of dramatic presentation in a given period. Questions of collaboration, revision, provenience, and interpretation many times require a profound knowledge of the writer under investigation and of the psychology of artistic creation. A knowledge of paleography is essential to establish linguistic correctness and approximate date, and in some cases, a study of handwriting in a particular period will help to interpret authentic readings. A wealth of philological and historical materials is needed, with special emphasis upon primary documents and the tools of descriptive bibliography (the art of examining, collating, and describing the actual make-up on a book).

Philology and linguistics

Since language is the medium of literature, the study of language is an important and logical approach to literature. A good knowledge of the history of a language as a whole is necessary for the adequate interpretation of any considerable portion or period of its imaginative writing. The study of the texture of a work of art — its diction, meter, style, euphony — is almost impossible without linguistics. Although the Dewey Decimal system places linguistics in a section separate from literary works, most scholarly and research library collections in this field are composed of a combination of both.

The word "philology" comes from the Greek, *logos*, meaning "the word." Broadly speaking, it is that branch of knowledge which deals with human speech and with all that speech discloses as to the nature and history of man. This area of study breaks into two divisions: that which deals with what is said (literary study) and that which deals with the instrumentality of its expression (linguistic study). The earliest scholarly work in this field lay in the area of literary philology. Language was considered a suitable subject for research only because it was an aid to the reading of literature; it was not considered a proper subject matter in itself. Therefore, no language was considered worthy of study which was not important for literary reasons, and the emphasis was placed upon Latin, Greek, and Hebrew since the main body of secular and sacred literature was written in those tongues. When, in the analysis of texts, attention was drawn to the importance of comparative philology, languages which were not prominent for literary achievement also became a part of the scholars' concern, and the way was opened for the scientific investigation of languages as such. In the nineteenth century this scientific study of language — linguistics — took its place beside philology as a scholarly discipline, and although European usage still retains the distinction between the humanistic connotations of philology and the scientific orientation of linguistics, the terms are virtually interchangeable in America.

Linguistic science is mainly concerned with studying the workings of language as a symbolic system of communication. The language data that a linguist examines are sounds, forms, relational groups of these, and meaning; and his methods, like those of other scientists, are descriptive, historical, comparative. A series of special-interest areas within the field of language study have thus come into being. The descriptive and historical study of patterns of speech is called morphology; the study of the use or function of the forms of language is called syntax; research in the origins of words is called etymology; and the study of meaning and change of meaning has been designated semantics. Stylistics takes as its field the whole domain of language phenomena, sounds, syntax, and vocabulary, and parallels the literary study of style.

Nineteenth-century linguists, by and large, devoted their attention to "dead" languages and set up correspondences between them. The regular practice, which is not completely superseded today, was to explain later stages of a language in the light of earlier: French on the basis of Latin, modern English as derived from Old English, etc. The twentieth-century contribution to linguistic study has been mainly in the addition of a "synchronic" and structural orientation. The synchronic view, according to J. C. McGuillard, "leads to scientific description of languages as working systems in a particular time and place: Classical Greek in Athens in the age of Pericles, Old High German in the ninth century, American English in the twentieth, etc.... The synchronic linguist therefore applies the structural method of description and classification."[19]

The importance of linguistic study to the interpretation and analysis of literature should not be underestimated. While it is possible to study literary genres and forms which cut across all linguistic boundaries, a sure knowledge of the writer's language is essential in almost all intensive study of literary works. The latent suggestions and overtones which are inherent in the subtle associations of words can be caught only when the language is truly understood, and linguistic methods have established texts far more accurately in the past century than earlier scholars were able to do.

---

[19] J. C. McGuillard, "Language," p. 75-6, in *Literary Scholarship; Its Aims and Methods,* by Norman Foerster *et al.* (Chapel Hill, The Univ. of North Carolina Pr., 1941).

They have offered data on the drastic changes which have occurred
in the denotation and connotation of words and have made possible
the interpretation of earlier writings in the light of their time and
place. Allusions, proper phraseology, the real language of the poet
have been recovered by verifiable means, instead of by the haphazard guessing which marked the subjective studies. While linguistic study of literature is external rather than internal, it is one
of the most central approaches to the understanding and appreciation of literary art.

For the student of philology and linguistics, certain types of
aids are essential. Dictionaries are the most obvious language
tool, but they do not constitute as simple a category as may at first
appear. The lexicons which provide an alphabetical list of the
major words in a language with their current meanings are well
known and probably need not be listed here, although it should be
remembered that dictionaries covering non-Western and older
languages are as important as those devoted to the major modern
languages which are more widely used. Other types of dictionaries
which are less familiar are also of importance to the scholar in
the field of language. There are the dictionaries based on historical principles which trace the changes through time in meanings
and uses of words; there are the etymological dictionaries which
trace the origins of words; and there are the dictionaries of slang,
dialect, regional idioms, and other variations from the standard or
literary form of the language. Grammars, particularly those devoted to the comparative study of several languages, are invaluable
in philological study. Specialized periodicals are especially important in the field of linguistics because, just as in the natural and
physical science fields, recent investigations are first reported in
the learned journals. Literary texts in different languages are
needed for analysis and comparison, and the classics of philological
and linguistic study themselves, even though they are directed
solely to the study of language rather than of literature, should be
represented. A selective list of some of the core books and periodicals representing each of the classes named above is given at
the end of this chapter. The list is suggestive, but by no means
exhaustive.

Textual analysis

The critical analysis of literary texts employs many different
methods and serves many different ends. In some cases, the scholar's concern is to establish an authentic text — to recapture as
accurately as possible the exact wording as intended by the author.
In other cases, the purpose is to establish absolutely the authorship

of a work and to discover the extent to which a particular text or parts of a text are the sole work of the supposed author, the result of collaboration, the interpolation of later revisers, or the work of an entirely different writer or writers. Sometimes the scholar is called upon to determine the authenticity of a particular edition or printing and employs his literary techniques to uncover hoaxes or to corroborate claims of authenticity. A large part of critical analysis is undertaken on the assumption that the text is authentic and by the author who is claimed for it, and seeks to interpret and clarify the meaning and purpose intended by the original creator. Scholars employ documentary analysis also in order to describe accurately a particular edition or printing (descriptive bibliography); to bring together the extant literature of a writer, a period, or a subject (enumerative bibliography); or to analyze factors which characterize different kinds of literary style.

As has already been mentioned, the methods of the historian are frequently used to assist the interpreter and critic of literature. The problems of authenticity — is the text the work of the author, is the form of the text the one he intended, and was this edition actually printed at the time claimed — involve questions of chronology and evaluation similar to those raised by the historian in his evaluation of the authenticity of historical records. A knowledge of the time and place is often essential to such analysis, since the interpretation of both internal and external evidence may depend upon historical context. The methods of book production, the practices of the compositors, the manner of presenting plays, the eccentricities of handwriting in the Age of Elizabeth have provided keys to the texts of Shakespeare, for example, which have unlocked many secrets of chronology, authenticity, and authorship.[20] In addition, scientific tools and methods have contributed to the establishment of authentic texts and the discovery of hoaxes. One of the most fascinating chapters in literary scholarship is devoted to the research which led to the uncovering of the Thomas J. Wise forgeries — research which utilized not only the standard methods of literary examination but even required an analysis of the chemical make-up of the book paper used in different periods.[21] The scholar today relies as much upon physical evidence as upon literary criteria to solve his research problems in literature.

---

[20] See J. Dover Wilson, *The Manuscript of Shakespeare's Hamlet and the Problems of its Transmission; an Essay in Critical Bibliography* (N. Y., Macmillan, 1934); or W. W. Greg, *The Editorial Problem in Shakespeare; a Survey of the Foundations of the Text* (Oxford, The Clarendon Press, 1942).

[21] See John Carter and Graham Pollard, *An Enquiry into the Nature of Certain Nineteenth Century Pamphlets* (N. Y., Scribner, 1934); or Richard David Altlick, *The Scholar Adventurers* (N. Y., Macmillan, 1950).

To assist these scholars, the library must provide a strong collection of original documents and early editions, the standard guides to historical research, and a wide sampling of materials relating to printing, book production, and allied fields. Many specialized reference tools of analytical and descriptive bibliography exist to which the literary scholar should have access. Guides to watermarks, to printer's signs and colophons, and to type fonts, for example, are indispensable to anyone concerned with verification of editions. Histories of bookmaking and printing, glossaries of printers' terms, and catalogs of early editions and the output of early presses are also valuable. For manuscript materials and literary works written before the invention of printing, textbooks of paleography and guides to manuscripts will supplement the types of tools already mentioned.

To provide the basic collections needed for this kind of scholarly research, the librarian should himself be a bibliographer. Since he will be called upon to build up a collection of rare and early editions, it is necessary that he be able to judge authentic texts and important items himself. He must not only supply the tools of analytical bibliography but be able to apply its principles. Such ability can be acquired only through highly specialized training, and no attempt will be made here to do more than indicate that this special field of librarianship exists for those who are equipped to work in it.

In general, the kind of documentary analysis which attempts to explain the author's meaning or anatomize his style has tended to be subjective and to rely on insights and a familiarity with literature. The library's obligation to the critic has been mainly one of providing him with the great works of literature for his judgment and appraisal. But such intangibles as literary style and emotional effectiveness have been subjected to objective measurement also. Edith Rickert, Elsa Chapin, and Russell Thomas, for example, have utilized a graphic method of poetry analysis which attempts to objectify the causes of subjective pleasure by reducing poetic form to visible symbols representing sounds, silences, and rhythmic variations.[22] Josephine Miles has employed the statistical method — frequency count — to the analysis of poetic words;[23] Caroline Spurgeon has done the same in her study of types of imagery.[24]

---

[22] Edith Rickert, *New Methods for the Study of Literature* (Chicago, Univ. of Chicago Pr., 1927); Elsa Chapin and Russell Thomas, *A New Approach to Poetry* (Chicago, Univ. of Chicago Pr., 1929).

[23] Josephine Miles, *The Vocabulary of Poetry; Three Studies* (Berkeley, Univ. of California Pr., 1946).

[24] Caroline Spurgeon, *Shakespeare's Imagery and What It Tells Us* (N. Y., Macmillan, 1936).

Rejecting the impressionistic report of stylistic devices, these
critics have organized the devices into manipulable categories
through which it is possible to see precisely what elements receive
the most attention, which words occur most frequently and in what
contexts, and the number and proportions of different types of con-
structions and formulations that are used for particular effects.
Such studies do not require different services from the library
than are called for by the more traditional critics; they are mentioned here merely to note an interesting development in contemporary scholarship.

Related to the exegetical studies are those which attempt to
trace the origin of literary works and to discover the source materials which have contributed to the work as we now know it. The
study of provenience, as this search for sources is called, is concerned with borrowings, both conscious and unconscious, and often
shades into the kind of biographical and psychoanalytical studies
which are mentioned above. The scholar concerned with the problem of provenience will be interested in comparative texts and
literatures and will require a wide representation of the literature
and folklore of all countries. He will need to have access to the
kinds of materials which will reveal the reading done by the artist
under investigation, and he will lean heavily on the kinds of biographical data which also interest the historian: diaries, notebooks,
personal records, and documents of many kinds. Finally, he will
need to check not only the acknowledged masterpieces of literary
invention, but the second- and third-rate materials as well, for out
of unlikely sources the artist has often been able to recreate a true
work of art.[25]

The real aim of all such scholarship, whether it is devoted to
establishing a chronology of works, increasing our knowledge of
the relationship of languages, or determining the exact wording of
a particular poem or play, is to deepen our understanding and increase our enjoyment of the great works of literature. The history
of a period, to the literary historian, is of importance as it illumi-
nates the imaginative writing which arose out of it. The permuta-
tions in meaning that words undergo is pertinent to the philologist
because it clarifies literary texts which would otherwise be mis-
interpreted and misunderstood. The establishment of an authentic
text is important if we are truly to know what the author originally
intended. Although the scholars frequently lose themselves in the
intricacies of their methodological problems, the librarian seldom

---

[25] See, for example, John Livingston Lowes's fascinating study of Coleridge's
sources in *The Road to Xanadu, A Study in the Ways of the Imagination* (Boston
and New York, Houghton Mifflin, 1927).

can forget that the primary segment of the literature collection is the literature itself and that the research scholarship of literature, however important, has its major contribution to make in promoting the educational values, the aesthetic appreciation, or the pleasure which the reader derives from his reading of the primary works themselves.

Materials for Education, Aesthetic Appreciation, and Recreation

It is almost impossible, in the field of primary literature, to separate those works which are read for recreation from those which educate or from those which exert their primary appeal on the level of the aesthetic. The reader of the novel, the play, or the poem may consciously use the work to serve one of these purposes, but he usually will be deriving the other benefits from it unconsciously. Or he may use the same work for one reason at one time, and for another reason at another time. Seldom does a really great work of literary art possess one, and only one, of these appeals. For in great art the strength of its recreational or educative powers lies in the selection, ordering, arrangement, and design of the appropriate materials — in short, in its aesthetic qualities.

To learn from literature, to appreciate literary art, or to use literature as recreation, the reader should turn to the primary works themselves. The librarian, therefore, in choosing appropriate titles for his literature collection which will serve these three functions, will concentrate his major efforts on the selection of novels, poems, and plays. The secondary works which are purchased to answer these needs should be seen, always, as ancillary to the primary literature.

It is probably not necessary to repeat that literary criticism is important in assisting the reader to appreciate literary art and to learn from it. The critical and evaluative works are useful for drawing attention to the art of a poem, the construction of a play, or the theme of a novel. Historical studies and biographical works can place a work in its context and open new avenues to appreciation and understanding. But each work should be seen in relation to the primary works with which it deals and should be judged not only on its own literary quality and the depth of its insights, but also on its effectiveness in leading readers to the primary work itself. Such secondary materials should not be selected as substitutes for the primary works of art, but as introductions or supplements to them.

There are many primary works whose sole purpose is to provide relaxation and entertainment — recreation in the sense of play and diversion. These are the works which cause one of the serious problems in book selection, since in the strict sense they do not qualify as literature although they ape the forms of literature and are used by readers just as literary works are used. To many readers *Suds in Your Eye* and *Huckleberry Finn* are both "funny" books; that the latter might be something more than that is a claim which arouses either disbelief or indifference. Many a reader prefers the straight melodramatic sleuthing of Perry Mason to the ratiocinative and philosophical detective work of Faulkner's Gavin Stephens. Most readers of Western stories do not want the gunplay interrupted by moral dilemmas like those in *The Ox Bow Incident*. The question which the librarian must face is: If a work possesses little or no literary quality and adds little or nothing to the readers' knowledge or understanding, is it still a justifiable library purchase because it entertains? And if the answer to that question is "yes," is there anything that the library is justified in rejecting, if diversion is a sufficient criterion?

The aims and objectives of the individual library will help to set the limits upon purchase in the field of entertainment. If the librarian feels that he is obligated to select from the field of literature those examples which represent the highest achievement for each genre, he may feel that temporary excitement, consolation, or amusement are insufficient reasons for devoting a heavy expenditure of money, time, and space to many of the most popular novels, poems, and dramas of the day. If the librarian feels that his most important function is to meet the demands of his present public, he may find that popularity is the most important criterion for selection. If he finds, on the other hand, that the library's primary purpose is to provide for the scholars of the future, he may decide that only those books should be purchased which represent a lasting artistic value.

But here a new criterion enters. There are values besides the aesthetic to which the scholars of the future may direct their attention. The current sociological approach to literary scholarship has brought to our attention the importance of the literature of the "masses" as well as of the court, of the popular as well as of the critically acceptable. Students of the future may well wish to have access to the ephemeral entertainments of our day as well as to the more serious and permanent works, and the scholarly library may feel the obligation to collect materials which are, paradoxically, far below the critical standards set by a library that caters to a more general audience. But whether the librarian is selecting for the contemporary reader or the future scholar, one question calls for an answer: what exactly are the values which readers derive from the literature they read on whatever critical level it falls?

The values of recreational reading

Popular literature is frequently referred to as "escape," indicating one important function served by such reading. The librarian should not be troubled by the designation; he should recognize that the library's provision of "escape" may be a valuable social contribution. There are many kinds of escape, and some may be more defensible, in social terms, than are others. The *katharsis* of which Aristotle speaks is, in its way, an escape, since the spectator (or reader) finds emotional release through vicarious participation. But the object of this escape was to provide a temporary withdrawal from everyday problems for the purpose of gathering new strength to face them, while the reading of much of the contemporary escape literature reflects merely a refusal to face reality, a permanent withdrawal into a fantasy world where problems are automatically solved. If the reader of such literature accepts the stories as a substitute for reality, he may so completely lose contact with the world in which he lives as to become a completely ineffective member of society, if not actually a burden to it. Certainly the question may be raised whether the temporary emotional release obtained from popular literature will not, in the long run, have to be paid for by an intensified sense of frustration and by the reader's having been rendered still more incapable of realizing emotional experience outside the stories. [26]
Yet much escape reading is an attempt not so much to flee reality, as to find a pattern which will give meaning to the world. In these instances, the reader does not refuse to face his problems but seeks rather for some method for adjusting to them. This use of popular literature may be unconscious on the part of the reader, but the continued popularity of many "inspirational" and "religious" poems, novels, and plays would seem to indicate that "pattern-seeking" more than "escape" is the motivation of much popular reading.
In either case, the kind of escape or pattern with which the reader is presented becomes a matter of great importance. To what does the reader escape, more than the fact of escape itself, is the question which concerns us.
For many readers books provide information about the world, a broader outlook, new horizons, perception into other lives and problems, and a guide to conduct. In popular literature they find a reaffirmation of basic human values: the triumph of bravery, loyalty, love, heroism. Indeed, the poesy and fiction which are least acceptable on a critical level frequently appeal most firmly to these ideals. In such writers as Edgar Guest, Ella Wheeler

---

[26] Herta Herzog, "On Borrowed Experience," *Studies in Philosophy and Social Science* IX (April, 1941), p. 71-72.

Wilcox, Grace Livingston Hill, and others like them, the reader
finds the assurance that love rules triumphant, that life is eternal,
that a purpose and plan prevail. To the disappointed, the disillusioned, the bereaved, and the rejected, this consolation is neces-
ary if they are to be able to accept their troubles, and on this basis
the literature of critical status too often fails them.

> It is a sobering experience for any poet to read the last
> page of the Book Section of the Sunday Times where corres-
> pondents seek to identify poems which have meant much to them.
> He is forced to realize that it is not his work, not even the work
> of Dante or Shakespeare, that most people treasure as magic
> talismans in times of trouble, but grotesquely bad verses
> written by maiden ladies in local newspapers; that millions in
> their bereavements, heartbreaks, agonies, depressions, have
> been comforted and perhaps saved from despair by appalling
> trash while poetry stood helplessly and incompetently by.[27]

The librarian of a publicly supported institution finds it difficult
to defend an attitude of intellectual snobbery about popular literature.
It is difficult to answer the defenders of this "appalling trash" when
they point out that such works are clean and not profane; that they
show the "better side of life"; that they make one want to "live better"
that they show that faith and trust in the Lord never fail; and that they
defend the morals and virtues which are the basis of the Christian
ethic. It cannot be denied that for many readers such books register
common experience in common terms, impart emotional satisfaction,
provide consolation, hope, and assurance. Why should the librarian
wish to remove these works from his shelves and to replace them
with books which often are filled with profanity, despair, disillusion-
ment, and the deliberate depiction of depravity and ugliness?

The answer lies in the broader goal which the library has set
for itself — not merely entertainment but enrichment, not pure diversion but recreation in its nobler sense. If the librarian thinks
of recreational reading in these terms, much of the popular literature of the day must be discarded. While the moral virtues which
are extolled in popular literature are ethically acceptable, they are
standardized and stereotyped to such an extent as to lose all spon-
taneity. The ideas in the novels or poems are already fully established, quickly identified and easily followed, so that comprehension
is simplified. No effort is required on the part of the reader; he
can suspend all intellectual activity because no new ideas and no
challenges to his intellect are presented. One objection to popular

---

[27] W. H. Auden, in *Poets at Work;* Essays Based on the Modern Poetry Collection at the Lockwood Memorial Library, University of Buffalo (N. Y., Harcourt,
Brace, 1948).

literature, then, is that it usually fails to provide the intellectual stimulation which the library wishes to foster and which good recreational reading can provide.

Another objection growing out of the stereotypic content and style of much popular literature is that it stifles the development of discrimination and taste. The constant repetition of matter and manner leads to a standardization also of the taste of the reader and to its gradual eradication. In the mass entertainment field, whether it be in book, radio, television, or film, it is often claimed that the audience dictates content, but it is also true that the taste of the audience is, in great part, created by the content of the media to which it attends. The library, by providing a sufficient number of materials below a certain standard, is partially responsible for the continued popularity of these materials and for the unwillingness — and subsequent inability — of readers to progress to more challenging and more profound reading.

A third objection raised against popular literature is that it deliberately appeals to the wishful self. These books do not so much satisfy popular taste as they exploit it with their emotional appeal of wish fulfillment. They console and soothe because they flatter the reader and extend false hopes to him. They allow him to identify with the success of the protagonist and to substitute the prettily patterned world of the story for the harsher reality of life. In other words, they do not help the reader adjust to the world but rather render him less capable of adjustment. If part of the library's obligation is to contribute to the creation of stronger and better citizens of our society, it cannot knowingly misinform and delude its patrons.

A final social critique of popular fiction concerns its ideological effects. In the poesy and potboilers of wide popularity the general tone is one of uncritical acceptance of the status quo which diligently avoids any inquiry into causes and solutions. By consoling and soothing its readers, this literature blocks any kind of social change which would lead to improvement; the kind of adjustment it promotes is that which accepts and submits. Its failure to criticize social realities and the soporific effect it exerts upon social consciousness create smugness and self-satisfaction rather than humility, tolerance, wisdom, and magnanimity.

These, then, are some of the objections to the public library's provision of those books which have no other claim to shelf space than popularity. The objections do not apply to all popular literature, and the student should not automatically equate best sellers with poor literature. But if any literary work, popular or not, exhibits these weaknesses the librarian should consider carefully his responsibilities in making it available to the public.

In providing recreational reading the public librarian should clearly define the sense in which he is using the term "recreation." A useful exercise for the student is an examination of several popular rental romances in terms of the ideals they foster (both overtly and implicitly), the literary style they exhibit, the picture of the world they portray, and the extent to which they supply any food for subsequent thought or contemplation. The important part of such a study is that *several* books be examined, for it is the repetition of the pattern which constitutes the danger of the mass-produced stereotype.

On the other hand, the administrator of a research collection may find that the very weaknesses of popular literature make certain titles essential. The scholar of the future will want to know many things about the literature of the present: not only how good it was but how bad it was; not only what was critically accepted but what was popular and widely read; not only what present-day readers escaped from, but what they escaped to. For purposes of the study of our society, the poorer fiction may be as important as the best; for an insight into the thinking of the common man the poesy rather than the poetry of our time may be of value; for a picture of the audience and its tastes, not only the artistic triumph but the box-office success. The very books which are rejected for recreational reading by the public library may be purchased and preserved by the scholarly library for the use of students of both literature and society.

The Problems of Establishing Criteria

In setting up standards for the selection of materials in the several subject fields, librarians have placed heavy emphasis upon such criteria as objectivity, factual accuracy, and clarity of expression. The primary materials of literature, however, are works of art which can not always be subjected to these tests. Factual accuracy, for example, is quite irrelevant as a test of many of the greatest works of poetry; objectivity would be a source of weakness rather than of strength in many of the world's literary classics; and clarity of expression as a standard would rule out some of the more important experimental works of the past and present whose importance to the development of literature is profound. Although these characteristics may be found in literary works, their absence does not necessarily detract from their value as literature.

The field of poetry in its more restricted sense is a particularly difficult one in which to establish objective standards, for poetry moves on many levels simultaneously and aims — usually — at affecting the reader emotionally as well as intellectually. Since poetry uses language, and since language is a means for conveying ideas, it is often difficult to evaluate poetry without overevaluating the ideas it contains, but it is not alone the thing said but the way of saying it which is the essence of poetry. Poetry uses language in such a way that what is said will have a peculiarly poignant effect upon the reader; what is said and how it is said are both important in real poetry. The means are the art, however; the thing conveyed is not. We find that those periods — like the eighteenth century — which are noted for the ascendancy of reason are not the periods of great poetry, and that there are those who feel, with Coleridge, that poetry gives most pleasure when it is only generally and not perfectly understood. The ideas in a poem are indissolubly united with its sensations and emotions, the rhythms of its speech, and the texture of its language. A prose paraphrase of the literal meaning of a poem will not only not be poetry, in most cases, it will not even be very profound prose. Those whose reading is usually confined to prose works often find themselves unable to discover in poetry the appeal and power that are claimed for it.

The most frequently encountered difficulties in the evaluation of poetry have been listed by I. A. Richards as a result of his experiments with student appreciation of poetry.[28] Among them he finds that making out the plain prose sense is often a major problem. The language of poetry is highly concentrated and sown with allusions; it breaks out of the standard patterns of prose construction and ordinary speech; and it often requires abandoning preconceptions for its acceptance. The average reader — and the librarian charged with the selection of poetry will more often than not be just an average reader — finds himself insufficiently flexible to cooperate fully with the poet. Good poetry demands that the reader possess what Richards calls "sensuous apprehension" — the ability to perceive the form and movement of the poem. It requires the capacity to visualize imagery. It forces the reader to set aside his stock responses, his personal connotations ("mnemonic irrelevances"), his presuppositions and preconceptions about poetry and its function. Even more difficult for most readers, the good poem — for that matter, good literature in any genre — will probably challenge the reader's convictions and prior beliefs.

A set of rules for judging whether a poem is good or not (or in library terms, whether a poem should be purchased or not) is almost impossible to formulate. The poets have been of no help to us at all; they have given us such highly subjective and personalized criteria as those of Emily Dickinson's, "If I read a book and it

---

[28]Ivor A. Richards, *Practical Criticism; A Study of Literary Judgment* (London, Routledge and Kegan Paul, 1929).

makes my whole body so cold no fire can ever warm me, I know
that is poetry. If I feel physically as if the top of my head were
taken off, I know that is poetry. These are the only ways I know it.
Is there any other way?" The librarian can be forgiven for hoping
that there are other ways, but most of the criteria that have been
enunciated, even when they appear to be more concrete, are almost
equally intangible in practical application. John Ciardi has set up
a list of ways to read a poem[29] which seems a little less amorphous.
But even he is reduced to such admonitions as "Read for delight,
not sense." (Note, however, that Ciardi is emphasizing individual
enjoyment of the poem and not the broader objective of library
selection.)

In the end it would seem that the best way to recognize good
poetry is to *read* good poetry; to steep oneself in the works of art
until one becomes an expert on them. The more good poetry one
knows the more touchstones he will have for comparison and judgment and the more capable he will be of overcoming the average
reader's difficulties and blocks to appreciation. Subjective judgments will not be eliminated, but they will be based on standards
inductively established. To multiply the number of specific cases
from which the principles are derived is the best way to minimize
errors and false conclusions.

The selection of fiction poses similar problems, although the
reading of prose ordinarily does not tax the reader with so many
challenges to his normal reading patterns. But literature, whether
in verse or prose, is characterized by the interrelation of matter
and manner; the fitting together of structural elements and meanings to produce a sense of harmony and order. Rhythm, figurative
language, the sound values of words, and devices for capitalizing
upon the connotative power of words by placing them in precon-
ceived designs and relational patterns are not exclusively the
characteristics of poetry. The use of such devices in imaginative
prose, however, tends to be more incidental, and the reader of
fiction often finds other values equal to those of style in judging the
worth of a novel.

Some of these values become of major importance to the librarian, especially in his selection of contemporary novels. Very
frequently the "worthwhile" books of a particular year or even
decade are not expected to reach the highest rank of the great literature of all time. Their importance lies in their statement of an
idea which deserves a hearing, or a point of view which will be of
value to certain readers, or in their treatment of a controversial
issue which may help to clarify the several aspects of the point in

---

[29]John Ciardi, "What Does it Take to Enjoy a Poem?" *Saturday Review of
Literature* XXXII (Dec. 10, 1949), p. 7-8.

question. Such novels as *Gentlemen's Agreement*, for example, or Helen MacInnes' *Neither Five Nor Three*, or Merle Miller's *The Sure Thing*, have something to say about contemporary issues. Twenty-five years from now the problems with which they deal may be completely solved, and their commentaries upon them may be of little value, since they do not contribute anything new to the artistic development of the novel form. But for today's audiences they do have a value and the librarian should be cognizant of it.

There are also novels which have a contribution to make to factual knowledge, in their detailed description of certain places, ways of life, or historical periods. There are others which are important because they represent a particular school of writing or a particular philosophy, or because they are an essential step in the development of a particular writer. And there are still others which have historical importance in social history or in the history of the novel even though they no longer affect current audiences as they did the audiences of their time. *Uncle Tom's Cabin, The Jungle*, and *Sister Carrie* will probably always be a necessary part of an American literature collection even though they are susceptible to severe stylistic criticism and to the charge that they no longer are able to stir a later generation of readers.

Since such a variety of values exists in fiction, strict standards of selection may be imposed without destroying the breadth of the collection or reducing the size of the audience to which it will appeal. The librarian can require that each book of fiction purchased make some positive contribution to the enlightenment and broadening of its readers, knowing that these objectives may be met in so many different ways that no reader need be deprived of the kind of reading which interests him. Few novels — even among the greatest — will answer all needs of all readers. But each novel which is accorded room on the library's shelves should be defensible on at least one of the following characteristics:

1. Its literary style

2. The profundity of its thought, or its power to provoke thought in the reader

3. Its significance in social or literary history

4. Its provision of factual information in a context which sharpens its meaning or underlines its human significance

5. Its clarification of problems of the past or of the present (although not necessarily their solution)

6. The quality of its insights into human character

7. Its ability to recreate vividly a time, place, attitude, or way of life

The novels which have been hailed as "great" by critical consensus will be found to possess more of these qualities than lesser novels, but a work need not possess them all in order to make a positive contribution. Good detective stories, fast-moving Westerns, and entertaining love stories can all be justified in terms of the criteria listed above, and if the criteria are carefully applied the librarian need not be embarrassed by the examples of these popular forms which he provides. As a test of this claim, the student should attempt to apply these standards to a list of novels with which he is familiar and in which he includes some of the popular novels of the day whose permanent critical standing has not yet been established. He will find that careful adherence to the standards will not weaken his coverage of fiction types but will strengthen the positive contribution that the fiction collection can make to the community it serves.

The question of censorship

The application of the suggested standards does not solve all of the librarian's selection problems. Few would argue with the suggestion that if a book contains some of the characteristics listed above it may be purchased, and if it exhibits none of them it should be rejected. But the additional question must be faced: what is to be done with books which are not merely lacking many of the positive qualities but which actually exhibit negative ones? The problem is complicated by the fact that frequently such books also contain some positive qualities, and the librarian must decide whether the good that the book may do outweighs the harm that it may do.

The underlying assumption in this discussion is, of course, that books do have an effect upon the people who read them. Conclusive evidence is difficult to find, but certainly librarians and other educators operate on the principle that reading does have an effect and that through judicious selection the librarian can control the effect along desirable rather than undesirable lines. Certainly this is the philosophy also of all censors — official and unofficial — whose work would be completely pointless if reading made no difference. Until it can be decisively shown that reading does not have an effect, all who are interested in either the promotion or suppression of reading will feel justified in acting upon the assumption that it does.

The problem of censorship of most concern to the librarian is that represented by outside interference with the selection of books which the librarian feels deserve representation on the shelves. If books fail to meet the standards set by the library's policy, the librarian himself rejects them — and considers this to be selection rather than censorship.[30] If a book is suppressed by legally established authority, the librarian as librarian will naturally accept the decision of the court (or other official agency) and abide by its regulations, even if he personally does not agree with the judgment. But most censorship problems in the library arise out of the unofficial pressures which seek to control library policy in order to serve some individual or group purpose outside the library's established obligation to its public.

The problems of censorship have already been alluded to in other chapters. They deserve mention again in connection with literature because it is here — especially in the field of fiction — that censorship pressures have most frequently been exerted. The special power of fiction to convince and to move the emotions and the large size of its audience have always made its control seem particularly desirable to those who would protect readers from "dangerous" content. It has been censured, therefore, not only on grounds of obscenity and pornography but also for advocating ideas which are considered subversive or which attack established institutions and philosophies.

It would be easy if the librarian could dismiss the attacks of the censors as the vagaries of crackpots and frustrated reformers. Certainly a list of books banned in the past invariably includes some of the accepted classics of the present, and to point to the public outcry which greeted such works as *The Scarlet Letter*, *Leaves of Grass*, *Tom Sawyer*, *Huckleberry Finn*, *Sister Carrie*, *The Sun Also Rises*, *All Quiet on the Western Front*, *An American Tragedy*, and *The Grapes of Wrath* would seem to imply that all censorship is stupid and detrimental to the production of great literature.

Not all attempts to control literature are prompted by ignorance or self-interest. Many intelligent people are seriously concerned with the possible harmful effects of certain books upon those who are insufficiently mature to use them intelligently or who deliberately misuse them. Indeed, if we accept the premise that reading can affect readers at all, we must recognize that bad as well as good effects are possible. It is logical then to assume that a publicly supported institution should not promote the kind of literature which is harmful to the community which supports it. And since it is a publicly supported institution, the public's right to "call the tune" can be rationalized with some justice.

---

[30] For a more detailed discussion of this distinction see Lester Asheim, "Not Censorship But Selection," *Wilson Library Bulletin* XXVIII (September, 1953), p. 63-67.

Actually, the public's will is reflected in the very fact of its support for the library and in its willingness to employ a professional librarian whose competence is presumed to be greater in the bibliothecal field than that of a citizen trained in some other profession. The authority for professional decisions in individual instances is, in effect, delegated to the librarian when he is appointed to his position, and the question which he must face is whether he has the right to shirk this obligation. He is responsible to his entire community; when he submits to the pressure of a single individual or group he is abandoning that responsibility, even though he may justify himself on the grounds that he is moved by the pressure of public opinion. An opinion expressed publicly is not necessarily the opinion of the entire public. Nor can the librarian shift his responsibility to individual members of the community with the argument that they are more in touch with the will of the public than he. There is no particular reason to believe that the corner grocer or the local dentist is better equipped to interpret the needs and interests of the reading public than is the librarian, who is — after all — also a member of the community, and more directly charged with the responsibility for making such an interpretation.

This does not mean that the librarian should ignore the expressed interests and wishes of his public. He should listen to the criticisms and suggestions of his library's users, but he should also weigh the merits of their arguments in terms of the objectives of the library and the values of the individual work. So long as the librarian lays claim to professional status, he must meet the obligation of making professional decisions. If he relinquishes that responsibility, he reduces himself from professional status to that of a skilled worker.

Miscellaneous Materials

Outside of the extraordinary materials mentioned in connection with the research collection — incunabula, manuscript materials, holographs, and other historical and biographical sources — there are few selection problems arising out of special format in the field of literature. The social sciences rely heavily upon documents and pamphlet materials; the art collection must concern itself with the question of prints, reproductions, and mounted pictures; the music collection is concerned with sheet music, scores, and recordings. But selection for the literature collection, even in the larger libraries, may be generally limited to the consideration of the traditional book and journals.

Recordings

Recently, however, nonmusical recordings have begun to represent, both in quantity and quality, an important contribution to the literature collection. Educational recordings have long been available, and occasionally a commercial recording company has released an isolated speech or reading which would be of interest. But today entire plays, versions of books, and readings of poetry can easily be obtained by even the smallest library. If a literary work is worth purchasing for the book collection, it is reasonable to believe that its value would be much enhanced — particularly in the case of plays or poetry — if its oral performance were also made available.

Since many of the major manufacturers of records include nonmusical releases in their catalogs, it is comparatively simple for the librarian to keep in touch with currently available materials. The most complete and up-to-date source of listings is probably the *Schwann Long Playing Record Catalog* (Boston: W. Schwann) which, under the heading "Spoken," provides a monthly guide to nonmusical recordings. Occasional articles, with selected bibliographies, also appear in general periodicals (see, for example, the *Saturday Review of Literature,* May 20, 1950).

The question of handling recordings, both musical and nonmusical, has already been raised in the chapter on "Music" (see p. 185). At this point it is necessary only to stress again the importance of making available to the users of the literature collection the materials which are pertinent to them. Certainly the reader who borrows Eliot's *The Cocktail Party* or Jeffers' adaptation of *Medea* in book form should have the opportunity to know that a recorded reading of the play also exists. Similarly, students of certain poets would be much aided by having the opportunity to hear the poet's oral interpretation of his work. Yet many libraries which keep their recordings together in a single department by format rather than by subject fail to list such holdings in the appropriate subject catalogs. If catalog cards for such recordings are not interfiled with the book cards, the patron must know of their existence beforehand if he is to find them. One of the purposes of the card catalog is to inform the user of materials in his field whose existence he is not aware of; therefore, the reasons for including recordings in the general catalog hardly need further discussion. Available library facilities and other administrative considerations may dictate whether recordings will be housed by format rather than by subject field, but whatever the decision as to handling, related materials should be indexed in those catalogs to which their potential users have access.

"Acting" editions

Acting editions of plays are another special kind of material used in the drama collection. Here the existence of little theater and amateur acting groups within the community will indicate the extent of the need for such editions and selection should be guided by the suitability of the plays for local production facilities. The problem of handling these materials is not a complex one; the major point to be remembered is that their users generally wish to know more than author, title, and subject and that the catalog of acting editions will probably have to be set up so that data are supplied concerning the number of acts and scenes, the number of characters, the kinds of audiences for whom the plays are suited, and some clue as to the complexity of production (extraordinary props, make-up demands, etc.). When the patrons' interests lie in reading current writing for the theater rather than in presenting plays, the regular reading editions of plays are more suitable and require no special handling.

"Little" magazines

In the field of literature a special kind of periodical publication exists which is neither popular magazine nor learned journal. This is the so-called "little" magazine, usually dedicated to the new and experimental forms of literary composition and the unknown writers who have not yet earned recognition in the established media. They are often deliberately unconventional and usually elect to represent a point of view or a school of literary thought which has not yet received scholarly or popular sanction. Because they are in rebellion against tradition and because they deliberately seek innovation and experiment, their content is frequently unintelligible to the average reader, and the writing in them is often below standard. They have been accused of exhibitionism, pretentiousness, and indiscriminate advocacy of protest for protest's sake, and all of these accusations can be supported by evidence from one or another of the little magazines which have been published or are currently being published

Because of these weaknesses, selection of the little magazine is more difficult than is the selection of periodical materials of a more conventional kind. In addition, most of them are short-lived, frequently as a matter of policy (to avoid becoming "satisfied") but more often because of shortage of funds or a loss of interest either on the part of their limited publics or of the publisher himself. It has been estimated that over 600 little magazines were published between 1912 and 1946, of which very few are still in existence.[31]

On the other hand, these publications have an important part to play in the development of new writing. Many of our leading writers were first published in the experimental magazines — about 80 per cent of the most important post-1912 critics, novelists, poets, and storytellers having had their first hearing in their pages.[32] They are also the forum for much of the influential critical discussion which accompanies the rise and fall of schools of literary thought and expression. They serve a two-fold purpose in the library: (1) They make available contemporary material of importance which can not be found elsewhere; and (2) They provide an indispensable collection of research material for later historians, biographers, and critics.

The research libraries will certainly wish to have a representative collection of some of the earlier little magazines and will strive to anticipate the needs of future scholars in their selection from contemporary publications of this type. The general libraries will probably have to be more selective in building a little magazine collection because of their limited appeal and the self-consciously unconventional character of many of them.

As in the case of any periodical collection, the extent to which magazines are indexed is a partial guide to their probable usefulness. An *Index to Little Magazines*[33] began publication in 1949 (covering 1948 publications) and may serve as a guide to some of the leading examples of the genre. The list of little magazines in the collection in the New York Public Library, compiled by Carolyn F. Ulrich and Eugenia Patterson and published in the *Bulletin of the New York Public Library* (January 1947), is much lengthier and gives fuller bibliographical information. The student will be interested also in the book by Frederick Hoffman and others[34] which gives the history of the major little magazines as well as the bibliography on which the Ulrich and Patterson list is based.

Paper-bound books

The showcase for new and experimental writing, which the little magazines have long provided, is now being made available also through the medium of the paper-bound book. Several series

---

[31] Frederick J. Hoffman, Charles Allen, and Carolyn F. Ulrich, *The Little Magazine; A History and a Bibliography* (Princeton, Princeton Univ. Pr., 1946).

[32] Charles Allen, "The Advance Guard," *Sewanee Review* II (July/Sept. 1943), p. 425-9.

[33] *Index to Little Magazines*, 1948- (Denver, Alan Swallow, 1949-).

[34] Hoffman, *op. cit.*

of collections of new writing have appeared in the soft-cover format and should be given as serious consideration by the librarian of the literature collection as any hard-bound book of literary work.

Most of these series began in the early 1950's and include such titles as *New World Writing* (New American Library), *Discovery* (Pocket Books), and *New Campus Writing* (Bantam). These and other interesting anthologies are listed under "Collections and Anthologies" in *Paperbound Books in Print* (R. R. Bowker), the most recent number of which should be consulted by anyone desiring to utilize the best in soft-cover publications to supplement the hard-cover book collection.

The use of paper-bound books need not be limited to the literature department of the library. There are many excellent nonfiction titles in different fields which are available in this less expensive format. The special advantage of paper-bounds, however, is that they provide ephemeral titles at a low cost, so that duplication of titles which are not expected to be permanent additions to the collection may be accomplished without too great a strain on the budget. The disadvantage of the paper-bound book is that it will not stand much handling and will have to be discarded after several circulations without affording the chance to rebind. In the case of many current fiction titles for which there is a short-lived but heavy demand, this is actually an advantage, and the addition of paper-bound editions of mystery stories, love stories, and other escape titles would seem to be an inexpensive way to fill this kind of demand without an excessive financial loss.

In general, libraries have been slow to use these inexpensive reprints, even to provide duplicates of titles in heavy demand. In some cases, librarians are loath to put even ephemeral books in the collection without fully accessioning, classifying, and cataloging them — a process which increases the actual cost of each title to the point where the advantage of low initial price is lost. Others find it hard to discard library property as freely as economy suggests, even in the case of worn volumes of inexpensive reprints. Still others cannot adjust to the unfamiliar format of the paper-bounds. Yet in most cases where the use of these reprints has been tried, the fears of those who hesitate to try them have not been realized. Patrons seem not to dislike the format and in some cases, even prefer it. Technical processes can be reduced to a minimum in dealing with these volumes without hampering library service. And constant discarding of worn copies soon becomes a painless process when it is seen that new titles can be so readily added.[35]

---

[35] "Public Library Use of Paper-bound Books," *PLD Reporter* Number 1 (September, 1954); "Paperbacks in the Public Libraries - A New Set of Handling Problems," *Publishers' Weekly* v. 168 (December 17, 1955), p. 2432-4.

It is not suggested that all libraries should use the paper-bound reprints in their literature collections. There are many valid reasons why certain libraries would find them less a solution to a problem than an added problem in themselves. But the student should find it an interesting exercise in policy making to weigh the advantages and disadvantages of the paper-backed books for different library situations. He should not either reject or accept them automatically, but should study the uses to which they can be put, the real cost as against the apparent cost, the possible patron reactions to them, and the kinds of procedures that may have to be introduced to handle them. In the practical library situation it is just such problems that will face him; he will be a better librarian if he learns early to study all sides of each problem instead of approaching it with firmly established prejudices, guesswork, or too-easy enthusiasm.

CONCLUSION

In the preceding pages an attempt has been made to touch upon the variety of purposes served by literature and the many audiences to which it appeals. It is hoped that the student will recognize that the very richness of the field imposes an obligation upon the librarian to define his library's objectives carefully and to interpret, evaluate, and use literary materials in the light of those objectives. It is not accidental that no prescription for enunciating objectives has been laid down. It is the purpose of this book to illustrate that hard and fast rules cannot be applied where such a variety of purposes and people can be served. If its users approach their library problems with questions instead of with ready-made answers, that purpose will have been achieved.

REPRESENTATIVE REFERENCE TOOLS IN THE FIELD OF LITERATURE

General Language and Literature

Bibliographies

Blanck, Jacob Nathaniel, comp. *Bibliography of American Literature*; comp. for the Bibliographical Society of America. 1955-
Vol. 1. Henry Adams to Donn Byrne.
The Cambridge Bibliography of English Literature. Bateson, Frederick Wilse, ed. 4 vols. 1941. (Reissued 1947)
Cross, Tom Peete, comp. *Bibliographical Guide to English Studies.* 10th ed. 1951.

English Literature, 1660-1800; A Bibliography of Modern Studies,
     comp. for *Philological Quarterly* by Ronald S. Crane and others.
     2 vols.
          Vol. 1. 1926-1938. 1950.
          Vol. 2. 1939-1950. 1952.
Kennedy, Arthur G. *A Bibliography of Writings on the English
     Language from the Beginning of Printing to the End of 1922.*
     1927.
────── *A Concise Bibliography for Students of English, Systemati-
     cally Arranged.* 3d ed. 1954.
Leary, Lewis. *Articles on American Literature, 1900-1950.* 1954.
     (Cumulates, and is continued by, "Articles on American Liter-
     ature Appearing in Current Periodicals," in the quarterly
     issues of *American Literature* magazine, q.v.)
Literary History of the United States. Editors: Robert E. Spiller
     and others. 1948.
          Vol. 3. "Bibliography."
Modern Humanities Research Association. *Annual Bibliography of
     English Language and Literature....*   1920-
Modern Language Association of America. "American Bibliogra-
     phy" in *Publications (PMLA)*: March issues, 1922-1931; An-
     nual Supplement, 1931-1947; April issues, 1948-
Modern Philology. (May issues since 1933)
Northup, Clark S. *A Register of Bibliographies of the English
     Language and Literature.* 1925.
Pollard, Alfred W., and Redgrave, G. R., comps. *A Short-Title
     Catalogue of Books Printed in England, Scotland & Ireland ...
     1475-1640.* 1926. Most comprehensive record of English books
     for this period, giving location as well as full bibliographical
     information.
Wing, Donald Goddard, comp. *Short-Title Catalogue of Books
     Printed in England, Scotland, Ireland, Wales, and British
     America ... 1641-1700.* 3 vols. 1945-51.

     Encyclopedias and Handbooks

Benét, William Rose, ed. *The Reader's Encyclopedia.* 1948. (Re-
     printed, with supplement, 1955)
Brewer, Ebenezer C. *Dictionary of Phrase & Fable.* Rev. and enl.
     1952.
────── *Reader's Handbook of Famous Names in Fiction, Allusions,
     References, Proverbs, Plots, Stories, and Poems.* A new ed.,
     rev. 1935.
Cassell's Encyclopaedia of World Literature, ed. by S. H. Stein-
     berg. 2 vols. 1954.

Hart, James David. *The Oxford Companion to American Litera-
ture*. 3d ed., rev. and enl. 1956.
Harvey, Sir Paul, ed. *The Oxford Companion to Classical Litera-
ture*. 1937. (Frequently reprinted)
—— *The Oxford Companion to English Literature*. 3d ed. 1946.
Magnus, Laurie. *A Dictionary of European Literature, Designed
as a Companion to English Studies*. 2d impression rev. with
addenda. 1927.
Moulton, Charles W., ed. *The Library of Literary Criticism of
English and American Authors*. 8 vols. 1901-05. (Reprinted
1935)
The New Century Handbook of English Literature, ed. by Clarence
L. Barnhart. 1956.
Peck, Harry Thurston, ed. *Harper's Dictionary of Classical Lit-
erature and Antiquities*. 1897. (Frequently reprinted)
Shipley, Joseph Twadell, ed. *Dictionary of World Literature*:
Criticism, Forms, Technique. New rev. ed. 1953.
—— *Encyclopedia of Literature*. 2 vols. 1946.
Thompson, Stith. *Motif-Index of Folk-Literature*. Rev. and enl.
ed. 1955- Vol. 1. A-C.
Walsh, William Shepard. *Handy-Book of Literary Curiosities*.
1893. (Reprinted 1925)
The Warner Library. 30 vols. 1917. (Earlier editions published
under title: *Library of the World's Best Literature*)

Yearbooks

English Association, London. *The Year's Work in English Studies*.
1919/20-
Yearbook of Comparative and General Literature. 1952-

Indexes

Essay and General Literature Index, 1900-1933; 1934-40; 1941-47;
1948-54- (For materials before 1900, see American Library
Association. *An Index to General Literature*. 2d ed. 1901)
International Index to Periodicals. 1907-

Biographical Tools

Burke, William J., and Howe, Will David. *American Authors and
Books, 1640-1940*. 1943.
Grismer, Raymond Leonard. *A Reference Index to Twelve Thousand
Spanish American Authors*; A Guide to the Literature of Spanish
America. 1939.

Kunitz, Stanley J., and Haycraft, Howard, eds. *American Authors,
1600-1900*; A Biographical Dictionary of American Literature.
1938.
—— *British Authors before 1800*; A Biographical Dictionary. 1952.
—— *British Authors of the Nineteenth Century*. 1936. (4th
printing, 1955)
—— *The Junior Book of Authors*; [An Introduction to the Lives
of Writers and Illustrators for Younger Readers, from Lewis
Carroll and Louisa Alcott to the Present Day]. 2d ed. rev.
1951.
—— *Twentieth Century Authors*; A Biographical Dictionary of
Modern Literature. 1942. (Supersedes *Authors Today and
Yesterday* (1933) and *Living Authors* (1931) by the same editors)
—— —— First Supplement. 1955.
Millett, Fred Benjamin. *Contemporary American Authors*; A
Critical Survey and 219 Bio-Bibliographies. 1940.
Who's Who among North American Authors; Covering the United
States and Canada .... 1921-1939. (Issued irregularly)
Who's Who among Living Authors of Older Nations .... 1931-1932.
1931.
Similar tools exist in other languages, and in English for writers of
non-English-speaking countries. See "Literature and Language"
section of Winchell's *Guide to Reference Books.*
See also current issues of *Wilson Library Bulletin* for biographies
supplementing *Twentieth Century Authors.*

Reference Histories

The Cambridge History of American Literature, ed. by William P.
Trent, John Erskine, Stuart P. Sherman, Carl Van Doren. 4
vols. 1931.
—— —— 3 vols. in 1. 1933. (Reprinted 1945)
The Cambridge History of English Literature, ed. by A. W. Ward
and A. R. Waller. 14 vols. 1907-16; vol. 15, General Index,
1927. (Reprinted frequently)
The Oxford History of English Literature; ed. by F. P. Wilson and
Bonamy Dobrée. 1945-
Sampson, George. *The Concise Cambridge History of English Literature*. 1941. (Reprinted 1953)

General Historical Treatments

(While not strictly "reference" books in the narrow sense, such
notable historical-critical studies as the following should be
familiar):

Brandes, Georg M. C. *Main Currents in Nineteenth Century Literature*. 6 vols. 1901-05. (Reprinted 1923)

Literary History of the United States. Editors: Robert E. Spiller and others. 3 vols. 1948.

Macy, John A. *A Story of the World's Literature*. 1950.

Parrington, Vernon L. *Main Currents in American Thought*; An Interpretation of American Literature from the Beginnings to 1920. 3 vols. 1927-30. (3 vols. in 1, 1930; reprinted 1939)

Saintsbury, George E. B. *A History of English Prosody from the Twelfth Century to the Present Day*. 3 vols. 1906-10. (Reprinted 1924)

Taine, Hippolyte A. *History of English Literature*. 2 vols. 1871. (Frequently reissued)

Poetry

Reference Books

Brewton, John Edmund, and Brewton, Sara Westbrook. *Index to Children's Poetry*. 1942. (Reprinted 1951)
—— —— 1st Supplement. 1954.

Bruncken, Herbert, ed. *Subject Index to Poetry*; A Guide for Adult Readers. 1940.

Granger, Edith. *Index to Poetry*. 4th ed. 1953.

MacPherson, Maud Russell. *Children's Poetry Index*. 1938.

Walker, John. *The Rhyming Dictionary of the English Language in Which the Whole Language is Arranged According to Its Terminations*; With an Index of Allowable Rhymes. Rev. and enl. by Lawrence H. Dawson. 1948.

Collections (Examples)

The Oxford Book of American Verse, chosen and with an introduction by F. O. Matthiessen. 1950.

The Oxford Book of English Verse, 1250-1918, chosen and edited by Sir Arthur Quiller-Couch. New ed. 1939.

Palgrave, Francis Turner. *The Golden Treasury*; Selected from the Best Songs and Lyrical Poems in the English Language. (Many editions available. Later editions usually include additional poems to bring collection up to date.)

Stevenson, Burton Egbert, comp. *The Home Book of Modern Verse* ... Being a Selection from American and English Poetry of the Twentieth Century. 2d ed. 1953.

—— *The Home Book of Verse, American and English*. 9th ed. 2 vols. 1953.

———— *The Home Book of Verse for Young Folks.* Rev. and enl.
ed. 1929.
Untermeyer, Louis, ed. *A Treasury of Great Poems, English and
American*; From the Foundations of the English Spirit to the
Outstanding Poetry of Our Own Time, with Lives of the Poets
and Hist. Settings Sel. and Integrated. Rev. and enl. 1955.
See also *Bookman's Manual*, 7th ed., 1954, p. 144-170.

Quotations

Bartlett, John, comp. *Familiar Quotations....* 13th and centennial
ed., completely rev. 1955.
Champion, Selwyn Gurney, comp. *Racial Proverbs*; A Selection of
the World's Proverbs Arranged Linguistically. 2d ed. 1950.
Hoyt, Jehiel Keller. *New Cyclopedia of Practical Quotations Drawn
from the Speech and Literature of All Nations*; Ancient and
Modern, Classic and Popular, in English and Foreign Text.
Comp. by Kate Louise Roberts. New 1947 ed. 1947.
Mencken, Henry Louis, ed. *A New Dictionary of Quotations on
Historical Principles from Ancient and Modern Sources.* 1942.
The Oxford Dictionary of Quotations. 2d ed. 1953.
Smith, William George. *The Oxford Dictionary of English Proverbs.*
2d ed. rev. by Sir Paul Harvey. 1948.
Stevenson, Burton Egbert, ed. *The Home Book of Proverbs, Maxims
and Familiar Phrases.* 1948.
———— *The Home Book of Quotations, Classical and Modern.* 8th
ed. 1956.
———— *The Standard Book of Shakespeare Quotations.* 1953.

Speeches and Recitations

Edgerton, Alice (Craig). *More Speeches and Stories for Every
Occasion.* 1936.
———— *A Speech for Every Occasion, New Speeches.* 1931. (Latest
edition, 1949)
Fanning, Clara Elizabeth, and Wilson, Halsey William, comps.
Toaster's Handbook; Jokes, Stories, and Quotations, comp. by
Peggy Edmund [pseud.] and Harold Workman Williams [pseud.].
3rd rev. ed. 1916.
Silk, Agnes K., and Fanning, Clara Elizabeth, comps. *Index to
Dramatic Readings.* 1925.
Sutton, Roberta (Briggs). *Speech Index*; An Index of 64 Collections
of World Famous Orations and Speeches for Various Occasions.
1935.

Fiction

Bibliographies and Subject Guides

Baker, Ernest Albert. *A Guide to Historical Fiction*. 1914. (New
edition planned)
Baker, Ernest Albert, and Packman, James. *A Guide to the Best
Fiction*; English and American, Including Translations from
Foreign Languages. New and enl. ed. 1932.
Coan, Otis W., and Lillard, Richard G., eds. and comps. *America
in Fiction*. 4th ed. 1956.
Dickinson, Asa Don. *The World's Best Books, Homer to Heming-
way*. 1953.
Fiction Catalog; A Subject, Author and Title List of ... Works of
Fiction in the English Language with Annotations. 1908 to date
through cumulations and supplements. Wilson.
Kerr, Elizabeth Margaret. *Bibliography of the Sequence Novel*.
1950.
Lenrow, Elbert. *Reader's Guide to Prose Fiction*; An Introductory
Essay, with Bibliographies of 1500 Novels .... 1940.
Logasa, Hannah, comp. *Historical Fiction and Other Reading Ref-
erences for Classes in Junior and Senior High Schools*. 5th
rev. and enl. ed. 1951.
Mish, Charles Carroll. *English Prose Fiction, 1600-1700*. 3 vols.
1952.
Nield, Jonathan. *A Guide to the Best Historical Novels and Tales*.
5th ed. 1929.
O'Dell, Sterg. *Chronological List of Prose Fiction in English
Printed in England and Other Countries, 1475-1640*. 1954.
Wright, Lyle Henry. *American Fiction, 1774-1850*. Rev. ed. 1948.

Handbooks

Haydn, Hiram C., and Fuller, Edmund, eds. *Thesaurus of Book
Digests*; Digests of the World's Permanent Writings from
Ancient Classics to Current Literature. 1949.
Keller, Helen R. *The Reader's Digest of Books*. New and greatly
enl. ed. 1929. (Frequently reprinted)
Magill, Frank N. *Masterplots*; Plots in Story Form from the
World's Fine Literature. 4 vols. 1949-1953. (First two vol-
umes also issued in 1952 in one vol. under title: *Masterpieces
of World Literature in Digest Form*. Issued in 10 vol. ed.,
1954)
Masterplots Annual Review. 1954-

Short Stories

Analytical Indexes

American Library Association. Editorial Committee. *Subject and Title Index to Short Stories for Children.* 1955.
Cook, Dorothy E., and Monro, Isabel S., comps. *Short Story Index.* 1953.
Cotton, Gerald Brooks, and Glencross, Alan, comps. *Fiction Index.* 1953.

Collections

The Best American Short Stories ... and the Yearbook of the American Short Story 1915-
The Best British Short Stories and the Yearbook of the British, Irish, and Colonial Short Story. 1922-40.
Prize Stories. The O. Henry Awards. 1919- (Formerly O. Henry Memorial Award Prize Stories)
See also the several anthologies by subjects, by types, region, etc., currently in print.

Drama

Bibliographies

Baker, Blanch. *Theatre and Allied Arts.* 1952.
Eldredge, H. J., comp. *"The Stage" Cyclopaedia*; A Bibliography of Plays. Comp. by Reginald Clarence [pseud.] . 1909.
Greg, Walter Wilson. *A List of English Plays Written before 1643 and Printed before 1700.* 1900.
—— *A List of Masques, Pageants, etc.* Supplementary to *A List of English Plays.* (See preceding entry.) 1902.
Hill, Frank Pierce, comp. *American Plays Printed, 1714-1830.* 1934.
New York. Public Library. *Foreign Plays in English.* 1920.
Roden, Robert F. *Later American Plays, 1831-1900.* 1900.
U. S. Copyright Office. *Dramatic Compositions ... 1870 to 1916.* 1918.

Analytical Indexes

American Library Association. Board on Library Service to Children and Young People. *Subject Index to Children's Plays.* 1940.

Firkins, Ina Ten Eyck, comp. *Index to Plays, 1800-1926*. 1927.
———— ———— Supplement. 1935.
Hyatt, Aeola L., comp. *Index to Children's Plays*. 3d ed., rev. and
enl. 1931.
Logasa, Hannah, and Ver Nooy, Winifred, comps. *An Index to One-
Act Plays*. 1924. (Contains plays published since 1900)
———— ———— Supplement, 1924-1931. 1932.
———— ———— Second Supplement, 1932-1940. 1941.
———— ———— Third Supplement, 1941-1948. 1950.
Ottemiller, John H. *Index to Plays in Collections*; An Author and
Title Index to Plays Appearing in Collections Published be-
tween 1900 and 1950. 2d ed., rev. and enl. 1951
Thomson, Ruth Gibbons. *Index to Full Length Plays, 1926 to 1944*.
1946.
West, Dorothy Herbert, and Peake, Dorothy Margaret. *Play Index,
1949-1952*. 1953.

Biographical Dictionaries

Fleay, Frederick Gard. *Biographical Chronicle of English Drama,
1559-1642*. 1891.
Matthews, Brander, and Hutton, Laurence. *Actors and Actresses
of Great Britain and the United States* .... 5 vols. 1886.
Nungezer, Edwin. *A Dictionary of Actors ... in England before
1642*. 1929.
Who's Who in the Theatre. 1912- (11th ed., 1952)

Yearbooks

The Best Plays and the Year Book of the Drama in America.
1899/1909-
Daniel Blum's Screen World. 1949-
The ...Film Daily Year Book of Motion Pictures. 1927-
Index to the Best Plays Series, 1899-1950. 1950.
The Theatre Book of the Year. 1942/43- 1951.
Theatre World. 1944/45-

Periodical Indexes

The Dramatic Index. 1909-1949. (Continues in *Bulletin of Bibli-
ography*)
See also: *International Index*; *Readers' Guide*; *New York Times
Index*.

Miscellaneous

Gilder, Rosamond, and Freedley, George. *Theatre Collections in Libraries and Museums.* 1936.
Hartnoll, Phyllis, ed. *The Oxford Companion to the Theatre.* 1951.
New York Theatre Critics' Reviews. May 27, 1940-
Simon's Directory of Theatrical Materials, Services & Information. 1955-
Sobel, Bernard, ed. *The Theatre Handbook and Digest of Plays.* Rev. ed. 1948.

Buying Lists

Freedley, George. "Two Hundred Dollar Budget for a Theater Collection," *Library Journal,* LXXVI, No. 19 (November 1, 1951), p. 1790-1791.
Myers, Kurtz. "Theater Records," *Library Journal,* LXXVI, No. 19 (November 1, 1951), p. 1763-1771.
Stallings, Roy, and Myers, Paul. *A Guide to Theatre Reading.* 1949.

Philology

Dictionaries - Historical Treatments

A Dictionary of Americanisms on Historical Principles; ed. by Mitford M. Mathews. 2 vols. 1951. (1-vol. ed., 1956)
Craigie, Sir William Alexander, and Hulbert, James R., eds. *A Dictionary of American English on Historical Principles.* 4 vols. 1938-44.
Murray, Sir James Augustus Henry, ed. *A New English Dictionary on Historical Principles.* 10 vols in 14 and supplement. 1888-1933.
Murray, Sir James Augustus Henry, ed. *The Oxford English Dictionary*; Being a Corrected Re-Issue with an Introduction, Supplement, and Bibliography of a New English Dictionary on Historical Principles .... 12 vols. and supplement. 1933.

Dictionaries - Current Usage

Fowler, Henry Watson, and Fowler, Francis George. *The Concise Oxford Dictionary of Current English.* 4th ed., rev. by E. McIntosh. 1951.
Fowler, Henry Watson. *A Dictionary of Modern English Usage.* 1926. (Frequently reprinted)

Horwill, Herbert William. *A Dictionary of Modern American Usage*.
2d ed. 1944.
Opdycke, John Baker. *Get It Right!* A Cyclopedia of Correct English Usage. Rev. ed. 1939.

Etymological Dictionaries

Partridge, Eric. *Name into Word*; Proper Names That Have Become Common Property; A Discursive Dictionary. 1949.
Skeat, Walter William. *An Etymological Dictionary of the English Language*. New ed., rev. and enl. 1910.
Weekley, Ernest. *An Etymological Dictionary of Modern English*. 1921.

Dictionaries of Synonyms

Crabb, George. *Crabb's English Synonyms*. Rev. and enl. Reprinted last, 1945.
Mawson, Christopher Orlando Sylvester. *Roget's Thesaurus of the English Language in Dictionary Form*. 1951.
Roget, Peter Mark. *Thesaurus of Words and Phrases* .... Enl. by John Lewis Roget. New ed. rev. and enl. by Samuel Romilly Roget. Rev. and authorized American ed. 1947.
Webster, Noah. *Webster's Dictionary of Synonyms*. 1st ed. 1942.

Slang and Dialect Dictionaries

Berrey, Lester V., and Van den Bark, Melvin. *The American Thesaurus of Slang*; A Complete Reference Book of Colloquial Speech. 2d ed. 1953.
Partridge, Eric. *A Dictionary of Slang and Unconventional English*. 4th ed. 1951.
Wentworth, Harold. *American Dialect Dictionary*. 1944.
Weseen, Maurice Harley. *A Dictionary of American Slang*. 1934.
(See also the general dictionaries, both for English and for foreign languages)

Some "Classics" in the Study of Language

Baugh, Albert Croll. *A History of the English Language*. 1935.
(Reprinted 1951)
Bopp, Franz. *Vergleichende Grammatik des Sanskrit, Zend, Griechischen, Lateinischen, Gothischen und Deutschen*. Six parts. 1833-52.
Grimm, Jakob. *Deutsche Grammatik*. 4 vols. 1819-37.

—— *Geschichte der Deutschen Sprache.* 2 vols. 1848.

Herder, Johann Gottfried. *Abhandlung über den Ursprung der Sprache.* 1772.

Johnson, Alexander Bryan. *A Treatise on Language.* 1836.

—— *The Meaning of Words.* 1854.

Korzybski, Alfred. *Science and Sanity;* An Introduction to Non-Aristotelian Systems and General Semantics. 1933. (3d ed., 1948)

Krapp, George Philip. *The English Language in America.* 2 vols. 1925.

Kurath, Hans. *Linguistic Atlas of New England.* 3 vols. in 6. 1939-43. (Linguistic Atlas of the U. S. and Canada)

Mencken, Henry Louis. *The American Language;* An Inquiry into the Development of English in the United States. 4th ed., cor., enl., and rewritten. 1936. "Proper Names in America": p. 474-554.

—— —— Supplement I-II. 2 vols. 1945-48.

Ogden, Charles Kay, and Richards, Ivor Armstrong. *The Meaning of Meaning.* 1923. (6th ed., 1944)

Rousseau, Jean Jacques. *Essai sur l'origine des langues.* 1781.

Sapir, Edward. *Language;* An Introduction to the Study of Speech. 1921. (Reprinted 1955)

Schleicher, August. *Compendium der vergleichenden Grammatik der indogermanischen Sprachen.* 2 vols. in 1. 1861-62.

Periodicals

The American Journal of Philology. 1880-

Etc., A Review of General Semantics. 1943-

The Journal of English and Germanic Philology. 1897-

Lexis. Studien zur Sprachphilosophie, Sprachgeschichte und Begriffsforschung. 1948-

Modern Language Association of America. *Publications of the Modern Language Association of America.* 1884/85-

Modern Language Notes. 1886-

The Modern Language Review. 1905-

Modern Philology. 1903-

Philological Quarterly. 1922-

Studies in Linguistics. 1942- (Issued irregularly)